Yale Historical Publications, Miscellany, 112

The Logic of Millennial Thought

Eighteenth-Century New England

James West Davidson

New Haven and London   Yale University Press

1977

Published under the direction of the Department of
History of Yale University with assistance from
the income of the Frederick John Kingsbury Memorial Fund

Designed by John O. C. McCrillis
and set in Baskerville Selectric type.
Printed in the United States of America by
The Vail-Ballou Press, Inc., Binghamton, New York.

Published in Great Britain, Europe, Africa, and Asia
(except Japan) by Yale University Press, Ltd., London.
Distributed in Latin America by Kaiman & Polon,
Inc., New York City; in Australia and New Zealand by
Book & Film Services, Artarmon, N.S.W., Australia; and in
Japan by Harper & Row, Publishers, Tokyo Office.

Library of Congress Cataloging in Publication Data

Davidson, James West.
  The logic of millennial thought.

  (Yale historical publications: Miscellany; 112)
  Bibliography: p.
  Includes index.
  1. Millennium—History of doctrines. 2. Bible.
N.T. Revelation—Criticism, interpretation, etc.—History—
18th century. 3. Religious thought—New England.
I. Title. II. Series.
BR520.D29   261   75-43315
ISBN 0-300-01947-5

For my parents

Contents

It was the best of times, it was the worst of times . . . it was the season of Light, it was the season of Darkness, it was the spring of hope, it was the winter of despair, we had everything before us, we had nothing before us, we were all going direct to Heaven, we were all going direct the other way. . . .

—Charles Dickens

Preface

This book is called *The Logic of Millennial Thought: Eighteenth-Century New England*, not *Millennial Thought in Eighteenth-Century New England*; which is to say there is a difference between writing about millennialism and writing about the logic of it. I did not realize quite how peculiar the latter perspective was until I had finished writing from its vantage point, and since prefaces are the place where the writer is allowed to warn prospective readers of his peculiar points of view, I will briefly enlarge the distinction.

On the most general level, this book is an exercise in understanding how familiar people think strangely. Historians will be well acquainted with many of the figures presented herein: the Mathers, Samuel Sewall, Jonathan Edwards, Timothy Dwight; they will also know (thanks to the growing bibliography on millennial thought) that these men shared with many of their contemporaries an absorbing interest in the prophecies of the Bible. Yet few historians, even those whose province is religious history, have read closely the Revelation to John or the many voluminous commentaries written about it by seventeenth- and eighteenth-century Englishmen. Thus, while we might be able to hold our own in a conversation with Samuel Sewall about whether sanctification evidences justification, we would most probably be lost if he asked our opinion on the seventh vial, or whether the 1,260 days were synchronous with the dejection of the witnesses. So the original question I tried to raise was this: granting New Englanders' strange interest in the prophecies, how did eschatology influence the way they looked at the rest of the world? Did the Revelation and the tradition of

ix

interpretation growing out of it have a logic of their own which disposed people to think or act in certain consistent ways?

A second constraint further shaped the direction of my inquiry. Historians who have previously discussed millennialism have distinguished in it more than one logic, and have suggested that one perspective gave way to another as the eighteenth century progressed. My own research led me to emphasize the continuities throughout the century rather than any shift in point of view, and that approach has shaped the final form of this book.

Although the chapters move in roughly chronological progression, their organization is primarily thematic. The first half of the study attempts to explore systematically some of the possible ways one might reconstruct a logic of eighteenth-century millennial thought. Chapter 2 examines the possibility that the particular sequence or chronology of millennial timetables might have influenced motivation and behavior, chapter 3, the suggestion that natural and supernatural events affected a believers' outlook, and chapter 4, the theory that a person's conversion pattern provided a perspective which significantly shaped his eschatological attitudes and actions. The second half of the book examines, through the events of the latter half of the century, some of the ramifications of the logic finally derived from the first four chapters. Chapter 5 focuses on the ways eschatology functioned, in the late 1750s and early 1760s, as a theodicy in a social as well as intellectual sense. Chapter 6 explores the relationship of the millennial outlook to the ideology of the American Revolution, and thus tries to define more precisely the political implications of eschatology as manifested in New England. Finally, chapter 7 describes the gradual rise of a coherent, rationalized postmillennial theology, and suggests as well how some of the basic premises of millennial logic might unconsciously foster a divisiveness and polarity quite at odds with the expressed ideals of millennial peace and harmony.

My initial interest in whether millennial thought possessed a logic of its own, and the fact that I did find a thematic unity in prophetic exposition throughout the century, have led to what I see as the particular perspective of this book. While in theory intellectual historians are interested both in how ideas shaped events and how events shaped ideas, this book is more concerned with how ideas shaped events, how eschatology influenced men's perceptions rather than how events changed the shape of eschatology. I say that this viewpoint may seem peculiar because intellectual historians, all professions to the contrary, usually spend more time discussing how events shaped ideas, in this case, how eschatology *was used* by various social groups (and being used, was changed), rather than how it influenced those groups. In the first instance, eschatology functions passively ("was used") and thus remains only a mirror reflecting concerns of the larger society or, at best, a tool that can be pressed into service to further those concerns. In the second instance, it functions actively as a significant determinant in the situation. I hope to explore these distinctions at greater length elsewhere; for now it is enough to mention them in passing, so that the reader may be alerted and may more critically judge whatever pitfalls and strengths lie in this approach.

Whatever the final merits of the work, I enjoyed writing it, thanks largely to the kind and generous advice I received along the way. I began research on the subject in a seminar paper written for David D. Hall at Yale University; he has been good enough to supply me with incisive comment and criticism even after he assumed other teaching responsibilities at Boston University. Sydney Ahlstrom and David Davis have also been most helpful in their discussions of the subject with me as I worked on this study in its original form as a Ph.D. thesis. To the Johns Hopkins University, and especially to Timothy L. Smith, I owe the opportunity of enlarging and revising the thesis in a stimulating and congenial scholarly setting, for which I am especially grateful. Above all, I owe a great debt to Edmund Morgan for his encouragement and detailed reading of the dissertation as it progressed. He has helped me in more ways than he probably suspects.

I would also like to thank the libraries of Yale, Harvard, and Johns Hopkins universities for their assistance, and especially the staff at the Beinecke Rare Book Library; also the libraries of the American Antiquarian Society and the Massachusetts Historical Society.

Needless to say, the reader is warned not to impugn any of the above-mentioned persons or institutions through the dubious process of guilt by association. I assume all responsibility for errors, sins of omission or commission, or any other faults the book bears.

PART 1: Unraveling the Logic

1

Revelation

Sometime near the end of the first century A.D., a little book began circulating among a number of Christian churches in Asia. Its author, who identified himself only as John, a servant of Christ, wished it to be passed from church to church and read aloud among gatherings of the faithful. Just who John was is difficult to discover. Some traditions claimed he was Jesus' beloved disciple John, son of Zebedee; others, that he had been an elder for some time in the church at Ephesus.[1]

Ultimately, his message mattered more than his identity. Whoever John was, he showed an acute awareness of the problems early Christians faced and the tidings they were longing to hear. For those who gave total allegiance to a crucified and risen Lord, living under the protection of the imperial rule of Rome was difficult indeed. Romans demanded more than political loyalty to the state. Subjects were required to participate in cultic rituals whose deities included the goddess Roma as well as a pantheon of past Roman emperors. At first, Christians were not hard put to decide how to deal with the conflict. Jews had always refused to participate in such idolatrous worship, and Rome yielded to their

1. The historical background of the Revelation can be found in Robert H. Charles, *A Critical History of the Doctrine of a Future Life*, 2d ed., revised and enlarged (London, 1913), chaps. 9-10, or in any competent introduction to the New Testament, such as Paul Feine, Johannes Behm, and Georg Kümmel, *Introduction to the New Testament*, trans. A. J. Matill, Jr. (Nashville, Tenn., 1966).

stubbornness by exempting them from the practice. Since Christians were initially regarded as a group of Jewish sectaries, they too were granted the exemption.

But the religion spread, and as Gentile converts began to outnumber Jews, Rome revised its opinion. Persecution of Christians began in earnest under the reign of Domitian, whose paranoia fed a demand for total obedience. Domitian preferred to be addressed as "*dominus ac deus noster*," which for Christians put the issue in the boldest possible relief. Which man were they to swear was "our Lord and God"—a crucified yet supposedly risen Jesus, or an emperor who had the power to persecute, imprison, and kill them if they did not?

John chose loyalty to Christ, and for his troubles was exiled to Patmos, a rocky Aegean island about five by ten miles long. But his faith was exceptionally strong; for many, exile, prison, or death was a frightening prospect. Was not compromise of some sort possible? Surely, if it were a case of life or death, paying lip-service to a Roman Caesar was the most sensible solution. Or perhaps it was wiser to give up belief in a risen Christ entirely. If He was indeed Lord over all the nations, why were Christians persecuted wherever they went? How was it that evil men like Domitian and Nero were allowed to reign unchecked? John was aware that these questions would inevitably be asked; and if his position in the church had been one of authority before his exile, he would naturally have felt a responsibility to strengthen the resolve of those who wavered. That was precisely the effect he hoped his book would have.

Its title is simply the *Apocalypse* (or *Revelation*) *to John*, *Apocalypse* being a transliteration of a Greek verb's substantive form meaning "an uncovering" (*Re-vel-ation*: *re* = un, *vel* = veil; hence, an unveiling). And so John begins:

> The revelation of Jesus Christ, which God gave unto him
> to shew unto his servants things which must shortly come
> to pass; and he sent and signified it by his angel unto his
> servant John: who bare record of the word of God and of
> the testimony of Jesus Christ, and of all things that he
> saw.[2]

John reports that he was "in the Spirit" one Sabbath morning, when he heard behind him "a great voice, as of a trumpet, saying, 'I am Alpha and Omega, the first and the last, and, What thou seest, write in a book, and send it unto the seven churches which are in Asia.'" The voice belongs to Christ, who then dictates a series of letters to the churches, admonishing obedience. But these are only a preface to greater disclosures of "things which must be hereafter" (Rev. 1:10–11).

Before the heavenly throne, John sees Christ, the Lamb who was slain, opening for him a book fastened by seven seals. Each seal reveals a vision. The first is of a white-horsed rider going forth to conquer; the second, a red horse and rider with power to take peace from the earth; the third, a pale mount with the power of death. To John, the visions signify present and future plagues unleased upon the world, and the fifth seal indicates the way troubled Christians react to them. Those who "were slain for the word of God" cry out, "How long, O Lord, holy and true, dost thou not judge and avenge our blood on them that dwell on earth?" The reply is, that "they should rest yet for a little season, until their fellow servants also and their brethren, that should be killed as they were, should be fulfilled" (Rev. 6:9–11).

And in fact, the Revelation predicts even greater calamities.

2. Rev. 1:1-2. The King James version is used to avoid confusion regarding prophetic terminology. The Revised Standard, for example, refers to "bowls" of wrath (Rev. 16), whereas the King James and all eighteenth-century expositors call them "vials."

After the seven seals, another series of visions begins, these under the auspices of seven trumpets. The trumpets predict that burning mountains will fall into the sea, the sun, moon and stars darken, and plagues of locusts descend. Witnesses for Christ will prophesy in sackcloth—the state of affliction—for 1,260 days, after which "the beast that ascendeth out of the bottomless pit shall make war against them, and shall overcome them, and kill them." Their opponents will leave their bodies in the streets, rejoice over their deaths, and mock them. Like the martyrs of the seven seals, their fate seems to be one of tribulation and trial.

But both visions end in triumph. The slain witnesses have the spirit of life breathed into them, and they rise from the dead to ascend into heaven. The martyrs killed under the seven seals are later seen dressed in white robes, rejoicing around the throne of God. Lest his readers have any doubts as to who these men are, John has an elder of heaven ask him, "What are these which are arrayed in white robes? and whence came they?" John gives the humble and proper response—"Sir, thou knowest"—and of course, the elder does: "These are they which came out of great tribulation, and have washed their robes, and made them white in the blood of the Lamb" (Rev. 11:1-13; 7:9-17).

But the Revelation to John goes beyond the mere reassurance that his persecuted comrades will ultimately reign with a triumphant Christ. The unveiling of future events is connected with the larger context of God's great battle with Satan. John sees a vision of a heavenly woman about to give birth to "a man child, who was to rule all nations with a rod of iron." But the woman is menaced. A great, red dragon with seven heads and ten horns stands before her, ready to devour her child as soon as it is born. He fails, and the child is taken up by God to his throne (Rev. 12:4-5). John's readers would have little trouble identifying the scene as a celestial representation of Jesus' birth. And shortly thereafter, the dragon is revealed as none other than "that old serpent, called the Devil, and Satan, which deceiveth the whole world." Although Michael and his angels have succeeded in banishing the dragon from heaven, he is still left free to roam the earth. There, with the assistance of three agents, he makes war on the "remnant" of the faithful church (Rev. 12:17).

The first of these agents is another seven-headed, ten-horned beast who emerges from the sea; the second is a similar creature who rises from the earth. In other visions, John sometimes seems to combine the two, and for those who later interpreted his book, all such beasts were representations of antichrist, Satan's principle agent on earth. A third enemy appears later, the whore of Babylon, whose full title is written on her forehead: "MYSTERY, BABYLON THE GREAT, THE MOTHER OF HARLOTS AND ABOMINATIONS OF THE EARTH." She rides atop one of the beasts, and John provides further clues to her earthly identity in a series of hints decipherable only by "the mind which hath wisdom." The most obvious clue is that "The seven heads [of the beast] are seven mountains, on which the woman sitteth," a reference to the tradition of Rome being founded on seven hills. Satan gives power to all three creatures, and they use it to impress simple multitudes by performing false miracles. Thus they attract many followers, and kill "as many as would not worship the image of the beast" (Rev. 13; Rev. 17).

So the lines are clearly drawn between the forces of the Lamb and those of the dragon. Those who swear allegiance to the evil powers have a mark put upon them, either in their right hand or on their forehead; and the servants of God are likewise sealed by an angel of the Lord (Rev. 13:15–17; 7:1–8). In this war, there is no neutral ground, and Christians will be deceiving themselves if they envision compromise as a possibility. Thus the Revelation castigates the church of

Laodicea for being "neither cold nor hot: I would thou wert cold or hot! So then because thou art lukewarm, and neither cold nor hot, I will spew thee out of my mouth (Rev. 3:15–16). God's patience has ended, and John moves from his vision of the beasts to the harvesting of history. Angels pour out the seven vials which contain the last seven last plagues.

Here the tempo increases as God's wrath spreads across the world. The first vial brings a plague of sores upon the men who bear the mark of the beast; the second is poured into the sea, and brings death to all that live there. The third turns rivers and fountains into blood, while the fourth causes the sun to scorch the earth. Yet the worshippers of the beast remain unrepentant, even when the fifth vial is poured onto the throne of the beast. Satan's kingdom is threatened but not destroyed. An angel pours the sixth vial on the river Euphrates, and from out of the mouths of the dragon, the beast, and the whore come three "unclean spirits like frogs," who go about the world assembling hosts for a battle at Armageddon. The last vial is poured into the air, and a great voice proclaims, "It is done." Thunder, lightning and earthquakes all signal the fall of Babylon. Princes and kings "who committed fornication and were wanton with her" weep and wail; merchants mourn when they see their trade in ruins; shipmasters and sailors cry with dismay when their source of profit is dried up (Rev. 18).

At the height of the crisis, an angel bids the faithful to "Come out of her, my people, that ye be not partakers of her sins, and that ye receive not of her plagues." As the saints gather, the heavens open and Christ appears seated on a white horse. This time, he is no meek Lamb, ready to endure persecution. His eyes are "as a flame of fire," his clothes "a vesture dipped in blood." The armies of heaven join in the ensuing war, and the beast is thrown alive into the lake of fiery brimstone. Finally Satan, the chief source of mischief, is seized by an angel and cast into the bottomless pit to be bound for a thousand years. Now the martyrs who had endured so much in earlier persecutions come to life and reign with Christ for the millennium: a thousand years when Satan and his evil forces are banished from the world (Rev. 18-19; 20:4-5).

The drama, however, is not quite finished. At the end of that time, Satan breaks free to gather his forces for one last battle led by his minions, Gog and Magog. Only then is he decisively defeated, and joins the beast in the lake of fire where they are "tormented day and night for ever and ever." And with Satan defeated, the world ends with the Last Judgment. The unfaithful are sentenced to the lake of fire, but those who suffered for Christ go to "a new heaven and a new earth: for the first heaven and the first earth were passed away" (Rev. 20:10; 21:1). The holy city, also called the New Jerusalem, descends from heaven. Together, the Lamb and his followers come to the city, where

> there shall be no more curse: but the throne of God and of the Lamb shall be in it; and his servants shall serve him: And they shall see his face; and his name shall be in their foreheads. And there shall be no night there; and they need no candle, neither light of the sun; for the Lord God giveth them light: and they shall reign for ever and ever. [Rev. 22:3-5]

So history ends well after all, despite the temporary appearance of desolation. The book closes with Christ assuring John that what he has seen is true, that the end is indeed near, and that the future should not be kept hidden from the faithful. "Surely I am coming soon," says Jesus, and John's fervent reply is, "Even so, Come Lord Jesus!" (Rev. 22:6-21).

To cynics John's version of history may seem a trifle neat. Like so many inept playwrights, he needed a *deus ex machina* to get his troubled characters out of a jam. Yet, somehow, the church survived without the help of a *deus ex machina.* Certainly John was sincere in believing that little time remained before Christ's second coming; but the Revelation helped sustain members of the earthly body of Christ even without help from heaven.

It did so in part because it made the lines of good and evil clear in an ambiguous world. Roman emperors were not men with whom compromise was possible. When wavering Christians considered swearing allegiance or participating in Roman cultic rites, they were forced to think not only of Rome, but of the seven-headed beast, the whore of Babylon, and—behind both—Satan the grand dragon, the ultimate source of evil. John's fantastic imagery wrought a horrible transformation in what might otherwise have seemed merely an unpleasant bureaucracy. And judging by the persistence of the church under continuing persecution, John's ministry was a successful one.

But successful at what price? Subsequent Christian tradition has insisted that ministry is twofold in character, combining the traits of both priest and prophet. And indeed, John's letters to the seven churches are examples of the combination at work. When he writes Ephesus, he can provide the comfort and assurance of a good priest: "I know thy works, and thy labor, and thy patience . . . [and that thou] hast borne, and hast patience, and for my name's sake has labored, and hast not fainted." And yet, right upon the heels of this comes prophetic admonition: "Nevertheless I have somewhat against thee, because thou has left thy first love. Remember therefore, from whence thou art fallen, and repent, and do the first works" (Rev. 2:2–7). The other letters follow the same pattern; the alternation of consolation and admonition, of the priestly and the prophetic, of mercy and judgment. John manages both to comfort the afflicted and to afflict the comfortable.

But the combination of these two traits is a precarious one for John, because it threatens to disrupt the clear lines he draws between the worlds of good and evil. To see the elect as simultaneously the comfortable and the afflicted, to see mercy and judgment as inseparable, is to grant an ambiguity in the nature of the faithful which does not rest well with a vision of all men marked on the forehead either with the seal of the Lamb or that of the beast. Mercy and judgment are dealt with much more easily if they are separated. Then Christ's role in his first coming can be interpreted as primarily one of mercy. Jesus is meek to the end, allowing himself to be crucified for the sins of those who believe in him. But his second coming is one of judgment. The time of mercy has past, and the formerly meek Christ now appears with the armies of heaven, ready to deal with the sins of the world in a radically different way.

Hence we find a tension in the Revelation that is illustrated, for instance, by John's vision of the slain martyrs. Resurrected, they appear in heaven gathered around the throne of God in white robes, "washed" and made "white in the blood of the Lamb." But just what does this mean? One traditional Christian answer is that the blood which Christ removes from the robe by shedding his own blood is the sin of the one who wears the robe. In that case, the mercy shown is also a judgment upon the unworthiness of the elect. But with John the case seems different. The blood here points not to the sins of the martyrs but to the sins of those who slay them. And if that is the case, mercy is easily separated from judgment, and comfort from affliction. For in the end, the acceptance of martyrdom earns mercy by virtue of the act itself, and judgment is saved for the sins of those who have slain in service to the beast. The perspective is simpler, clearer, and infinitely more comforting—at least to those wearing the white robes.

THE PRESENT PROBLEM

This book concerns eighteenth-century New England, not first-century Asia Minor. Yet the background is necessary because, in this case, eighteenth-century New England is closer to the first century than to the twentieth. When the world did not end as soon as John hoped, the church had to decide whether or not to accept his book as a true revelation. That took several centuries, with eminent men arguing on either side of the question; but both Athanasius and Augustine included it in the canon, and serious opposition diminished. New England Protestants, like the great majority of Christians before them, believed that the Revelation was indeed from Christ, and that it predicted events which at the time they were revealed had not yet taken place.

To anyone interested in pursuing the social implications of religious thought, New Englanders' acceptance of the Revelation raises two basic questions. First, was this belief an important part of their religion? Some Christians, Calvin among them, agreed that John had been inspired, but professed that they hardly knew what to make of his book.[3] Did New Englanders actually give serious attention to it? And secondly, if they did, how did that attention affect their view of the world around them and especially of their fellow men?

A preliminary answer to the first question can be given merely by looking at the lives of three eminent New England divines whose careers spanned the period we are investigating. If the writings of Cotton Mather, Jonathan Edwards, and Timothy Dwight are any indication, study of the prophecies

3. For Calvin's views, see Heinrich Quistorp, *Calvin's Doctrines of the Last Things* (London, 1955).

was a major activity of eighteenth-century theologians. To say that prophetic thought was important to these men is not to say it was also important to most New Englanders—or even to most ministers. But Mather, Edwards, and Dwight were influential men, and the following sketches, brief as they are, indicate that the effects of prophetic thought on broader attitudes bear further investigation.

Cotton Mather is familiar to many as one of God's most strenuous creations; what has been less appreciated until recently is that much of that strenuousness was motivated by an interest in biblical prophecies.[4] Mather often had a sneaking suspicion (and sometimes not so sneaking) that God might be using him as a principal instrument in fulfilling the Revelation. In 1691, he published the first of many sermons dealing with *Things To Be Look'd For*, a survey of colonial and international events which hinted at how close the world was to Christ's second coming. The following year, *A Midnight Cry* painted Christ's arrival in vivid terms. Jesus would "become Visible unto this lower World, and make the Sky to rattle with his rapid peals of Thunder, the Mountains to tremble before his Lightnings, and the Hills and Rocks to melt at the presence of his Majesty," and would also "by a terrible *Conflagration* make a *New Earth*, whereon the *Escaped Nations* are to walk in the *Light* of that *Holy City* [the New Jerusalem]." Nor was this a dream for the distant future. Mather was convinced that the world was "doubtless very near the Last Hours of that *Wicked One*," and his own calculations indicated that antichrist might fall as soon as 1697.[5]

Long hours of study stood behind this conclusion. Cotton, like his father Increase, was familiar with writings on the Re-

4. Robert Middlekauff's excellent study, *The Mathers* (Oxford, 1971), clearly indicates this central concern, not only in Cotton, but also in his father Increase and grandfather Richard. For Cotton, see especially chapter 18, but also all of book 3.

5. Cotton Mather, *A Midnight Cry* (Boston, 1692), pp. 23, 24.

velation from the early church fathers down to the numerous seventeenth-century commentaries. Often he would copy relevant portions of these tracts and discuss their merits in his "Biblia Americana," a six-volume manuscript dealing with critical issues raised by the Scriptures. He compiled his own detailed scenario of the end of history in another unpublished manuscript, "Triparadisus."[6]

Prayer was also a part of Mather's concern for the coming Kingdom, and the sabbath a particularly appropriate time for such activity. Sunday was the seventh day of the week, when God had rested after creating the world, and thus "a Peculiar Type and Sign of the Blessed *Millennium*," when the world would finally be at rest. Both before and after dinner (when he was not at church), Mather would study prophetic commentaries, read Scripture, make "suitable Ejaculations," and sing a hymn on the subject, concluding with a prayer while he was "Prostrate in the Dust . . . for *Zion in the Dust*, and for the Hastening of the Day of God."[7] He called the whole process "Indefatigable Sabbatizing," and indefatigable it was. As 1697 approached, he resolved to set time aside for daily prayer on the subject, just as the prophet Daniel had done.[8] He was so successful with these "extraordinary Supplications" that he often received what he called "Particular Faiths" from God—an assurance that a wish strongly prayed for would be granted. Thus he reported that Christ had "informed, inclined, and assisted" him "to foresee, and putt on that Work of His."[9]

6. "Biblia Americana," MS, Massachusetts Historical Society, Boston; "Triparadisus," MS, American Antiquarian Society, Worcester, Mass.

7. *The Diary of Cotton Mather for the Year 1712*, ed. William R. Manierre II (Charlottesville, Va., 1964), p. 69. See also the *Diary of Cotton Mather*, Collections of the Massachusetts Historical Society, 2 vols.; 7th ser., vols. 7–8 (Boston, 1911–12), 1:337 (hereafter cited as Mather, *Diary*).

8. Mather, *Diary*, 1:261.

9. Ibid., p. 261.

Mather's response to this revelation was to engage in greater and greater activity. In addition to the numerous publications touching the subject, he began to hold meetings in his study once every two weeks for a *"select"* group of Christians who were interested in the "Approaches of the Kingdome of our Lord Jesus Christ." He somehow took time ("a few leisure Minutes in the Evening of every Day") to learn Spanish in three weeks in order to prepare a pamphlet on the articles of the Protestant faith. His hope was to help spread the true gospel throughout Spanish America, as prophesied in Scripture.[10] A similar interest prevailed toward the Indians, only in this case he relied on others to do the translating. And since the Revelation predicted that in the last days the Jews would recognize Christ as their Lord and Saviour, Mather was always on the lookout for news of conversions, and composed manuals to promote them. Of course, God would see that most Jews remained blind to the faith until just before the very end; but the trickle of converts would still help Christians in their *"Looking Out,* for the blessed Revolution which is to come."[11]

An end to all things did not come in 1697, but Mather was not discouraged. Prophetic calculations were difficult to get exactly right. Further research convinced him that the time would not come until around 1736; later he moved the date to 1716. At times his meditations rose to ecstatic heights in anticipation of the Holy Spirit which angels would spread throughout the world: *"They are coming! They are coming! They are coming! They will quickly be upon us; and the World shall be shaken wonderfully*!"[12] Disappointment came

10. Ibid., pp. 284–85.

11. Hence Cotton's perverse logic, not to mention tact, when he told Jews, "One thing that satisfies us Christians, in the truth of Christianity, is your obstinate Aversion to that Holy Religion." *The Faith of the Fathers* (Boston, 1699), p. 3; *American Tears* (Boston, 1701), pp. 57 ff.

12. Mather, *Diary*, 2:366.

again in 1717, but not disillusionment. Until his death in 1728, he continued to pray and hope for the arrival of Christ's kingdom.

Mather's death was followed the next year by that of another influential minister, Solomon Stoddard; and Northampton chose his grandson, Jonathan Edwards, to replace him. Like Mather, Edwards made prophecies the subject of private study as well as public discourse. Early in his career he composed a list of "Books To Be Inquired For" which included "The Best Exposition of the Apocalypse"; and by the summer of 1723, he decided the subject merited enough attention to warrant keeping a separate notebook on it. Thus his "Notes on the Apocalypse" was begun.[13] Edwards added to this for the rest of his life, working out his own theories about various prophecies and often copying excerpts from the other sources he read. Since many of the prophetic commentaries were not easily available in New England, he drew upon Matthew Poole's *Synopsis Criticorum*, a survey in Latin of forty divines' positions on the Revelation.[14]

Stoddard's death meant more time had to be spent in pastoral duties, and Edwards soon found himself in the midst of an awakening greater than any his grandfather had managed. News of it spread, and Londoners like Isaac Watts and John Guyse saw the revival as a token of even greater ones promised in the prophecies. The Boston ministers who wrote a preface to the *Faithful Narrative* agreed, calling it "an Earnest of what God will do towards the Close of the Gospel

13. Edwards's list of books is quoted in Stephen Stein, " 'Notes on the Apocalypse,' by Jonathan Edwards," 2 vols. (Ph.D. diss., Yale University, 1970), 1:*49*. Edwards's "Notes" will soon be published in the Yale Edition of his works. Stephen Stein's thorough research into Edwards's apocalyptic views has been of great help to me, and his work on the "Notes" provides Edwards scholars with an important but hitherto neglected source.

14. Stein, "Notes," 1:*99*.

Day."[15] And when similar awakenings spread across New England in 1740, Edwards's hopes soared. Christ's original mission had been accomplished in the Old World, so it made sense that his second, spiritual coming would commence in the New. And in that case, would not the "most likely" place be New England? It seemed probable that the revivals were "the dawning, or at least a prelude, of that glorious work of God, so often foretold in Scripture, which in the progress and issue of it shall renew the world of mankind."[16]

Hence Edwards, like Mather, was always on the lookout for tell-tale signs of the times. He admitted he "had great longings for the advancement of Christ's kingdom in the world"; and that he was "eager to read public news-letters, mainly for that end, to see if I could not find some news favorable to the interest of religion in the world."[17] The "Notes on the Apocalypse" dutifully recorded advances and setbacks of the Protestant interest in Europe as well as in America: Spain's trade seemed to be languishing; a new poll tax in France caused "surprise and consternation among the people"; a Jesuit house was struck by lightning and the library consumed.[18] Similarly, Edwards's correspondence with Scottish ministers discussed such standard prophetic questions as whether the French loss at Cape Breton signaled the pouring of the sixth vial; or what the slaying of the witnesses referred to.[19]

15. For Watts and Guyse, see their preface to *A Faithful Narrative*, 3d ed. (Boston, 1738), p. iii. The Boston ministers wrote a separate preface for the same edition, from which they are quoted, p. iv.

16. *Some Thoughts on the Revival of Religion*, in *Works of Jonathan Edwards*, Perry Miller and John Smith, gen. eds., 4 vols. (New Haven, 1958–   ), 4:353. Hereafter cited as Edwards, Yale *Works*.

17. Diary, in *Works of President Edwards*, 4 vols. (reprint of the Worcester Edition; New York, 1849), 1:19. Hereafter cited as Edwards, *Works*.

18. Stein, "Notes," 2:324, 327, 321-22.

19. Letters of January 21, 1747 and March 5, 1744, in *The Works of President*

These letters also sparked more concrete action. A number of Scots sent over a proposal designed to hasten the coming kingdom by holding a series of public prayer meetings, and Edwards agreed to spearhead a similar effort in New England. He hoped the "disposition to such prayer" created by the meetings would "gradually spread more and more, and increase to greater degrees; with which at length will gradually be introduced a revival of religion." Others would then be awakened, and "in this manner religion shall be propagated, until the awakening reaches those that are in *the highest stations*, and until *whole nations* be awakened. . . . "[20] The concert of prayer never succeeded in kindling revivals as large as the earlier ones, but the prayer meetings continued to be held in some New England congregations for more than fifty years.[21]

The magnificent scope of the drama fascinated Edwards, and he preached a series of thirty sermons for half a year in 1739, tracing the divine plan all the way from Adam's creation and fall down to the present times and the coming millennium and final judgment.[22] The idea of such a grand history intrigued him, and near the end of his life, he accepted the presidency of the College of New Jersey only on the condition that he be granted enough free time to write

> a great work, which I call a *History of the Work of Redemption,* a body of divinity in an entire new method, being thrown into the form of a history; considering the affair of Christian Theology, as the whole of it, in each part, stands in reference to the great work of redemption

Edwards, Sereno Dwight, ed., 10 vols. (New York, 1830), 1:230, 214ff. Hereafter cited as *Works* (Dwight ed.).

20. *A Humble Attempt to Promote Explicit Agreement and Visible Union of God's People in Extraordinary Prayer*, in Edwards, *Works*, 3:432–33.

21. *Works*, (Dwight ed.), 1:245–46.

22. *History of the Work of Redemption* in Edwards, *Works*, vol. 1.

> by Jesus Christ; which I suppose to be, of all others, the grand design of God . . . particularly considering all parts of the grand scheme, in their historical order. . . . This history will be carried on with regard to all three worlds, heaven, earth, and hell; considering the connected, successive events and alterations in each, so far as the scriptures give any light. . . .[23]

The college was ready to grant the request, but Providence proved unwilling. Edwards died in 1758 from an inoculation against the smallpox, before he could finish his cherished project.

At that time, his grandson Timothy Dwight was only six years old; but if we can believe his biographers, he had already been reading the Bible for two years. The early interest stayed with him: his first published work was a *Dissertation on the History, Eloquence, and Poetry of the Bible*, delivered publicly upon receiving his master's degree from Yale. Its conclusion was draped in millennial metaphors, a rhetorical technique that was to serve him well in the years ahead. "Nothing gives greater weight and dignity to Poetry than Prophecy," he explained. "The Prophecies are always certain, the events referred to the future; their Hero is the Messiah . . . — the Empire, that of the Universe, its extension immensity, its duration eternity."[24]

Dwight was soon trying his own hand at poetry, adding plenty of "weight and dignity" by the use of prophecy. He loved millennial conclusions, and often his narrators are off wandering in secluded glens, only to see "an awful form" advance: a goddess wearing white robes who smiles sublime and then presents a vision of the future. In "America," one of his

23. *Works*, (Dwight ed.) 1:564–70. Stein argues that this refers not simply to a republication of the 1739 sermons but to an entirely new version utilizing researches in the "Notes on the Apocalypse." Stein, "Notes," 1:*83–84*.

24. Dwight, *Dissertation* (New Haven, 1772), pp. 15–16.

earlier creations, she describes first "Discord thundering from afar," where "warring millions roll in dread array"; but then "white-robed peace begins her milder reign." The gospel spreads, the arts flourish, the entire world is converted, and the millennial reign begins: "Th' Almighty Saviour his great power display/From rising morning to the setting day."[25] And in a later poem, "Greenfield Hill," Dwight treats his reader to essentially the same scene. This time, the vision is provided by the "Genius of the [Long Island] Sound," but it is the same joyous parade of religion and knowledge across the globe.[26]

These millennial hopes were more than convenient poetic visions. Dwight was a chaplain for American forces during the Revolution, and his watchful eye found parallels between scriptural prophecy and the revolutionary conflict. The defeat of Burgoyne in 1777 seemed remarkably like Hezekiah's victory over his Assyrian foes. If Americans remained faithful to God, their "armies would be crowned with health, success and glory, . . . Independence and happiness fixed upon the most lasting foundations; and that *kingdom of the Redeemer* . . . highly exalted, and durably established, on the ruins of the kingdom of Satan."[27] When victory came at Yorktown, Dwight was ready with another sermon—and a prophecy from Isaiah 19. Isaiah predicted that "they shall hear the name of the Lord from the West," and who else could "they" refer to but the inhabitants of Europe—and especially Britain, that favored nation of God who for so many years had strayed from righteousness? Meanwhile, as great as the colonial victory might seem, it was "to be viewed only as a preparation for others of higher impor-

25. Dwight, *America* (New Haven, 1780), p. 12.
26. Dwight, *Greenfield Hill* (New York, 1794), pp. 150–66.
27. Dwight, *Sermon upon the General Thanksgiving* (Hartford, 1778), p. 16.

tance," which would ultimately lead to the commencement of the millennium around the year 2000.[28]

Of course, Satan still raged, and today Dwight is better known for his war on infidelity than he is for his paeans to the American Revolution. But in both cases, he saw the conflict in terms of a larger history of redemption. In his famous speech, *The Duty of Americans at the Present Crisis*, the emphasis was not on current events embroidered by prophecy, but the other way around.[29] Thus Dwight examined the threat of atheism and the Bavarian Illuminati as indications of whether or not the fifth vial had been poured out. In similar fashion, his review in 1800 of the past century pointed toward the more important events of salvation history. As evil as Roman Catholicism had been, developments in the past hundred years proved that the antichrist of the prophecies was "far more justly applied to the collective body of modern Infidels."[30]

The threat of atheist and idolater alike demanded a forceful countereffort by Christians to spread the kingdom. Hence Dwight's involvement in the growing missionary effort had definite millennial overtones. "The day, in which these blessings are to be ushered in, has arrived," he told the American Board of Commissioners for Foreign Missions. "Forget, then, the little period which intervenes between us and this glorious day. Convey yourselves on the wings of anticipation to the dawn of this Great Sabbath of time."[31] Dwight's career

28. Dwight, *Sermon Preached at Northampton . . . Occasioned by the Capture of the British Army* (Hartford, 1781), pp. 3, 11, 19, 27.

29. Dwight (New Haven, 1798). The prefatory note (as well as the rest of the speech) makes this quite clear.

30. Dwight, *A Discourse on Some Events of the Last Century* (New Haven, 1801), p. 36.

31. Dwight, *A Sermon Delivered in Boston . . . Before the American Board of Commissioners for Foreign Missions* (Boston, 1813), p. 32.

at the close of the eighteenth century was motivated as much by "Indefatigable Sabbatism" as Cotton Mather's was at its beginning.

Preliminary evidence, then, indicates that at least some New Englanders gave much more than passing attention to the prophecies. And in fact, Mather and Edwards were hardly alone in their interest. One purpose of this work is to document more fully the prophetic speculation of less prominent men. But the accomplishment of that task inevitably leads to the second and more interesting question: granting New Englanders' concern for the subject, did it affect in any significant way the rest of their lives?

The answer to that requires a good deal of mental exercise, and understandably so. To many historians, the prophetic tracts of eighteenth-century scholars seem strange—if not in their metaphor, at least in their logic. The conflagration and Last Judgment may be familiar as theological concepts, or antichrist and the beast as literary symbols, but we hardly take them as accurate representations of events and forces in the future history of mankind. Thus it is not easy to imagine what logical connections might have been made, or conclusions drawn, by those who took the prophecies seriously.

A small example of the vagaries of eschatological speculation can be found in an after-dinner conversation between two lay students of the Revelation, Samuel Sewall and Paul Dudley. That evening they were engaged in "Discourse about the Body," and what its state would be at the final judgment. Dudley thought that when the dead were resurrected, "the Belly should not be raised, because he knew of no use of it." Sewall countered with the argument that since Christ was perfect, and *He* had a belly, so too would the saints. Dudley was not satisfied; it seemed to him several parts of the body would be of little use:

Dudley:	What use of Tasting, Smelling?
Sewall:	Tis possible the bodies of the Saints may have a Fragrancy attending them.
Dudley:	Voice is Laborious.
Sewall:	As much Labour as you please, the more the better, so it be without Toil, as in Heaven it will be. I dare not part with my Belly. Christ has redeemed it, and there is danger of your breaking in further upon me, and cutting off my Hand or foot.

Apparently Sewall himself was not completely satisfied with his answers, and only the next day did he think of a clinching argument: "This morning [it] comes to my mind, I can't believe the blessed Womb that bore our Saviour, will always be buried."[32] What historian could anticipate the logic in *that* reasoning!

Yet even this fails to convey the strangeness found in the meticulous texture of prophetic exposition. Sewall again serves as a good example. Historians have often treated his prophetic tract, *Phenomena quaedam Apocalyptica*, by quoting the description of Plum Island:

As long as *Plum Island* shall faithfully keep the commanded Post; not withstanding all the hectoring Words, and hard Blows of the proud and boisterous Ocean; As long as any Salmon, or Sturgeon shall swim in the streams of *Merrimack*; or any Perch or Pickeril, in *Crane Pond*; As long as the Sea-Fowl shall know the Time of their coming, and not neglect seasonably to visit the Places of their Acquaintance; As long as any Cattel shall be fed with the Grass growing in the Medows, which do humbly bow down themselves before *Turkie-Hill;* As long as any Sheep shall

32. *Diary of Samuel Sewall*, Collections of the Massachusetts Historical Society, 3 vols.; 5th ser., vols. 5-7 (Boston, 1878-82), 2:430 (hereafter cited as Sewall, *Diary*).

walk upon *Old Town Hills*, and shall from thence pleas-
antly look down upon the *River Parker* and the fruitful
Marishes lying beneath. . . . So long shall Christians be born
there; and being first made meet shall from thence be
Translated, to be made partakers of the Inheritance of
the Saints in Light.[33]

Unquestionably, historians have been right in giving the passage prominence. This is Sewall's prose style at its finest, and
its lyricism is directed toward something any modern reader
can appreciate: the concrete beauty of Turkey Hill, sheep
and cattle.

Unfortunately, the Plum Island passage is hardly characteristic of the subject matter found in the *Phenomena*. A more
representative choice would be the following:

I was now about to have passed on to the Sixth Vial; but
am interrupted by some of my Friends, who suppose that
not one of the Vials is yet poured out. To which Objection, I have nothing more satisfactory to myself, to say,
than what I writ in answer to Mr. *Benjamin Eliot*, April 7,
1685. Some object, that *Revel.* 11.19. & *Rev.* 15.5 intend the same Thing: and the Witnesses are not yet risen,
and therefore there is no Vial as yet poured out. Vide
Med. lib 3. cap. 6. P. 735. *Answ.* See *Med. Synchron.* 5.
Sect. 3 P. 534. The word *Temple*, in both places signifies
the Reformed Church fashioned according to the Com-
mandment of Christ, and his Apostles; and separated
from that sorry earthly heaven comfortable to the inventive fancys of men. But these two Scriptures have respect
to very different *Times*, and Conditions of this Church.
The Opening mentioned Rev. 15.5 precedes that mentioned Rev. 11.19. some hundreds of Years. The Temple
Rev. 15.5 is the *Temple* of the *Tabernacle* of the *Testi-*

33. Samuel Sewall, *Phenomena*, 2d ed. (Boston, 1727), p. 63.

mony. Tabernacle intimating its ambulatory, and moveable condition, taken down in one place, and set up in another, according to the holy, wise, and soveraign Pleasure and Providence of God: And this may be spoken of in contradistinction to the Temple Rev. 11.19, wherein God will settle his Abode, Psal. 46.4.[34]

For us, the passion behind Plum Island is easily evident; but there is passion behind these lines too. Something moved Samuel Sewall to spend long hours poring over the Bible, weighing the opinions of other authorities, writing his friends for their opinions. Because of the strangeness, we must infer the passion; and having done that, somehow attempt to fit this strange part of his world into the more familiar aspects of eighteenth-century life. What connections are there between the passion for the seven vials and the concrete world of Plum Island?

PAST INTERPRETATIONS

One answer historians have given is that there are no important connections. Ola Winslow, in her typically excellent biography of Sewall, devoted a scant four-page chapter to the *Phenomena*, considering it as part of "an intellectual life apart from [his] daily busyness." The text of it, she said, "is as coldly removed from the life of his time (or anyone's time) as the title might suggest."[35] Basically, she saw Sewall's concern with the Revelation as only a hobby on the side. Another biographer seemed almost embarrassed by the *Phenomena*, and assured his readers, despite what they might think about Sewall's fantastic ideas, that "all transcendental beliefs are in some sense 'fantastic'; that some of the most fantastic have figured in man's greatest accomplishments; and that in

34. Ibid., pp. 18–19.
35. Ola Winslow, *Samuel Sewall of Boston* (New York, 1964), p. 153.

the absence of a better means of evaluation, one must look to results."[36]

In some cases, these answers may be no answer at all, merely a dodge of the problem. It is always easier to attribute actions to more familiar and understandable motives. Yet a more sophisticated point is at stake. Is it not possible to face the problem squarely, admit that prophetic speculation was a significant part of many people's lives, and still claim that it affected their behavior in no important way? The Revelation packed a good deal of imagery into a small number of pages; the sketch which began this chapter hardly does justice to the plethora of beasts, candlesticks, and thrones. In addition, books of the Bible like Daniel, Joel, and Isaiah provided additional obscure texts. With so many vague symbols around, why not suppose that expositors picked the ones that suited their purposes, or interpreted the various visions according to the exigencies of current events? Theologians have been able to justify a wide variety of doctrines by citing Scripture, and surely if any book bids fair to be used in an arbitrary way, it is John's Revelation.

If this is the case, then historians ought to use millennial tracts in the same way that psychiatrists use Rorschach inkblots. The blots may tell a psychiatrist much about his patient, but only if they are so amorphous that any meaning may be read into them. Thus when the psychiatrist prepares his diagnosis, he will not list certain blots as *causes* of the patient's malady. In the same way (so the argument might go), millennial tracts could prove to be quite useful as an indication of a person's social stance, but it would be a mistake to see them as a determinant of that stance.

One study that implicitly adopted this attitude was Kenneth Silverman's biography of Timothy Dwight. Silverman

36. T. B. Strandness, *Samuel Sewall: A Puritan Portrait* (East Lansing, Mich., 1967), p. 107.

perceptively noted that there was a strange combination of gloom and hope in Dwight's writings, calling it "his dooms-day rhetoric of broken cisterns" and his "birthday rhetoric of rising empires." He realized that the rhetoric was prophetic in tone, but argued that, basically, it was shaped by the "political and social realities" of the time. "To fully understand [Dwight's] writings, one must translate the broken cisterns into Jefferson or Shays, the rising empires into Washington or Eli Whitney." Thus, these contradictory stances "cannot be explained merely by his having entertained varying theories of history. They resulted from real upheavals in his time."[37] During the patriotic days of the Revolution, Dwight was optimistic about the future; but then Jefferson and infidelity threatened, and he became gloomy. With the Second Great Awakening, things began to look up, and so too did Dwight's interpretations of the prophecies. With "infidelism all but vanquished, he postponed the millennium to sometime around 2000." But not for long. "As the religious revivals changed Dwight the Calvinist into Dwight the enlightened Protestant, the War of 1812 changed him back. It renewed his dormant chiliasm. He gave scriptural prophecies a fatalistic, contemporary reading. . . ."[38] But then, the new health of religion and the settlement of the disestablishment controversy brought out "the long inactive optimistic half" of Dwight, and for the rest of his life he remained faithful to this vision.[39] Thus are prophecies pulled out and polished up according to their fitness for the varying circumstances.

Certainly this hypothesis must be taken seriously. Even contemporaries were aware of the ambiguities of the prophecies. Stanley Griswold, a Connecticut minister who differed with Dwight in matters of politics, also objected to the way

37. Kenneth Silverman, *Timothy Dwight* (New York, 1969), pp. 7–8.
38. Ibid., pp. 113, 137.
39. Ibid., p. 151.

he and others used prophecy. "It has been greatly disgraced
by men's undertaking to construe it *beforehand*," he said.
"If, for instance, all that has been said about the *Revelations
of John*, is to be credited, a more wild, incoherent book
never was written." Some people assumed they could discover God's meanings before the event, but actually they
were only spouting their own "jargon and nonsense."[40] Obviously, we must be ready to admit the possibility that this
strange part of New England lives did not significantly affect
more mundane social relationships.

But there is a reply to this position. Surely the language
and concepts which men inherit actually limit and influence
their response to the world as much as they reflect it. As
Quentin Skinner has remarked in another context, "the
models and preconceptions in terms of which we unavoid-
ably organize and adjust our thoughts will themselves tend to
act as determinants of what we think or perceive."[41] In that
case, prophetic thought deserves to be treated as more than
an obscure religious hobby or an interesting cultural mirror.
And in fact, a number of historians have claimed that understanding millennial thought is a crucial part of understanding
both the intellectual and social history of eighteenth-century
New England.

One of the distinctions these historians have stressed is that
of pre- and postmillennialism. Premillennialists believed that
Christ's coming would take place before—and in fact would
inaugurate—the thousand years of peace and prosperity on
earth. Postmillennialists believed that, even though the spirit
of Christ would be abundant during the millennium, his

40. Griswold MSS Collection, Sermon no. 542, Houghton Library, Harvard University. For an earlier, English example of skepticism, see William Lamont, *Godly
Rule* (London, 1965), p. 21.
41. Quentin Skinner, "Meaning and Understanding in the History of Ideas,"
History and Theory 7, no. 1 (1969):6.

physical Second Coming would not occur until afterward, at the general judgment. In a pioneering study of Jonathan Edwards's eschatology, C. C. Goen concluded that Edwards was the first American to adhere to the postmillennial point of view, which he discovered in the works of English commentators Daniel Whitby and Moses Lowman.[42] Although this "new departure" might not have seemed significant at first, Goen pointed out a number of implications that he felt were important. If the millennium began without Christ, then there was no need to wait for his coming to bring in the kingdom. Action was possible immediately. Furthermore, Edwards's reading of the Revelation construed the terrible prophecy about the slaying of the witnesses as having already taken place, whereas many commentators had previously thought it still in the future, indicating a time of trouble ahead for the church. If Edwards's reading was right, then the faithful had less reason to fear the coming of the kingdom, and would work harder to help usher it in. Thus the postmillennial reading of history became "an integral part of the optimistic activism which was destined to crown with success the 'errand into the wilderness.'"[43]

Goen and others saw this shift as important for several reasons. First, it indicated the connection that was to develop between religious millennialism and more progressive views of man. Though Goen admitted that direct evidence was lacking, he concluded, "it is difficult to believe that Edwards's historicizing of the millennium did not furnish a strong impetus to utopianism in America."[44] In an article published several years earlier, Stow Persons had attempted to point out more specifically the connections between the religious

42. C. C. Goen, "Jonathan Edwards: A New Departure in Eschatology," *Church History* 28, no. 1 (1959):25–40.
43. Ibid., p. 39.
44. Ibid., p. 38.

and the secular ideas of progress. He argued that the two concepts could not be linked merely because of a similarity in
form. Rather, he said, the American Enlightenment initially
rejected the Calvinist view of history in favor of a cyclical approach. But since "the implicit conservatism" of this model
proved a hindrance during and after the Revolution, a new
synthesis emerged. In it, "the idea of progress drew from millennialism its sense of the irreversible secular trend of the
historical process, and from the moralism of the cyclical
theory the assumption that the role of the individual in history was purposive and creative."[45] Another historian,
Ernest Tuveson, also argued that "the idea that progress is
the 'law' of history, that it is ordained, was religious before it
was secular." The basic attributes of an "idea of progress"
could be found "in the [post] millennialist commentaries a
century before Condorcet and Saint-Simon."[46]

The millennial quest supposedly inspired changes in religious as well as secular thought. Although Edwards did not
know it, his millennialism was "of a piece" with the liberal
theology which matured in the nineteenth century. It gave
"encouragement" to the idea that human effort could affect
history, and hence it was "a natural ally to the new doctrine
of human ability which had already begun to make inroads
on the older Calvinism."[47] In contrast to the optimistic, active postmillennialists, premillennialists were gloomy. Said

45. Stow Persons, "The Cyclical Theory of History in Eighteenth Century
America," *American Quarterly* 6, no. 2 (1954):163. Goen's article showed that
Persons was wrong in seeing Edwards and his followers as premillennialists (Per-
sons, p. 149).

46. Ernest Tuveson, *Redeemer Nation* (Chicago, 1968), p. 39. Tuveson's terminology is different but the distinction the same. He called premillennialists "millenarians" and postmillennialists "millennialists." Tuveson traced the European
religious roots of the idea of progress in *Millennium and Utopia* (Berkeley, Calif.,
1949).

47. Goen, "New Departure," pp. 38–39.

Tuveson, "This school believes that 'It is not the intention of God to convert the world before that [second] advent. . . . No radical spiritual change in the condition of the world will take place, on the contrary, it will grow worse and worse, under the present dispensation.' "[48] The faithful could only "separate from an incurably evil world."[49]

These studies raised some crucial issues, but they did not provide a detailed examination of eighteenth-century millennial thought. Tuveson's work treated several centuries, and limitations of space prevented Goen and Persons from doing more than hint at significant trends. Alan Heimert's *Religion and the American Mind* did more than hint. Over five hundred tightly packed pages trace the effects of religious divisions in America from the Great Awakening to the American Revolution, and more briefly on down to the election of Jefferson. Arrayed on opposite sides of the fence are two groups, the Liberals and the Calvinists. Edwards was the acknowledged leader of the latter, and his millennial views provided Heimert with a key to understanding social developments in America after 1740. "The heart and soul of Calvinism," he concluded, "was not doctrine, but an implicit faith that God intended to establish this earthly Kingdom—and to do so within the eighteenth century."[50]

Heimert agreed with Goen that, indeed, Edwards's millennialism was a significant departure. Declensions and jeremiads characterized early eighteenth-century New England, and in a basically pessimistic stance, the Mathers used their chiliasm as the ultimate rhetorical device for bringing worldly colonists to their religious senses.[51] In contrast, "perhaps Edwards'

48. Tuveson, *Redeemer Nation*, p. 34. Tuveson here quoted and accepted a definition in the *Princeton Review* 55 (1879):415.

49. Tuveson, *Redeemer Nation*, p. 35.

50. Alan Heimert, *Religion and the American Mind* (Cambridge, Mass., 1966), p. 66.

51. Ibid., pp. 59–60. Perry Miller also takes this viewpoint in *The New England Mind: From Colony to Province* (Boston, 1961), pp. 187–88.

most impressive achievement was to purge Calvinist millenarianism of all those seventeenth-century elements which were
symptoms of cosmic despair."[52] One reason for this optimism was, as Goen had pointed out, a reinterpretation of the
passages concerning the slain witnesses. But Heimert believed
the experience of the Awakening confirmed and emphasized
the postmillennial belief that the kingdom need not be inaugurated by the supernatural appearance of Christ; and that
this had larger implications in terms of a postmillennial view
of nature and supernature.

According to Heimert, premillennialists saw the end of
time in essentially disjunctive terms. "Cataclysm, providential
judgments, a personal second coming—all . . . represented
dramatic interference in the course of history, abrupt rever-
sals of its flow." Edwards's "high cosmic optimism" was
possible because the millennium did not need a great conflagration and miracles to bring it about. It could be accomplished by natural causes, and especially by "the use of
human instrumentalities."[53] Tuveson proposed the same hypothesis. Postmillennialists believed that "God does not work
through wonders and marvels, but by the established laws of
nature, physical and human. . . . He works with and through
men and their institutions to regenerate the kingdoms of this
world," and thus there was no need for "the *deus ex machina*
of the [pre] millenarians."[54] Edwards all but removed Armageddon from the road to the millennium, whose fulfillment
came in a series of gradual, natural steps which constituted a
"nearly lineal progress."[55]

52. Heimert, *Religion and the American Mind,* p. 64.
53. Ibid., pp. 65, 59.
54. Tuveson, *Redeemer Nation,* pp. 36, 38.
55. Heimert, *Religion and the American Mind,* p. 66. Tuveson's progressivism,
however, might put more emphasis on the cyclical element (*Redeemer Nation,*
p. 33).

Thus Heimert, like other historians, argued that, far from being inconsequential, prophetic thought heavily influenced the outlook of an eighteenth-century New Englander. If he were a premillennialist, he tended to be pessimistic, less active, socially conservative, and inclined toward supernatural and cataclysmic solutions. If he were a postmillennialist, he tended to be optimistic, active, socially progressive, and inclined toward natural, gradualistic solutions.[56] The scheme is logical and neat. It has the virtue of explaining prophetic thought without dismissing it, according it the importance which Mather, Edwards, and others wished to give it in their writings. One question remains, however; and that is, does the theory represent the true picture adequately? Astute readers who have noticed that this is the introduction to the book and not the conclusion, may suppose I have some doubts. The more detailed reasons for them are revealed in subsequent chapters; at this point, only a more general suspicion is discussed.

That suspicion arises partly because the scheme outlined is logical and makes eminent sense. What seems at first a virtue may in the end prove a liability. This is not to say that historians have failed by drawing lines too clearly, by making shades of gray into black and white. Heimert's book, to use only one example, is replete with "to be sure" qualifiers.[57] Nor is it to say that the historian's explanation itself ought to be illogical

56. See also David Smith, "Millenarian Scholarship in America," *American Quarterly* 17 (Fall 1965):535-49. Smith also supports these distinctions. Charles Sanford's *Quest for Paradise* (Urbana, Ill., 1961) is not discussed here because his categories are quite different and suffer from an attempt to work all of Western history into a framework of psychic desire for peace and rest in Nirvana. A valuable beginning bibliography is available in Leroy Froom, *The Prophetic Faith of Our Fathers*, 4 vols. (Washington, D.C., 1946-54), especially vol. 3.

57. E.g. "To be sure, Winthrop did not phrase his argument against Calvinism explicitly in terms of undermining the cosmic support of evangelical optimism." Heimert, *Religion and the American Mind*, p. 72.

and make eminent nonsense. It is, however, possible to write logically about a past figure's illogical conclusions and actions. And as we have seen, eighteenth-century prophetic expositors often thought in strange ways. Perhaps if *we* knew for a fact that the world was going to become more and more sinful, and that Christ alone could save it through his second coming, our logic would lead us to gloomy inactivity. But did premillennialists in New England think that way too? There is good evidence they did not.

In effect, historians must take themselves seriously if they wish to argue that ideas as well as events influence a person's construction of his world: they must realize that they, too, are affected in the same way. When Quentin Skinner spoke, in the passage quoted earlier, of "preconceptions" which tended "to act as determinants of what we think or perceive," he was discussing the problems of historians, not millennialists. In the same article he went on to make another point. He argued that scholars must beware of beginning the history of an idea by setting out "an ideal type of the given doctrine," because it all too easily becomes an entity in itself.

> The reification of doctrines in this way gives rise in turn to . . . a form of non-history which is almost entirely given over to pointing out earlier "anticipations" of later doctrines, and to crediting each writer in terms of this clairvoyance. So Marsilius is notable for his "remarkable anticipation" of Machiavelli; Machiavelli is notable because he "lays the foundation for Marx." . . . And so on.[58]

In the case of millennial thought, the danger is that, even if we avoid substituting our own logic for that of eighteenth-century New Englanders, we use instead the logic of doctrines which Edwards and others were supposedly "anticipating."

58. Skinner, "Meaning and Understanding," pp. 10–12.

Then, their prophetic expositions are seen as being important primarily because they are forerunners of the idea of progress, later radical religious utopianism, or Jeffersonian democracy. When Goen concluded, "Though Edwards knew it not, his historical millennialism was of a piece with the liberalizing thought which came to full flower in the following century," he said something that is more useful for understanding nineteenth-century liberal thought than for discovering Edwards's own intentions. Goen properly made the distinction clear in his clause, "Though Edwards knew it not." But it is less clear in Heimert's discussion of Edwards's radicalism. At one point, Heimert first quoted Edwards's belief that God's great design had to do with rational creatures and not animals or "lifeless things," and then claimed that this "principle" was "Edwards' special contribution to radicalism." The statement pretends to tell us something about Edwards, but does it? If he did use the principle for radical purposes, it does; but if his "contribution" was only to enunciate a principle others would later use (in this case, "his ideological heirs, the spokesmen of the early American democracy"), it may indicate something about later radicals but leaves us uninformed about the reason why Edwards made the statement.[59]

If prophetic expositors in eighteenth-century New England are to be understood properly, the connections between prophecy and the more concrete world must be their own, and not ones formulated by twentieth-century logic or nineteenth-century millennialists. Perhaps to attempt a complete escape of our own "models and preconceptions" is to attempt

59. Heimert, *Religion and the American Mind*, p. 64. One might also be tempted to wonder who in eighteenth-century America *did* think God's great design was directed primarily toward animals and lifeless things.

60. Skinner, "Meaning and Understanding," p. 53. Peter Berger discussed the connotations of ecstasy in similar terms, in *Invitation to Sociology* (New York, 1963), pp. 136–38.

the impossible: a perspective of history above time, vouch-safed only to God—or through the ecstasy of revelation, to men like John. The historian's means are more modest; and any "re-velation," unveiling of the past, will not come from being in the spirit on the sabbath. Yet the root of the word *ecstasy* is the Greek *ekstasis*, a stepping outside of oneself; which may well indicate a process worth pursuing. If, as Quentin Skinner noted, it is a commonplace "that our own society places unrecognized constraints upon our imaginations," then "It deserves . . . to become a commonplace that the historical study of the ideas of other societies should be undertaken as the indispensable and the irreplaceable means of placing limits on those constraints.

Strange as prophetic expositors may seem to historians, both groups would agree that one can understand the present only by getting outside of it. Men like Mather, Edwards, and Dwight attempted to get outside of theirs by viewing the world from the perspective of God's history of redemption, and we turn now to look more closely at the consequences of their efforts.

2

Chronology

DECIPHERING THE OBSCURE

The argument thus far has led to two not very helpful conclusions: first, biblical prophecies seemed important to many eighteenth-century New Englanders; and second, prophecies and expositions of them are strange to us. Obviously, we cannot draw any conclusions about the larger significance of prophetic thought until we make more intelligible the logic and terminology of eighteenth-century interpreters. To accomplish this requires a careful, sometimes arduous, reading of the tracts and sermons dealing with the obscurities in the Revelation and other prophetic writings. Precisely because the subject matter is obscure and unfamiliar, the danger of misinterpreting what New Englanders wrote on the Revelation is as great as the danger of expositors misinterpreting the Revelation itself. A few examples sufficiently indicate the need for caution.

Naturally, the historian interested in millennial thought will want to know how far ministers and theologians thought God had progressed in his grand scheme of salvation. Was the world nearing its end, with Christ's second coming imminent? Longer treatises often discussed in detail prophetic numerical allusions, such as the 1,260 days of the woman in the wilderness or Daniel's seventy weeks. In that case, the writers' speculations were usually clear enough; but not all sermons were as specific. Sometimes New England preachers would merely assure their readers that they were living in the "last

times" or the "latter days." Nicholas Noyes, in 1698, referred
to the times as "these last ages of the professing world"; and
not many years later Benjamin Colman claimed that certainly
"we live in the *last Days*."[1] The phrase sounds quite eschatological and expectant; yet Colman's italics indicated a biblical
origin that made its exact meaning ambiguous. The Apostle
Paul had originally used the term in referring to his own
times, a fact which the context of the biblical passage made
clear. Hence later scholars generally concluded that "the
whole days of the Gospel, since that glorious triumph of
[Christ's resurrection] . . . be upon the Scripture's reckoning
the last times."[2] Another respected interpreter explained that
"the latter times" could mean either the period just before
Christ's coming, or else, more generally, the Christian era,
since "the *times* wherein *Saint Paul lived*, and all the times of
Christianity [were] the *last times*, and so stiled in Scripture."
Even when the phrase meant the last times in a more limited
sense, it could still encompass a period of several hundred
years.[3]

Colman's use of biblical phraseology throughout his sermons
was, of course, standard practice. For New Englanders, scriptural passages strengthened the sermon's argument; for modern readers, they sometimes confuse the meaning, especially
when prophecies are involved. The Revelation talks of darkened suns, falling stars, slain and resurrected witnesses. The
meaning of these phrases is not immediately clear; yet considering the distinctions historians have drawn, it is crucial to
know whether or not New Englanders believed the sun would
really darken, or the witnesses would literally rise from the

1. Nicholas Noyes, *New England's Duty . . . to Be a Mountain of Holiness* (Boston, 1698), p. 7. Benjamin Colman, *Practical Discourses* 2d ed. (Boston, 1747),
p. 339.

2. Robert Fleming, *The Fulfilling of the Scriptures* (Boston, 1743), p. 492.

3. Joseph Mede, *Apostacy of the Latter Times* (London, 1641), p. 66.

dead. Expositors claimed that they preferred to take the literal sense of Scripture wherever possible, but often enough they found sufficient obstacles and had to opt for a "figurative" or "mystical" sense. Joseph Sewall preached a sermon on the suddenness of Christ's coming, and noted Peter's statement "that in that Day, *The Heavens shall pass away with a great Noise, and the Elements melt with a Fervent Heat*." The passage augurs catastrophe on a wide scale; fortunately Sewall explained that scholars differed on its meaning. Some, indeed, felt that it indicated the substance of the world "shall wholly perish"; yet others thought it meant only the destruction of Jerusalem and the Jewish nation. Sewall himself seems to have thought the prophecy might have a double application, the destruction of Jerusalem being a prefiguring of the final "Day of Universal Doom; when in a literal sense, the Elements shall melt with fervent heat."[4] Other ministers were not always as helpful as Sewall, and sometimes—especially in sermons rather than formal expositions—they contented themselves with biblical allusions unadorned by further explanation.

In any case, it seems evident that the first step in unraveling the meaning of millennial thought consists of trying to establish more clearly the particular order and nature of events which New Englanders (and the English expositors they consulted) thought the Scriptures foretold for the latter part of the "last days."[5] The best way to interpret the strangeness of millennialists and their sermons is by watching *them* interpret the strangeness of the original biblical prophecies.

The prophecies were, in fact, almost as strange to them as

4. Joseph Sewall, *The Certainty and Suddenness of Christ's Coming* (Boston, 1716), p. 3.

5. New England divines were quite conscious of the work their English predecessors and contemporaries had done in apocalyptic matters. It has proved impossible to cover all of the English millennial tracts that New Englanders used, but I do include here the sources cited most often.

they are to us. Some divines thought them so mysterious that they were better left alone, one noting that Calvin "had Expounded all the Books of the Scripture except the Revelation, which his not doing of, was an excellent commentary."[6] In New England, Benjamin Colman did not disapprove of all speculation, but he felt that God had purposely hidden the times of prophecies' accomplishments, in part "to teach us *Modesty* in our *Enquiries* after them."[7] Another New Englander, perhaps reacting to one of Cotton Mather's hopeful sermons, made the point even more strongly by listing in the *New England Courant* a number of predictions by European fanatics which had since proved wrong but in their time had captured the fancies of "whole Hords of the Vulgar." As further ridicule, he included the case of a canny Scotsman who had first predicted that only ninety-two years remained before the end of the earth, and then later complained to the king when His Majesty refused to grant him lands for a term of five hundred years. "God a my soul!" the king was quoted as saying, "that is Four Hundred Years more than the World shall last, and would you hold my Lands in the world to come?" The writer to the *Courant* concluded that Christians ought to be less solicitous about establishing the world's final hour and more about leading holy lives.[8]

It was natural enough that those who wished to leave prophecies alone felt they were obscure, but even those who wrote expositions admitted the fact. Countless introductions stressed the difficulties of making sense of the Revelation, and only with diffidence hazarded guesses about events yet to be fulfilled. Some of this, of course, was rhetoric of the humble-pie variety, trotted out for the introduction and for-

6. Thomas Philpot, *A Defence of the Illustrations*, preface; bound with *A New Systeme of the Apocalypse* (London, 1688).

7. Colman, *Practical Discourses*, p. 341.

8. Anonymous letter, *New England Courant*, September 18, 1721.

gotten once the writer had plunged into the heady conjectures of the text. Henry More, an English interpreter, made only a perfunctory nod in the direction of prophetic obscurity, and even before the preface was out, claimed that, although he found nearly eighty flaws in Grotius's commentary, he doubted "any one should be able to find one in my whole Exposition"![9] But such confidence was not usual, and for a good reason: everybody acknowledged that prophecies by their very nature were meant to be obscure. Any modern reader who is used to thinking of prediction as being valid only if it is made specifically and before the event, can certainly see how prophetic forecasts were easily malleable in imaginative hands. But were all these eminent divines so obtuse that they failed to notice how convenient it was to have a vague prophecy ready to fit the circumstances?

In fact, they were not. They believed that in human hands at least, prophecy was not to be confused with prediction. The essence of any prophecy—in Greek as well as Christian tradition—was that its true meaning would be hidden from men until after its accomplishment. Isaac Newton, the man who excelled all others in predicting the motions of the solar system, made the distinction quite clear in his own study of the prophecies:

> The folly of Interpreters has been, to foretel times and things by [prophecies], as if God designed to make them Prophets. . . . The design of God was much otherwise . . . he gave [them] not to gratify men's curiosities, by enabling them to foreknow things, but that after they were fulfilled they might be interpreted by the event.[10]

The observation was a commonplace among prophetic expos-

9. Henry More, *Apocalypsis Apocalypseos* (London, 1680), p. xv.
10. Isaac Newton, *Observations on the Prophecies of Daniel and the Apocalypse of Saint John* (London, 1733), p. 251.

itors, one New Englanders knew was "agreed upon by all sober Divines and Christians."[11]

Why, then, did so many sober ministers persist in trying to unravel what they agreed were unravelable mysteries? In the first place, the Revelation and other prophecies were accepted as part of Holy Scripture, and Scripture was designed by God to be of use to his people. Men ought not to reject out of hand that which God had so graciously bestowed: had not Jesus himself closed the Revelation by saying, "Blessed is he that keepeth the sayings of the prophecy of this book"? So it was entirely natural for Samuel Lee, like many others, to argue that God "thought meet to write these things, and who art thou, vile worm, to say to him *what dost thou*?"[12] In addition, many centuries had passed since John received the Apocalypse, and expositors were convinced that, indeed, many of the prophecies had already been fulfilled, thus being legitimately "interpreted by the event." As Newton and others pointed out, Daniel had prophesied a time at the end of the world when "many shall run to and fro and knowledge shall be encreased." Since this and the rest of the prophecy referred to the "last age" of the world, Newton wrote, "it makes for the credit of the Prophecy, that it is not yet understood. But if the last age . . . be now approaching, as by the great successes of late Interpreters it seems to be, we have more encouragement than ever to look into these things."[13]

Of course, these justifications did not solve the problem; they merely changed the question. If the only prophecies that could be known were ones that had been fulfilled, how did one decide which these were? Supposedly the events themselves would make that obvious, but as John Danforth noted,

11. John Higginson, "Epistle Dedicatory," p. 6; in Noyes, *New England's Duty.*

12. Samuel Lee, *Dissertation Concerning the Place and State of the Dispersed Tribes of Israel* (London, 1677), p. 126.

13. Newton, *Observations*, pp. 250–51.

"The Diversity of Conjecture about the meaning of some of the abstruse *Hieroglyphicks* of Heaven . . . in the Writings of *our Worthies*, shews 'em still to be men, and that as yet they know but in part." Anyone who browsed through Matthew Poole's *Synopsis* of the various interpretations knew that Danforth was right.[14] What may have been an offhand comment actually struck right at the central issue: diversity seemed to prove that interpreters were, after all, still only men, and what they had hoped could pass as infallible truth obviously was in part based on private wishes or imperfect knowledge.

Again, the problem was not one that expositors overlooked. In apostolic times, Peter had warned his fellow Christians that "no prophecy of the scripture is of any private interpretation"; and the Revelation contained a final admonition that "If any man shall add unto these things, God shall add unto him plagues that are written in this book." But recognizing the problem was easier than actually doing something about it; and that was why Joseph Mede's little book, *Clavis Apocalyptica* (issued in 1627 and translated into English by order of Commons in 1642), made more than the usual stir. The *Key to the Revelation*, along with subsequent studies, established Mede as a major prophetic interpreter. Increase Mather echoed the sentiments of many when he said that, out of all the interpreters he had consulted, Mede "excells all."[15]

There were several reasons for this attention and respect. Unlike most other expositors, Mede devoted the majority of his life to the study of the prophecies. Born in 1586, he learned Hebrew while still quite young, and in 1602 entered Christ's College, Cambridge. In temperament he was ex-

14. John Danforth, *Judgment Begun at the House of God* (Boston, 1716), p. 94. Matthew Poole, *Synopsis Criticorum Aliorumque Commentatorum*, 2 vols. (London, 1669–76).

15. Increase Mather, *Dissertation Wherein the Strange Doctrine* . . . (Boston, 1708), p. 109.

tremely shy and abhorred controversy; consequently, he
never made a reputation as a polemicist or defender of the
faith. Problems with stuttering, which "rendered his expression painful to himself, and less pleasing to others," closed
the possibilities of a brilliant preaching career, and Mede
settled down to a life of study as a fellow at Christ's College.
His own diffidence caused him to publish only two more
works during his career, but after his death in 1638 (very
likely hastened by remedies which passed for medicine in
those days) his letters and unpublished manuscripts were
gathered together and published in the collected *Works of the
Pious and Profoundly Learned Joseph Mede*, the majority of
which was devoted to prophetic speculation.[16]

Mede won attention partly because this kind of speculation
was novel at the time. Augustine had begun a long tradition
which interpreted the thousand years of Satan's binding as
beginning at the time of Christ's resurrection, and hence
already past. Mede's new conclusions were soon abroad "by a
rumour spread of his opinion, concerning the glorious Kingdome of Christ here on earth, which many hundred yeares
agoe was cryed down, as the Errour of the Millennaries."[17]
Although a few other theologians had made conjectures
about a millennium still to come, Mede was the first eminent
Englishman to revive the belief that the martyrs' thousand-
year reign would take place on earth before its final destruction.[18] The *Clavis* first voiced these speculations in 1627, but

16. John Worthington, ed., *Works of the Pious and Profoundly Learned Joseph
Mede*(London, 1672). I have drawn most biographical information from the *Life*
included in this edition. It seems to confirm the title of the collection. See also
Richard G. Clouse, "The Rebirth of Millenarianism," in Peter Toon, ed., *Puritans,
The Millennium and the Future of Israel; Puritan Eschatology 1600–60* (Cam-
bridge, Eng., 1970), pp. 42–65.

17. William Twisse, in the preface to Mede, *Apostacy of the Latter Times*.

18. John Piscator had already suggested a future reign in heaven; and John
Henry Alsted had moved that to earth but put it after the Last Judgment. See
Twisse's preface to Mede, *Apostacy*.

even fifteen years later, when Commons received a report on the advisability of having it translated, a London minister concluded,

> though Master *Medes* opinion concerning the thousand years of the seventh Trumpet be singular from that which hath beene most generally received by Expositors of best esteem, and I conceive hath no just ground, yet he therein delivers his judgement with such modestie and moderation that I think the Printing of it will not be perillous.[19]

Mede's writings were soon winning converts with increasing speed, but not primarily because his novel ideas of the millennium proved irresistible. As we shall see, a good deal of variety still existed on that score. What gained Mede a respect that went beyond the initial interest in his new ideas was the nature of the "Key" he provided for interpreting the prophecies. Too many scholars failed to consider the internal evidence and order of the Revelation, he argued; they assumed that the events followed one another in the order in which they appeared in John's book. But surely that was a naïve assumption: even the slightest look at the narratives of contemporary chroniclers and historians showed that one hardly ever used such a rule when writing history. Narratives usually had a section dealing with the doings of kings and politics, followed by another covering religious history for the period, and so forth. Since the events in the Revelation were more obscure, the first task was to find where such divisions occurred, in order to "synchronize" the various prophecies that referred to the same time periods.[20]

19. Joseph Mede, *The Key of the Revelation* (London, 1643). The pagination of this report is unclear, since in the Yale University Library copy, the unnumbered page has been torn from its original place. The *Key* itself is divided into two parts, each separately paginated, although bound as one volume.

20. Mede may well have coined the term. His editor noted that "The glory of the First discovering these *Synchronisms* is peculiarly due to Mr. Mede"; and the *Oxford English Dictionary* lists his work as the earliest incidence of "synchro-

Accordingly, Mede presented a series of seven key synchronisms which helped to make sense out of the Revelation. The woman remaining in the wilderness for 1,260 days, for instance, referred to the same time period as the 1,260 days when the witnesses were prophesying in sackcloth, and the forty-two months when the beast was said to rule. When these synchronisms had been identified, it became clearer that the bulk of the Revelation was "distributed into two principall prophecies, either of which proceedeth from the same time, and endeth in the same period."[21] The first was the book that John saw, which was bound with seven seals and contained the visions of the seals and the trumpets. These dealt primarily with political and secular events from the days of John to the Last Judgment. The remaining prophecies were taken from the "little book" mentioned in Revelation 10, and covered the same time; only they referred more particularly to the story of the church and its struggle with the beasts, consummated by the pouring of the seven vials.[22]

To modern eyes, the results of Mede's system seem prosaic enough; but to expositors who delved through the many pages of the Pious and Profoundly Learned *Works*, it seemed as if Mede had gone a long way toward establishing a firm ground for prophetic explanation. Here was a system which could answer the accusation that prophecies were continually subject to the private whims of interpreters. The synchronisms kept such whims in check; but "without such foundation," Mede concluded, "thou shalt scarce draw anything out of the Revelation . . . which resteth upon divine authority, but [rather] upon begged principles, and meere humane conjectures."[23]

---

nize" (although other writers had used various forms of the root and combination—always within a prophetic context—as early as 1588).

21. Mede, *Key*, pt. 1, pp. 2, 13.

22. Ibid., p. 13.

23. Ibid., p. 27.

Readers of the *Key* found the tools used to arrive at these synchronisms equally impressive. Since Mede had an acquaintance with the Hebrew, Greek, Syriac, and Chaldean languages, he was able to compare original texts, and "he found by good experience that some Scriptures do excellently illustrate others where the like Expressions are to be found." This linguistic approach led him to assert what modern biblical scholars now accept: that "the Style of the New Testament doth frequently imitate the Construction and Propriety of the *Hebrew* in the Old." Furthermore, Mede logically assumed that since the prophetic symbols were originally taken from a culture quite different from his own, the best interpretations of such phrases would come from men of the same culture. Thus he studied Chaldean paraphrases of Scripture (in the Targum) and came to some revealing conclusions. When the biblical prophets, for instance, announced that God's judgments were "to come upon all the *Cedars* and *Oaks*, Esay [Isaiah 3] . . . the *Targum* instead of mentioning these tall and goodly Trees has . . . Princes of the People and Rulers of Provinces."[24] To further buttress his arguments, Mede in 1632 expanded the scope of the *Clavis* to include a wealth of historical evidence based on his familiarity with Roman history and the customs of the "Ethnick Antiquities."[25]

In short, Mede's rigorous and scholarly method impressed scholars, and they, too, concluded that a system of interpretive rules was the thing needed to systematize prophetic study. Without such guidelines, argued one English minister, everyone would be forced to "look upon the Prophecies as things of no Authority, which may be applied to any event according to the cunning and fancy of an Interpreter."[26] A French Protestant, whose commentary was read by English

24. John Worthington, general preface, in Mede, *Works*.
25. Clouse, "The Rebirth of Millenarianism," p. 60.
26. Peter Allix, *Two Treatises* (London, 1707), p. viii.

and New Englanders alike, amplified the argument by comparing prophetic methods with those used in other scientific endeavors:

> When we are to learn crabbed and abstruse Sciences, we begin with Common Notions, and with principles which are the most evident: and so we proceed by degrees till we have advanced into, and have conquered that which is more sublime and difficult. . . . And if we take the same course in our search into the *Apocalyptic Mysteries*, there will remain little but what we may master and unravel.[27]

As a result of this attitude, others were soon following Mede's example.

Some scholars chose to set out their axioms in advance, so that the exposition could proceed in an orderly fashion. William Whiston, professor of Mathematics at Cambridge and popularizer of Newton's scientific discoveries, provided his readers with a series of "preparatory *Observations* as will be of great use all along": a preface that took fully a third of the book. One of Whiston's primary concerns was to put the results of historical and scientific research to work in order to make chronological predictions in the prophecies more exactly translatable into specific terms. Hence, his rules established such propositions as:

> Jewish Prophecies use a *year* for a *year*.
> Christian Prophecies use a *day* for a *year*.
> The Stile of both follow the custom of the Age and Nation of each Prophet.
> Prophecies often use the past tense for the future.
> Prophecies sometimes Disorder'd in our present Copies;
> If the true Order were restor'd they would then be much easier.[28]

27. Philpot, *A New Systeme*, preface.
28. William Whiston, *Accomplishment of Scripture Prophecies* (London, 1708), table of contents.

The end results of this precision were undoubtedly deceptive in their exactness, but at least they were formulated by a rigorous mind. Not all expositors had equal talent, and some similar attempts resulted in a series of dubious propositions. The general formulations by Peter Allix sounded suspiciously like the specific points he later planned to prove. ("A Prophecy which supposes the distinction of the People into two Kingdoms, cannot be supposed to be fulfilled, but at a time when they are actually distinguished into two Kingdoms.")[29]

More often, interpreters did not bother to codify their premises, and merely produced them as the various occasions warranted. Thomas Goodwin agreed with other interpreters in asserting that prophecies often had two fulfillings, the first being a weaker forerunner of the later accomplishment. Increase Mather noted the commonplace that the literal meaning of a prophecy must always be taken "if it will stand with the Analogy of Faith," and quoted a "Law of opposites" which demanded that parallel incidents (ones which "opposed each other, like the first and second Resurrection in the Revelation) must be interpreted in similar ways, either literally or allegorically.[30]

The upshot of all this theorizing was both reassuring and disquieting. Prophetic scholars had dealt with a most serious problem and emerged confident that their methods had provided an objectivity able to rise above private whims. They could now clothe their speculations with a vocabulary of abstruse concepts and seeming exactness which at times rivals the jargon of a modern social scientist. ("The preconsideration of the ruine of the *Roman* Empire conducts to the expectation of the great devastations and confusions in the Papal. The fuller indagation of these periods belonging to another

29. Allix, *Two Treatises*, pp. x–xi.

30. Thomas Goodwin, *Exposition of the Revelation* in *Works* (Edinburgh, 1886), 3: 155–56; Increase Mather, *Dissertation Concerning the Future Conversion* (London, 1709), p. 19.

paper; I return to Israel.")[31] Yet the solution was still a disquieting one, perhaps precisely because it worked so well in
theory. General rules, even if they were derived correctly,
had to be applied to specific cases. To prove their real worth,
they would have to succeed at untangling the mystifying collection of prophetic allusions in a way that everyone could
agree upon; otherwise, the accusation of the skeptics could
be applied with equal force to the rules and applications
themselves.

This objection, in its more sophisticated form, was one that
most expositors were less able to deal with, perhaps in part
because most of them failed to perceive the force of it. Unfortunately, historians cannot afford to overlook the problem,
although for different reasons. For if all the divines failed in
their efforts to establish a uniform interpretation of the Revelation, does this not imperil the attempts of scholars to
find any consistent eschatological social outlook among eighteenth-century interpreters? If the canons of interpretation
succeeded only in producing conflicting scenarios of the last
days, then perhaps the historians who saw millennial tales as
mere Rorschach blots have an excellent case after all.

DIVERSITY IN OLD AND NEW ENGLAND

As we have seen, England produced a host of expositors
who proposed their own solutions to the prophetic puzzles. Thus New England divines had at their disposal—and
used—many of these commentaries as guides in preparing
their own opinions. What they found when they examined
the interpretations available to them was not the unanimity
everyone hoped that a strict use of rules would produce. If,
as many suspected, these were the days when knowledge was
indeed "running to and fro" over the globe, it was, in its

31. Lee, *Dissertation Concerning the Place and State*, p. 121.

haste, being careless about how the searchers of Scripture were enlightened.

Mede, whom everyone respected, had ventured one version of the drama. It opened with the first six seals, which were the judgments of Christ upon the pagan Roman empire. The first was obviously the blow struck against its power by Christ's resurrection itself, and from thence, the empire fell slowly but surely, as internal slaughters, wars, pestilence, and famine were meted out periodically under the seals.[32] The last of these encompassed an even greater seven-fold plague, described by the seven trumpets. This consisted of a long series of invasions, from the barbarian Huns and Vandals down to the Saracens, Arabs, and Turks.[33] This dreary procession of secular history ended with the seventh trumpet's thousand-year reign. Meanwhile, the open-book prophecy explained what had been going on at the same time in the church. The dream about the heavenly woman giving birth to a son meant, not Christ himself, but the "*mysticall Christ, or Christ formed in his members.*"[34] The faithful, though threatened by the red dragon of pagan Rome, were delivered by Constantine, clearly the meaning of the child's being caught up to God's throne. Despite this good fortune, the woman was still driven into the wilderness, where she waited for 1,260 days; and of course, the Whore of Babylon who kept her there was none other than the Roman Catholic church.

Mede's synchronisms had made it clear that these 1,260 days were the same time in which the witnesses were prophesying in sackcloth, and this fitted admirably into his scheme. But what was meant by their slaying and resurrec-

32. Mede, *Key*, pt. 1, pp. 40–67.

33. Of the seven trumpets, the last three were specifically called "woe trumpets." This could be confusing at times, since, for example, the Saracens and Arabs might be said to be either under the fifth trumpet or the first woe trumpet, and the Turks under either the sixth trumpet or the second woe trumpet.

34. Mede, *Key*, pt. 2, p. 37.

tion at the end of that period? Mede thought these events were still to come, but he was convinced that such words as *slaughter* and *death* were to be interpreted "metaphorically or analogically."[35] The same held true for their resurrection, "because no resurrection properly so called can be before the coming of Christ under the seventh Trumpet." Since the witnesses' revival came under the sixth, Mede interpreted their death as a "dejection of them from the office and place which they a little while had gotten in the reformed Church." In some cases, persecution by Catholics would mean death for individuals, but as a whole the prophecy referred to the political misfortunes of the church. After the three and a half years when they lay symbolically dead in the street, "a great commotion of the Nations, and alteration of Politique affaires" would take place, "whereby indeed a way is opened for the Witnesses, and power given them of reviving, with so great increase of dignitie and authoritie."[36]

Mede had to deal with one more set of plagues: the pouring of the seven vials. The Revelation made it clear that they destroyed the Roman Catholic whore, but exactly what each stood for was less certain. Mede guessed that the first had been poured when Wyclif and Huss bore witness to Rome's sin, and the second, when Luther once again revived the true faith. Queen Elizabeth's statutes against Catholics in England seemed the likeliest candidate for the third; but "the rest," concluded Mede, "remain to be poured out." He conjectured that the fourth, poured on the sun, would perhaps refer to Rome's loss of influence over the German empire. After that, the witnesses would be resurrected and the fifth vial emptied on Rome itself, the seat of the beast. The sixth vial would signal an end to the desolation by the Turks, whose stronghold was the Euphrates River. And since they were also

35. Ibid., p. 14.
36. Ibid., pp. 15, 24–25.

responsible for the sixth trumpet, their downfall would mark the end of that period.[37]

At the same time, the Jews—so long scattered and dispersed throughout the world—would be converted and return to their original home. Just how this improbable event would be accomplished was the source of much speculation among divines. Mede's own theory was that their conversion would be, like the apostle Paul's, accomplished by a miracle. "That of the *Jews* may be like it; *viz.* That though many were present with S. *Paul* at that time, yet none saw the apparition of Christ, nor heard him speak, but *Paul* alone."[38] And one way or another, the Jews would make their way home, perhaps aiding in the defeat of the Turkish foe at the same time.

All that remained before Christ's earthly triumph was the seventh vial, which Mede predicted would dramatically inaugurate the millennial reign. And this would be "not with a humane arme now any more, but with a heavenly and thunder striking revenge." At that point, Christ would appear "from heaven in flaming fire," and the ensuing conflagration would act to refine the world until it became a new heaven and earth.[39] Revelation 20:5 referred to a "first resurrection," which Mede believed was the beginning of the Last Judgment. His first inclination had been to interpret it as "*a rising of the Church from a dead estate* . . . yet afterward more seriously considering and weighing all things, I found no ground or footing for any sense but the Literal."[40]

This interpretation suggested that the thousand-year reign was to be enjoyed by immortal martyrs alone, raised early from the dead as a reward for their sufferings through persecution. But Mede felt the situation was more complicated:

37. Ibid., pp. 115–20.
38. Mede, *Works*, pp. 766–67.
39. Mede, *Key*, pt. 2, p. 121; Mede, *Works*, pp. 613–18.
40. Mede, *Works*, p. 770.

the Revelation spoke not only of the New Jerusalem but also of "Nations that are saved" which would "walk in the light of [the] New Jerusalem."[41] Thus he made a distinction between the risen martyrs who reigned in the new heavens and those "faithful servants of God who shall be found here alive at Christ's coming." The latter, though they would escape the fire, would still remain to live out their mortal lives on the new earth.[42] At the end of the thousand years, their progeny would face the forces of Gog and Magog, when Satan was let loose for the last time.

Where these evil forces would come from was a problem, and Mede hazarded a guess that America might do. It was a place remote from the central drama, and perhaps the conflagration would not have reached there, leaving the land as an unrefined blot in an otherwise blissful world. Mede's friend William Twisse liked the idea, and commented that "the grounds you go upon, for aught I see, are as good as the world can afford." Despite what optimists might think, the Indians appeared to be prime candidates for Satan's final army. And ironically, "Were it not for Christians that live amongst them, they could neither have notice of the glory of new *Jerusalem*, nor ever in all likelihood attain either to the Art of Shipbuilding and Navigation, or Art military, to fit them for such an Expedition as you speak of." Mede was diffident about these conjectures, calling them mere "Fancies"; but Twisse thought they were "sage conceits."[43]

Mede urged caution on one other subject, and that was the presence of Christ during the thousand years. "No doubt" it would be "glorious and evident," he said; "yet I dare not so much as imagine (which some Ancients seem to have thought)

41. Rev. 21:24.
42. Mede, *Key*, preface; Mede, *Works*, p. 604.
43. Mede, *Works*, p. 809; see also pp. 574–76.

that it should be a *Visible Converse* upon earth."[44] Christ's proper place was on his kingly throne in heaven. What Mede meant by a visible appearance was the same thing he meant when discussing Christ's appearance to the Jews at their latter-day conversion; his literal second coming would take place only when Gog and Magog were vanquished and the universal resurrection accomplished. Then the wicked as well as those other saints who had not been raised earlier would come forward to be judged, and the final scene would be played out as writers had traditionally imagined it.

The scheme was a grand one, backed by years of study; it no doubt helped to shape the general contours of prophetic interpretation in the following years. Certainly Mede was instrumental in Protestant efforts to put the millennium back in the future. Only a few years after the English translation of the *Key*, John Lightfoot felt compelled to speak against "the millenary opinion which I cannot but judge erroneous," which he was afraid might "go on altogether uncontrolled."[45] But Lightfoot was fighting a losing battle. Expositors generally accepted the idea of a future reign, as well as Mede's central division of the Revelation into the simultaneous prophecies of the sealed and the little opened books.

But beyond these general areas, it was not easy to find agreement.[46] One of the most troublesome problems was trying to fathom the specific meaning of the seven vials. Thomas Goodwin, writing not long after Mede's work first appeared, followed him more closely than anyone else, but still disagreed

44. Ibid., p. 603.

45. *The Whole Works of the Rev. John Lightfoot* (London, 1882), 6:165.

46. A few interpreters even challenged some of Mede's general points. William Whiston claimed that it was wrong to limit the sealed book to secular affairs and the little open book to ecclesiastical ones (*Essay on the Revelation* [London, 1706], pp. 42-61). Peter Allix thought the great master did well enough with John's prophecies but had misread Old Testament predictions by depending too much on rabbinical traditions (*Two Treatises*, p. 66).

on details. (He thought, for instance, that the third vial probably referred to the defeat of the Spanish Armada.)[47] Others
were more cautious in their hopes. Samuel Lee, a divine who
spent part of his later life in New England, wrote in 1677
that not one of the vials had yet been poured. Three years
later, Henry More agreed with him, arguing that Mede had
mistakenly placed the plagues under the sixth trumpet, whereas they rightly belonged to the seventh.[48] Thomas Philpot
also thought them still to come, but had a different list of
calamities for each.[49] He argued strongly for his system partly in order to refute a treatise by another French pastor who
argued that *all* the vials had been poured out.[50]

To complicate matters, the slaying and rising of the witnesses had to be fitted in somewhere. Fortunately, virtually
everyone agreed that the prophecy warranted a metaphorical
reading. "Their resurrection is not from a natural death," reasoned Goodwin, and "therefore such not their killing."[51] But
when would this take place? Some (Goodwin, More, and
Jurieu among them) agreed it would be in the midst of the
pouring of the vials; others (like Philpot and Benjamin Keach)
hoped for a resurrection before any of them had been loosed.
But to divide interpreters into two camps on this point is
deceptive. Although both Goodwin and More placed the
resurrection in the midst of the vials, since their schedules of
specific vials differed, Goodwin left the resurrection for the

47. Goodwin, *Works*, 3:101-08.

48. Lee, *Dissertation*, p. 115; More, *Apocalypsis*, p. 249. Whiston also judged
them yet unpoured.

49. E.g. the first simply meant a loss of papal revenues, and Rome's fall had
been placed earlier, under the third vial. Philpot, *A New Systeme*, pp. 253 ff.
and 98.

50. Pierre Jurieu, *The Accomplishment of the Scripture Prophecies* (London,
1687).

51. Goodwin, *Works*, 3:164.

future, while More set it at the remarkably early date of 1517 and the Reformation.[52]

Nor were opinions any more unanimous about the particulars of Christ's arrival. Whiston and others rejected Mede's belief that the extension of the seventh trumpet spanned the entire millennial reign, but this change was one of detail rather than substance. Whiston still had a dramatic conflagration, not to mention his own theory on its ignition by the fiery tail of a passing comet.[53] If anything, Whiston's version of the fire was even more spectacular than Mede's, since he did not exempt any part of the earth from the flames. But another interpreter, Drue Cressener, went in the other direction by supposing that the fire itself would be restricted to the center of sin, Italy, and would continue throughout the thousand years as "the means of keeping [the inhabitants] in a more constant and strict observance of their Duty."[54] Other expositors challenged the notion that any fires at all would come before the millennium. "I know it is supposed by some that the Conflagration will be but a *Purgation,* and not a *destruction* of the creatures," said William Allen, alluding to Mede's theory. But he felt that the Apostle Peter had "put the matter beyond all doubt or dispute," that the conflagration would occur not for purposes of purification at the first resurrection, but for destruction "at the last judgment of ungodly men." Henry More came to the same conclusion in his own studies.[55]

But while More and Allen agreed about the conflagration, they had radically different notions about the millennium it-

52. Ibid., p. 154; More, *Apocalypsis,* pp. 111, 154 ff.; see also Benjamin Keach, *Antichrist Stormed* (London, 1689), pp. 156 ff.

53. William Whiston, *A New Theory of the Earth* (London, 1696). Whiston's theory is discussed at greater length below, chapter 3.

54. Drue Cressener, *The Judgments of God upon the Roman Catholic Church* (London, 1689), pp. 288–301; 301.

55. William Allen, *Of the State of the Church in Future Ages* (London, 1684), p. 296. More, *Apocalypsis*, p. 259, and chronological chart, p. 256.

self. Allen saw it as virtually paradisiacal. The Bible had said
that all creatures would find deliverance from the bondage of
corruption; since this did not seem to come at the Last Judgment, Allen argued, "then there is no time can be assigned
for it so likely, as the time of Christ's universal kingdom upon
earth." Thus, he predicted that the soil would be more fertile
in those days, and that perhaps even Isaiah's prophecy about
the lion lying down with the lamb could be taken literally.[56]
More's view was less exalted. Satan certainly would be bound
for a thousand years, but the chains the angel would use were
the powers of legislation, "which are bonds and iron chains
to tye up the wicked from doing mischief." These laws would
be so "rigid, severe and inviolable" that no one would dare to
do anything "really Profane, Wicked, or Antichristian."[57]

Thus, for More, Christ's coming to earth was only a spiritual
one. True, the martyrs would be raised before the millennium,
but they would live with Christ in heaven, not on earth.[58]
Philpot echoed More's definition of the kingdom as a spiritual
reign: "Whensoever the Jews come to be brought home, and
all *Nations* converted; it will then appear so clearly, that Jesus
Christ is come into the world, that if he should descend from
heaven unto the Earth, we could not be more convinced."
This position went a step beyond Mede's interpretation, since
Christ's presence would be exemplified solely by this "deliverance of the Church from all her Enemies, not by a personal
reign, either on an earthly throne or from a visible perch high
in the heavens."[59] At the other end of the spectrum of
opinion was Jeremiah Burroughs, who thought there was "a
Probability [that Christ] in his Person GOD and MAN . . .
shall reigne upon the Earth, here in this World before that

56. Allen, *State of the Church*, pp. 296, preface, 299.
57. More, *Apocalypsis*, pp. 205–07.
58. Ibid., p. 207.
59. Philpot, *A New Systeme*, pp. 117, 112.

great and Solemne Day."[60] It was a glorious thought—and Goodwin too may have flirted with it—but most expositors steered clear of such extravagant hopes.[61]

Any New Englander, then, who was at all familiar with the range of opinions expressed by English and French divines, knew that the following conclusions had been reached: The witnesses had been slain and had risen. The witnesses had not been slain and had not risen. The seven vials had all been poured. Some had been poured. None had been poured. The first resurrection was a literal one, of the martyrs themselves. It was a spiritual and political one. The day of judgment began before and ran through the thousand-year reign. The day of judgment was after the thousand-year reign. The conflagration would engulf the entire earth. It would engulf some of the earth. It would engulf only Italy. It came before the millennium. It came after the millennium. It lasted through the millennium. At Christ's second coming, he would reign personally on earth. He would appear supernaturally but not reign on earth. His coming was only spiritual, evidenced through the glorious state of the church. The millennium was a paradise where risen saints lived in a fertile, renewed land. It was a time not dramatically different from the present, except that evil men would be kept in line by strict laws.

What did New Englanders make of all this? Few of them had the time to devote their lives to the study of prophecies, as Mede had done; nor were there as many line-by-line paraphrases of the Revelation. Yet ministers often evidenced an intense interest in the subject, and their treatises and sermons gave some idea of the varying viewpoints they held.

Historians are probably most familiar with the eschatologi-

---

60. Jeremiah Burroughs, *A Glimpse of Sion's Glory* (London [?], 1641), p. 27.
61. Goodwin moves toward this opinion in *A Glimpse of Sion's Glory*, in *Works*, 12:71; though compare with his later sermon *The World to Come*, in *Works*, 12:96, where he draws back.

cal opinions of Increase and Cotton Mather, who have generally been cast in the roles of archtypical premillennialists of
the period before the Great Awakening.[62] Certainly their
literal interpretation of the prophecies supports this notion.
Both of them agreed that the only possible way to account
for the resurrection of the martyrs was in an actual, bodily
sense. Increase cited his already mentioned "law of opposites"
to prove that since the second resurrection was literal, so also
was the first. Cotton set forth the other alternatives available
and eliminated all of them. He called "absurd" the opinion of
some that a "work of *Sanctification* upon the *Soul*" was
what was meant. More sensible was the conjecture that "'the
Church then shall continue in a state of Glorious rest and
peace'"; yet that too strained the sense of prophecy by
assuming that the martyrs lived only through the spirit of
their successors.[63] In assuming this double resurrection, the
Mathers likewise accepted Mede's conclusion that Daniel's
"Day of Judgment" was the same period as John's thousand
years.[64] But while Mede thought that only the saints and
martyrs would be resurrected, the Mathers optimistically assumed that all good men would be raised, leaving only the
damned to be judged at the end of time.[65]

As for those who would be living on earth at Christ's coming, the situation was less clear. Certainly there would be a
conflagration at his arrival, touched off by the flames in which

62. Robert Middlekauff discusses their eschatology with a good deal more
sophistication in *The Mathers*. Owing to the limited scope of this work, it will be
impossible to discuss all of the changes in their views, which Middlekauff covers in
some detail, especially in chapters 10 and 17.

63. Cotton Mather, "Problema Theologicum," MS, American Antiquarian Society, pp. 59 ff., 62.

64. Ibid., p. 56; Increase Mather, *Dissertation Concerning the Future Conversion*, pp. 23–24, 18.

65. Increase Mather, *Dissertation Concerning*, pp. 16, 18; Cotton Mather, "Triparadisus," MS, American Antiquarian Society.

Christ would be surrounded. In fact, Increase pointed out
that, actually, there would be *"Two Conflagrations* as well as
Two Resurrections," the first inaugurating the millennium.[66]
He remarked that Mede's ideas about America as an unburned
refuge for Gog and Magog were "ingenious, and may probably prove true." Where the fires did ravage, living saints would
"be *caught up into the Air*" and thus escape the fate of ungodly men. Cotton was, earlier in his career, "less sure"
whether saints would be saved in that way, but later accepted
the idea more readily. Nor would he fully commit himself on
the extent of the conflagration, arguing that it was impossible
to tell whether it would spread beyond Italy and the Roman
territories.[67] As for America, he seemed more hopeful than
his father. Possibly it might be used as a shelter for saints during the fire; and whatever happened, it would certainly "not
be cast off" when Christ conquered the rest of the world.[68]

Both Cotton and Increase waxed ecstatic about the rewards
in store for the saints after the conflagration. For them, the
millennium was no mere flourishing of the gospel state. An
age of miracles was dawning, said Cotton, and the end result
would be a paradise much like the one William Allen had
described.[69] People would not be subject to sin or temptation, and the church would be free of sectarian contention.
Infirmities of the body would be a thing of the past, for no
one would experience hunger, thirst, or pain. Cotton noted
with approval Drue Cressener's theory that the fiery vapors
and ashes from the fires in Italy would cool to a temperate

66. Increase realized the theory implied that inhabitants of America would have
no contact with the renovated world; yet he seemed to contradict himself in the
same treatise by arguing that "there will be a most glorious Conversion of all the
Nations on the earth, which shall escape that Deluge of Fire." *Dissertation Concerning*, pp. 32–33, 30.

67. Ibid., p. 15; Cotton Mather, "Problema," pp. 79–80; "Triparadisus," pt. 3.

68. Cotton Mather, *Theopolis Americana* (Boston, 1719), pp. 47–50.

69. Cotton Mather, *Things for a Distressed People* (Boston, 1696), p. 36.

warmth and promote fertility in areas farther away, just as
Vesuvius had in the past.[70] Unfortunately, Christ would not
live on earth, but Increase did hope for an occasional visit
from Him. Cotton surmised that the reign with the martyrs
would be in "Regions of the Air," so that those living on earth
could see Him anyway. When those living on the New
Earth died, they would be "Translated" to the New Heavens—
although this might not be until the end of the thousand
years. For Increase, even this was superfluous, since the living saints would be made immortal "instantly" at the Second
Coming.[71]

It was certainly a world to look forward to; Cotton especially could not refrain from calculating the years that remained. Both he and Increase thought Whiston had been right
in arguing that the vials all had to come under the seventh
trumpet and thus remained to be poured. But surely that
would begin soon. Despite Cotton's disappointment in 1697,
by 1710 father and son were affirming that the sixth trumpet
had passed, leaving only the seventh to sound.[72] What encouraged both of them were Whiston's computations, which
gave "greater light" to chronological obscurities than did any
others. What was more, although Whiston often disagreed with
Mede, in this particular case both of their calculations indicated that 1716 might inaugurate the precipitous fall of antichrist. Disappointment seemed only to whet Cotton's hopes.
As he approached the end of his life, he became surer and
surer that "all that has been *foretold* in the *Scripture of Truth*,
as what must come to pass before *the coming* . . . is, as far as

70. Increase Mather, *Blessed Hope* (Boston, 1701), p. 11; Cotton Mather,
"Problema," p. 79.

71. Cotton Mather, "Problema," pp. 79–80; Increase Mather, *Blessed Hope*,
p. 136.

72. Increase Mather, *A Discourse Concerning Faith and Fervency in Prayer*
(Boston, 1710), p. 97; Cotton Mather, *Theopolis*, p. 4.

we understand, Fulfill'd: I say ALL FULFILL'D!"[73] He had to do some juggling to come to this conclusion, including abandoning his earlier belief that the Jews would be converted as a nation before Christ's arrival; but his hopes outran his caution, and he died convinced that millennial fires were imminent.

No doubt all this provides good evidence that the Mathers promulgated a typically premillennial outlook in colonial America. Both of them stoutly defended Christ's supernatural appearance, a bodily first resurrection of the martyrs, and the conflagration. But their own testimony indicated that their defenses were so ardent because their opinions were hardly universal. In "Problema Theologicum," Cotton ticked off the many eminent British and European divines who had believed that the thousand years began not long after Christ's death. In "Triparadisus" he argued hotly in favor of a premillenial conflagration, noting that he would have been shocked to find one particular "learned man" denying this, had not such opinions been "so common among learned Men, that they are no longer to be wondered at." Increase acknowledged that there were "many learned and judicious Authors who take the *First Resurrection* in a *Political Sense*, as if it were of the same Nature with the Resurrection of the Witnesses."[74] Throughout, no New England divines were mentioned by name, but the Mathers definitely had some of their fellow clergymen in mind.

Cotton's "Problema" is a case in point. Though never printed, it circulated among interested New England ministers. Originally, the manuscript had been a letter to Nicholas Noyes, pastor at Salem, but Cotton revised it by excising the per-

73. Increase Mather, *Dissertation Wherein the Strange Doctrine*, p. 93: Cotton Mather, "Triparadisus," pt. 3, chap. 12, p. 28.

74. Cotton Mather, "Problema," p. 17; "Triparadisus," pt. 3, chap. 1. Increase Mather, *Dissertation Concerning the Future Conversion*, p. 20.

sonal addresses. The material crossed out indicates that in arguing that Christ would return before the thousand years, he
was trying to make a "proselyte" out of Noyes. His first version read, "If you will not be thus persuaded, You must be so
Charitable as to give me your Help, in answering the ensuing
Arguments."[75] Noyes never published a formal treatise on
the Revelation, but there is evidence that he was a man "deep
studied in the Revelations," and that he did indeed differ
with the Mathers.[76]

Noyes published some of his ideas in a sermon entitled *New
England's Duty and Interest to be an Habitation of Justice*,
bearing a preface by John Higginson, one of the few ministers
old enough to remember the time when John Cotton advised
Oliver Cromwell "that to take from the Spaniards in America
would be to dry up the sixth vial of Euphrates, which was
one thing put Him on his Expedition to Hispaniola."[77] The
particular predictions which interested Noyes were those promising a "Restauration, Reformation, and Blessing" to formerly degenerate churches. This, he assumed, was what the
resurrection of the witnesses referred to—an interpretation
which in itself was standard enough. But Noyes's discussion
of the restoration of the witnesses merged into a description
of the millennium without any mention of Christ's coming or
an attendant conflagration. Righteousness would spread over
Asia, Europe, and America, as "the Kingdoms of the world
[became] the Kingdoms of Our Lord." The metaphors referred to the state of the church instead of Christ himself: it
was "his day," not "his coming"; and it was compared with
Luther's original revolt, as a "*Second Reformation*, which,
when it cometh, will carry all before it."[78]

75. Sewall, *Diary*, 2:118; Cotton Mather, "Problema," p. 23.

76. John Barnard, "Sketch of Eminent Ministers in New England," Collections
of the Massachusetts Historical Society, 1st ser. (Boston, 1809), 10:168.

77. Sewall, *Diary*, 1:437.

78. Noyes, *New England's Duty*, pp. 64–68.

In discussing the extent of the millennial empire, Noyes had to deal with conjectures about America's fate. He treated with sarcasm Thomas Burnet's theory that the Indians were not descended from Noah. The savages ought to feel beholden to Burnet, jibed Noyes, because "he let them descend from Adam; and did not bring them out of the Slime, as he doth Gog and Magog." Mede's theory was more formidable, and even more distasteful. That America should be headquarters for Gog and Magog, or Hell itself, Noyes found "worse and worse still!" This was treading on tender ground, however, since only the year before, his friend Increase Mather had drawn that gloomy conclusion:

> I know there is a blessed day to the visible Church not far off; but it is the Judgment of very Learned men, that in the Glorious Times promised to the Church on Earth, *America* will be Hell. . . . I am very afraid that in the process of Time, New England will be the wofullest place in all America.

Noyes's response was tactful; yet behind the tact there perhaps lay a slight reproof. "I believe some *monitory Expressions* of men much better than myself; have been wrested beyond their Intention," he said, "and that the same persons hope better things concerning New England . . . and I believe that they are as good friends . . . as any in the Land."[79] Noyes was indeed walking a tightrope. He avoided committing himself to any particular solution, no doubt partly out of scholarly caution, but also quite probably because another friend and fellow expositor, Samuel Sewall, had asked why America might not be "the New Jerusalem, or part of it."

Sewall studied the prophecies as much as anyone in New England, as just about any of his acquaintances must have known. There was scarcely any way to know him and not

79. Ibid., pp. 69–78; Increase Mather, *A Discourse Concerning the Uncertainty of the Times* (Boston, 1697), p. 35.

realize it. He made a regular practice of carrying pamphlets and books with him on his visits, and often his friends found an apocalyptic tract in their hands at his departure. A dozen of his *Phenomena* were packed off to Barbados and Mexico, one to the governor, John Cotton's book "on the Vials" to Ebenezer Pemberton, copies of Willard's prophetic *Fountain Opened* to "as many as were in Council", and on and on. If he was not discussing resurrected bellies with Mr. Dudley, he might well be asking Mr. Bolt "whether [Negroes] should be white after the Resurrection" (Bolt thought it absurd—the body would be "void of all Colour"); or pleading with Mr. Brinsmead to pray for the drying up of the Euphrates. Even his artillery company could not escape his eschatology. Captain Sewall awarded crack marksman John Noyes a silver cup engraved with *"Euphratem Siccare potes,"* so every time Ensign Noyes dried up his own cup, he could wish the same might happen to the Euphrates under the sixth vial![80]

Sewall's main interest lay in championing one particular cause, that the pouring of the sixth vial referred to a diminishing of the antichristian empire in America; and he went about it in his usual energetic way. The theory was a novel one: although expositors were able to disagree on just about any detail one of the few things virtually all of them assented to was that the sixth vial encompassed the end of the Turkish woe and the conversion of the Jews. Since Sewall wished to include America in the prophecy, he accordingly suggested that one of the topics for debate at the Harvard commencement of 1696 might be "Res Antichristiana in America, Est Euphrates ille Apocalyptica in quam Angelus Sextus effundit phialem suam?" When that proposal did not take, he proceeded to print up "a pretty many copies" of the question to send to his friends. The result was a set of "long and elaborat Answers by way of Opposition." Sewall replied to these

80. Sewall, *Diary*, 2:140, 253, 305; 1:69; 2:55.

and then sent to the press his formal rebuttal, the *Phenomena quadaem Apocalyptica*.[81]

The conclusions he drew from his interpretation were hopeful for America. If indeed the Jews' conversion was to come at the same time, then this would fit nicely with John Eliot's old theory that the Indians were descended from the Ten Lost Tribes of Israel. The obvious deduction was that America "stands fair for being made the Seat of the Divine Metropolis." This was not a mere expression of New England local pride, since Boston and its environs was not the proposed site. Sewall's candidate was Mexico, and his quaint arguments made it clear that England was still the center of the world for him:

> The situation of [the old] Jerusalem is not so Central; but that a Voyage may be made from *London*, to *Mexico*, in as little time, as from *London*, to *Jerusalem*. . . . If the City of the Great King should be sat on the Northern side of it [Mexico] : Englishmen would meet with no Inconvenience thereby; and they would find . . . they might visit the Citizens of the *New-Jerusalem*, and their Countrymen, all under one.

Barbados and Jamaica stood ready to welcome travelers on the way to Mexico, and the "New English Tirzah" would also be happy for a visit.[82]

Although Sewall's initial proposals had met with great opposition, not everyone disagreed with them. Both Nicholas Noyes and Cotton Mather respectfully mentioned the theory in their sermons, although they stopped short of endorsing it. Sewall received further comfort when Timothy Clark, only a few years later, pointed out that "a Line drawn to the Comet

---

81. Samuel Sewall, *Letter Book*, Collections of the Massachusetts Historical Society, 2 vols.; 6th ser., vols. 1–2 (Boston, 1887), 1:227–28.

82. Sewall, *Phenomena*, pp. 1–2, 45.

[recently observed] strikes just upon Mexico." Sewall excitedly discussed the rumors of a revolution there, and after
himself seeing the results on Clark's globe, concluded, "Our
Thoughts being thus confer'd and found to jump, makes it to
me remarkable."[83] But even more immediate reaction came
from John Wise. Some of his parishioners had been considering a move to the Carolinas, and Wise was considering going
with them. If the increasing number of British settlements
near Spanish strongholds indeed signaled the beginning of the
sixth vial, then the ideas in the *Phenomena* seemed to be sur-
prisingly confirmed. Wise thus thought that he himself might
be able to contribute more directly to antichrist's downfall
by joining the attack. Sewall thanked him for his compliments
("I plainly saw that you had overvalued the crazy fining Pot,
when as you ventured to pour into it so many great Hyper-
boles of Praise") and then gave his own diplomatic and more
moderate reply to Wise's proposal. Certainly, he had been
glad to hear of the British settlements and hope that the
Romish territories would

> fall flat as ever Jericho did. But now as to this or the other
> Officer in the Army, it matters not much where he [is]
> placed, provided he be in the Post where his General has
> set him. And your Fathers and Brethren in the Ministry
> who know your Circumstances, and the condition of the
> Church in Chebacko, can best adjust that for you. . . .[84]

Wise, apparently convinced, remained in New England to
fight his own wars there, much to the later distress of the
Mathers.

Whether Wise agreed with the larger contours of Sewall's
interpretation is not known, but if he did, that would only

83. Sewall, *Diary*, 2:53.

84. Sewall, *Letter Book*, 1:196. See also the *New England Historical and Genea-
logical Register* (Boston, 1876), 30:64.

have added to his disagreements with the Mathers. Sewall was less convinced by Whiston than either Cotton or Increase, and had not moved the vials to the future. Instead, he followed Mede's scheme and argued that five had thus far been emptied. And where Whiston was convinced that the witnesses had already been slain, Sewall continually argued it was "past doubt" with him that this was not so. This conclusion had larger implications; for if the witnesses had not risen, it was a mistake to think, as the Mathers did, that 1716 would be a signal year in the war against the beast. "As for 1716," he wrote to one correspondent in New Hampshire, "it is the year that excellent Mead pitched upon above four score years agoe, as appears by his setting up the Ten Kings Ano $\frac{456}{1260}$] 1716. But being arrived at it, I can't receive the consolation that some doe."[85]

Sewall knew that other divines shared in the hopes for 1716. Noyes was convined that the witnesses had been slain, although his calculations were slightly different from Mede's or Whiston's. Pastor John Williams, famous for surviving capture by the French and Indians, wrote Sewall of his enthusiastic hopes; and Jeremiah Dummer reported from England that the "Apocalyptical Men" there thought there was a "Comfortable Prospect" of antichrist's ruin.[86] Sewall answered them all the same way, sticking to his point on the witnesses, noting that Mede had given his opinion "with a great deal of Modesty," and afterwards wishing that "they who so confidently and peremptorily fixed and proclaimed 1716 as the Year of Jubilee would make some Apology for themselves, lest otherwise they become guilty of depreciating the Prophesie."[87] He had support from his son Joseph, who preached a sermon from Habakkuk at the beginning of 1717:

85. Sewall, *Phenomena*, p. 20; *Letter Book*, 1:374; 2:53.
86. Sewall, *Diary*, 2:99; *Letter Book*, 2:63, 83.
87. Sewall, *Letter Book*, 2:63–65, 78, 83.

"For the vision is yet for an appointed time, but at the end it shall speak, and not lie: though it tarry, wait for it; because it will surely come, it will not tarry." The approving father commented that "Possibly some might not be well pleased, But others think people had been long enough held with the too Confident Affirmations that have been advanced."[88]

Thus the temporary disappointment of the Mathers' hopes served only to confirm Sewall in his opinions. As the years went on, and Cotton seemed to stress more and more the imminence of Christ's coming, Sewall noted with disapproval his "vehemently insisting on the Conflagration, so that he seems to think there is no general Calling or Convertion of the Jews, Or that it is already past and gone."[89] This scrap of evidence is tantalizing, since it implies that Sewall may well have agreed with those who placed the fire at the end of the millennium. He did not discuss the conflagration else-where, but there are hints that his millennial world differed materially from the Mathers' fire-refined, paradise state. The Mexican New Jerusalem appeared a little more down-to-earth than an immortally populated city in the clouds. And when Benjamin Wadsworth observed that Europe was a likelier location because of all the splendid buildings, Sewall replied that "the Beauty and Grandeur of the New Jerusalem will consist chiefly, in Humility, Purity, Self-Denial, Love, Peace, and Joy in Believing." As for Europe's splendor, "what signify the most sumptuous and magnificent Buildings of Europe? God will as readily Tabernacle in our Indian Wigwams, as enter into them."[90]

Saying this did not necessarily mean that love, peace, and joy would be the only qualities present: conceivably, immortal saints and glorious thrones might be a part of the new

88. Ibid., p. 65.
89. Ibid., p. 263.
90. Ibid., p. 201.

worlds too. But that was not how William Williams of Hatfield interpreted the *Phenomena* when Sewall sent him a copy. Williams's reading on the subject was less full—he was not acquainted with Mede's opinion on Gog and Magog in America—but he said he agreed with Sewall's view that the New Jerusalem meant "the Spiritual glory of the Church in purity, holiness, and peace." And this definitely did not mean "glorified Saints descending from Heaven and assuming their bodies," since to Williams's way of thinking there were a number of flaws in that hypothesis. If only immortal saints lived in the New Jerusalem, then why did the Scriptures describe that time as one when men would still live under the covenant, be guaranteed freedom from persecution, and have the gospel available to those who still thirsted for it? These were things only mortals needed; and thus the Revelation "doth not speak of a bodily but a political [first] resurrection, and that the church which hath been persecuted and slain under Antichrist shall revive again, and be brought into a prosperous and flourishing condition."[91]

Williams may have been a relatively new convert to the theory at the time he wrote Sewall in 1728, but Benjamin Colman had long before declared his support.[92] As early as 1707, Colman stressed that God purposely hid the time of Christ's coming in order to "teach us *Modesty* in our *Enquiries* after them." He noted with disappointment (and perhaps with reference to Cotton's hopes in the late 1690s) that "Some good Men have been too *Curious* and *Positive* . . . and have been rebuked for their bold Conjectures, by living to see themselves confuted." Nevertheless, there were some facts which the prophecies had disclosed. Christ would not come until the very end of the world. Before then, antichrist would fall from his great power; there would be "a further Enlarge-

---

91. Ibid., pp. 250–52.
92. Williams said he had held his views "for several years." Ibid., p. 250.

ment of the Kingdom of Christ, and the Conversion of the Jews"; and in addition to that, "a Time also of the Church's *Peace* and *Tranquility*, *Purity and Holiness*, beyond what has hitherto been known." In other words, Christ would not appear until after a *"a great and general Desertion"* from God's ways at the end of the millennium, when he would conquer Gog, Magog, and Satan once and for all. Colman insisted that the times of all these events "no man can proportion or adjust," and that however pleasant it would be to hope that God would use miracles to bring about the changes, "yet this also is secret to him."[93]

Given Benjamin Colman's better-known disagreements with the Mathers, it is perhaps not surprising to see him at odds with them again. More illuminating is the position taken by the impeccably orthodox author of the *Compleat Body of Divinity*, Samuel Willard. Along with the Mathers, he was one of the most prolific writers of his day; and one of the books Samuel Sewall was constantly bestowing on his friends was *The Fountain Opened*. Willard believed, like all other New Englanders, that the millennium was yet to come: Christ the fountain had been opened first in the Gospel, but there was also a "more particular" time of His benefits approaching.[94] Yet however great the benefits of the coming millennium, they would not be splendid enough to rival the qualities of the eternal heavenly paradise. Scripture, Willard admitted, sometimes seemed to refer to the millennial church as part of "the Triumphant state," but strictly speaking, the millennium remained within the realm of the Church Militant.

> There must also be an allowance made for our supposing the Spirit of God, who condescends to speak to us in our own Language, to use Hyperbolical expressions, and set forth the better condition of the *Militant* church upon

93. Benjamin Colman, *Practical Discourses* (London, 1707), pp. 416–20.
94. Samuel Willard, *The Fountain Opened* (Boston, 1700), pp. 106–14.

> Earth, with words borrowed from the state of Glory
> to which it shall at length arrive. . . .

Willard, in taking the time to make these distinctions,
seemed to be industriously engaged in laying to rest the opinions of St. Augustine and Thomas Brightman. But since no
one in New England held Augustine's or Brightman's opinions,
we may rightly suspect that the methodical divine had more
relevant targets in mind. Increase and Cotton Mather's descriptions of saints refined and made instantly immortal
by the conflagration sounded suspiciously like prophetic
interpretations which confused the Church Triumphant
with the Church Militant. And Willard also seemed to deny
the possibility of a paradise on earth when he argued that
"the gradual Communications of this good to the Church"
throughout time would in the last days "arrive to a fulness,
not of absolute, but comparative perfection."[95] Yet the
Fountain could hardly be called a definite repudiation of
the Mathers' chiliasm.

Willard made his position plainer the following year, in
The Checkered State of the Gospel Church. The title itself
foreshadowed the sermon's thesis that it was sheer vanity to
"expect all light in the Church of God in this world." True
enough, a time was coming when "the priviledges of the
Church both spiritual and temporal shall be great to admiration, but still it will have a mixture of darkness in it."[96] Of
course, one way to escape this conclusion was to deny that
the millennium would be part of the Church Militant. If the
Church Triumphant began at judgment when the saints were
raised, and the Last Judgment actually encompassed the
millennium as the Mathers believed, then there would be no
contradiction in a worldly paradise. But Willard specifically

95. Ibid., pp. 115, 118.
96. Samuel Willard, *The Checkered State of the Gospel Church* (Boston, 1701),
p. 22.

denied such a thesis. The millennium would "not be after the great and last day of Judgment is begun," he said. "Some have not only conjectured, but also confidently asserted this; but I cannot be of their perswasion." One reason they were mistaken came "from their supposing the time [of the millennium is] not yet as begun, and [their] thinking it hard to believe that the Judgment shall be deferred a thousand years from the beginning of it." But Willard reminded his listeners (not to mention the Mathers) that a thousand years was only a day in the Lord's sight.[97]

And as if that had not been clear enough, Willard continued to hammer away at his point from another angle: what was meant by the Second Coming? The Scriptures said the thousand years would begin with "a bright appearing of Christ, by which the destruction of Antichrist will be wrought." But this was hardly part of the day of judgment; merely an "earnest" of it. Paul had indeed written in his letters to the Thessalonians that Jesus would slay "the lawless one" "with the breath of his mouth and destroy him by his appearing and his coming," but "some have (I think) needlessly applied [it] to his coming to the last Judgment; for there are other comings of his in the *Power of his Kingdom*." Jesus very likely would not appear "to the lower world in his Humanity" until the final judgment.[98]

Thus Christ's coming was figurative, and not inaugurated by a catastrophic conflagration. In fact, the glorious times might well "begin ere we are aware of it; inasmuch as it is rationally to be supposed that this light will have its gradual increase, & not attain to its Meridian at once, as the darkness into which the Church went, in its retirement into the wilderness, was gradual." Even during the thousand-year reign, the church would have its enemies in the world; it was just that

97. Ibid., pp. 52–53.
98. Ibid.

they would be kept under control. And were there any further proof needed, the final appearance of Gog and Magog "indisputably" made it clear "that the Church will all this while remain in a condition which renders them in themselves liable to the malices of adversaries."[99] In short, it would have been hard for Willard to have been more firm in his opposition to the Mathers' eschatology.

A GLOOMY REASSESSMENT

What can we deduce after wading through all these apocalyptical conjectures? One conclusion at least is clear: the boundaries of millennial thought are certainly more complicated than the traditional pre- and postmillennial classifications indicate. Except for a few cases like Jeremiah Burroughs and possibly Thomas Goodwin, expositors never believed that Christ would literally descend for a bodily reign for a thousand years on earth. Indeed, if any major distinction were to be made between a pre- or postmillennial eschatology, it would be more properly based on the question of whether or not the Last Judgment encompassed the thousand-year reign. Willard, for one, made this clear in his discussion of the differences implied in viewing the millennium as part of the Church Militant or the Church Triumphant. Consequently, the more crucial question was the meaning of the first resurrection. If it was a literal one, then it inaugurated the Last Judgment, still considered only a day because (as Increase argued, using the same Scripture Willard cited to prove the opposite point) one day is as a thousand in God's eyes.[100] Thus Daniel Whitby, whom some have called the first English postmillennialist, chose to state on his title page that the millennium was "not a Reign of Persons Raised from the Dead, but of the Church Flourishing gloriously for a Thousand Years

99. Ibid., p. 58. See also Willard, *Fountain Opened*, p. 117.
100. Increase Mather, *Dissertation Concerning the Future Conversion*, p. 14.

after the Conversion of the Jews," rather than phrasing the issue in terms of Christ's second coming.[101]

Furthermore, New Englanders were no more successful than their English counterparts in attempting to agree on an objectively based interpretation of the prophecies. Historians have generally taken the Mathers' views as representative, partly because Increase and Cotton as a rule beat everybody else to the press, and partly because the debate itself was often abstruse and allusive. In fact, the Mathers were quite unable to impose their brand of chiliasm on everyone else— much to their distress. Cotton lamented that "mankind will have no more [apprehensions?] of any mighty and sudden change . . . coming upon the world," in part because expositors were "deluding them into an Imagination, of *Happy Times* to arrive, and be Long Enjoy'd by the church of God upon Earth, before the coming of the Lord. In a word, *All fast Asleep!*"[102] Thus Jonathan Edwards's interpretation of the first resurrection as political and Christ's coming as figurative was by no means novel: it had the support of eminent men like Benjamin Colman and Samuel Willard.

Yet for all their diversity, expositors did agree on some points; and these are perhaps as interesting as their differences. No one, for instance, denied the general meaning of the seven vials, or the death and resurrection of the witnesses. The vials were plagues that God poured out in order to destroy antichrist; and the witnesses were resurrected in a metaphorical and political sense rather than a literal one. But if this was the case, what becomes of the thesis that the premillennialist

101. Daniel Whitby, *A Treatise of the True Millennium*, in *A Paraphrase and Commentary on the New Testament* (London, 1727). Whitby's book is a further indication that a political interpretation of the first resurrection was present before the Awakening. I have not treated it in my discussion of English expositors here because there are other earlier examples of similar positions, such as Henry More, and because early eighteenth-century New Englanders did not depend on it as a guide. For a more detailed discussion of Whitby's views, see below, chapter 4.

102. Cotton Mather, "Triparadisus," pt. 3, chap 7.

view of the end of history was an incurably gloomy one? If the vials were poured out only one at a time, would that not indicate gradual improvement in the condition of the world? And if the churches, as witnesses for Christ, were elevated to positions of dignity and authority *before* He came, how could things be said to decline into a last, sinful state?

Thomas Goodwin, who believed in a corporeal first resurrection, argued that the raising of witnesses would be a forerunner of the actual millennium: "So glorious shall the condition of these witnesses be, in comparison of what it was before, that it shall justly be counted a heaven, if compared with their former best condition before their killing." William Allen had forecast a paradise state, but still held that prophecies often had gradual fulfillment; and that the seven vials were means by which "the Beast is gradually brought down." Samuel Lee thought antichrist had been in a "waining, withering State ever since the days of Luther," which made good sense, since God's purpose was "to manage the ruine and extirpation of the Churches Enemies by degrees; not all at once."[103] Even the Mathers seemed ambiguous on this point. Cotton—at least until the last few years of his life—believed there would be "symptoms" of the coming time which were hardly bad news for the church. More than once he "wrestled with the Lord" until He revealed "that a mighty Convulsion shall be given to the French Empire" and that England, Scotland, and Ireland would be "speedily Illuminated, with glorious Anticipations of the Kingdome of God." Increase noted that when the seventh trumpet sounded and the pouring of the vials began, the kingdoms of the world would "*Gradually* become the *Kingdoms of Christ*, until the whole World is become Christendom."[104]

103. Goodwin, *Works*, 3:193; Allen, *Of the State of the Church*, p. 33; Samuel Lee, *Dissertation*, pp. 113-14, and *Ecclesia Gemens* (London, 1677), p. 8.

104. Cotton Mather, *Diary*, 1:207-08; Increase Mather, *Dissertation Wherein the Strange Doctrine*, pp. 92-93 (his italics), also pp. 99-102.

Nor does the evidence support the notion of the inactive premillennialist who passively waited for Christ's catastrophic arrival. A mere glance at Cotton Mather's frenetic career is enough to scotch that generalization. And Cotton's eschatology provided an eminently logical incentive for his activity. Had he not believed that the conflagration was imminent, he would have deceived himself into a lethargic expectance of good times: "In a word, *All fast Asleep!*" Of course, this answer fails to deal with a more refined version of the argument: that the nature of the activity provoked by catastrophism was fundamentally different from that aroused by gradualism. I shall deal with this in the following chapters.

But exploding these stereotypes only presents another quandary. The evidence just given seems to suggest that it was wrong to criticize historians for viewing Jonathan Edwards's ideas as anticipations of later optimistic theories of history. Perhaps far from being the first major forerunner, Edwards was only one in a steady line of those who believed in a gradualism much like the one incorporated by the secular idea of progress. But that would hardly do justice to these expositors; for all their professed beliefs in the gradual fall of the beast, they spoke of difficult and gloomy times ahead. Goodwin may have believed that the vials betokened a slow decline of the beast, but he also thought that "that last scattering [of the church] will be so great a one as all the faith you have will be put to it." William Allen still included the climactic battle of Armageddon, as did Samuel Lee.[105] And no talk of gradual revolutions could eliminate the Mathers' belief in the conflagration. Nor was this confusing attitude confined to those who believed in a literal first resurrection inaugurated by the fire. Samuel Willard spoke of "the last and worst times, preceding the great Reformation which is

105. Goodwin, *Works*, 3:118; Allen, *Of the State of the Church*, pp. 119-50; Lee, *Dissertation*, pp. 118-19.

expected"; and Sewall apparently thought the good times would be directly preceded by those of "Unparallel'd Severity."[106]

All this leads to our own gloomy conclusion. With the end of the chapter in sight, millennial scholars and their ways of thinking seem, if anything, even more confusing than before. This much seems certain: interpreters failed to find meaning in history through an agreement on the order and arrangement of its last events; and as a result, New England parishioners could hardly have held very consistent or coherent opinions. Indeed, Increase Mather confessed as much in a sermon to his flock which touched briefly on his belief in the literal first resurrection. He mentioned that he had discussed the subject in a dissertation printed the year before in London, but did not elaborate on the point, since he thought "it to be a Problem fitter for Scholastical Argumentations, than to be handled in the Pulpit before a Popular Auditory."[107] Insofar as scholarly study attempts to unravel millennial logic through an understanding of chronology and specific events, it fails as much as expositors of the Apocalypse failed in their own quest for meaningful agreement.

But perhaps that quest was not the most important one for millennialists. As hotly as Increase defended the literal first resurrection, he seemed to feel that other things deserved to be stressed when preaching a practical sermon. If the particular details of the last days were not paramount, then possibly the general ways and means which God used to act in history might be. Perhaps the new departure of post-Awakening Calvinism was a basically different attitude toward the mechanisms of the church's salvation—a view of history which managed to purge New England millennialism of its strange

---

106. Samuel Willard, *Peril of the Times Displayed* (Boston, 1700), p. 14; Sewall, *Phenomena*, preface.

107. Increase Mather, *A Discourse Concerning Faith and Fervency*, p. xvii.

combination of simultaneous gloom and optimism. Assessment of the validity of this conjecture demands an understanding of the boundaries that New Englanders set, both
before and after the Awakening, between the natural and the
supernatural powers God used for his providential action in
history.

3

Judgment

Anyone who has even a passing acquaintance with Christian apocalypse knows that John did not choose to end his world with a whimper. Christ's return to judge the quick and the dead provided a spectacular, supernatural climax to the long drama of redemption. Nor did John confine his miraculous imagery to descriptions of the very end of time. The visions of the holy war throughout history depended heavily on the language of the supernatural and the violent. The sixth seal predicted a "great earthquake" after which "the sun became black as sackcloth of hair, and the moon became as blood; And the stars of heaven fell unto the earth." The trumpets comprised a whole string of prodigies, including hail and fire mixed with blood, the burning of a third of the earth, seas turned to blood, and fiery mountains thrown into the seas. The vials of wrath catalogued similar woes, and in all, the Revelation mentioned falling stars at least three times and great earthquakes at least four. Strangely enough, John remained mute on the subject of the conflagration, noting only that the old earth would "pass away" (Rev. 21:1) to make way for the new heavens and earth.

But other Old and New Testament scriptures provided ample reinforcement. Peter's oft-quoted second epistle described the "day of the Lord" which would come like a thief in the night, when the heavens would "pass away with a great noise and the elements . . . melt with fervent heat" (2 Peter 3:10). Old Testament prophets employed similar imagery, noting that the earth would "reel to and fro like a drunkard" and the mountains melt like wax before the fire. Matthew and Mark reported that Jesus himself gave a long list of signs preceding his second coming, including famines and earthquakes, false prophets performing deceptive wonders, and the usual darkening of the sun and moon, and falling of stars.[1] In short, the Bible provided ample material for those inclined to make use of the violent, the catastrophic, and the supernatural. Were eighteenth-century ministers so inclined?

The question is a logical one to ask at this point. If the previous chapter was correct in concluding that eighteenth-century millennialists could not easily be classified according to their chronologies of events predicted for the latter days, then we are forced to look elsewhere to discover the elements of a millennial logic which either united believers in a common eschatological perspective or divided them into opposing camps. This chapter begins by considering the possibility that a person's attitudes and actions varied according to how much he emphasized the supernatural aspects of God's plan of redemption. An expositor who often relied on a miraculous interpretation of the prophecies might well behave differently from someone who believed that biblical predictions would be fulfilled naturally.

Yet it is not always easy to imagine what these differences would be—or perhaps too easy. There are several ways one might reconstruct natural and supernatural logics, each of them plausible enough yet at the same time contradictory in their conclusions. Here, for instance, are two hypothetical models that attempt to distinguish certain kinds of millennial attitudes. They both begin by differentiating between a miraculous and a natural accomplishment of the prophecies, but end with different sets of millennial psychologies.

1. Isaiah 24:20; 34:4; Micah 1:4; Matthew 24; Mark 13.

Hypothetical Reconstruction No. 1: For medieval man, a supernatural end to the world provided an eminently satisfying moral conclusion to history. The final conflagration, the Second Coming, all the attendant earthquakes and famines, were parts of an immutable guarantee that no matter how much the wicked seemed to triumph in the present age, God would supernaturally set the scales of justice aright at the Day of Judgment. But with the advance of science, the wonders of eschatology were tamed and made regular along with the rest of the world. No longer was there a need to have supernatural forces effect the conflagration and final convulsions: natural processes could account for the events just as well. But this inevitably raised the specter of a mechanistic, meaningless end to the world. If the chain of cause and effect which led to the cataclysmic finale proceeded apace regardless of how the moral world behaved, could the final destruction of the world properly be called a judgment? Divines as well as natural scientists would be faced—no matter how they attempted to hide it—with the prospect of nature deprived of mind and catastrophe robbed of its meaning.[2]

Hypothetical Reconstruction No. 2: A supernatural end to the world meant that only God could purge the evils from the existing vale of tears. If antichrist could be defeated only with the aid of divine earthquakes, and if the millennium could begin only with the help of a miraculous conflagration and literal resurrection of martyrs, there would be little incentive for believers to redeem the world themselves. The only course open would be to wait patiently and passively

2. This is essentially the theory presented in Perry Miller, "The End of the World," *Errand into the Wilderness* (Cambridge, Mass., 1956), pp. 217-39, a superb essay that studied the apocalyptic genre while providing yet another example of it. Miller argued that the men who formulated or accepted the new naturalistic theories realized, with sometimes unconscious dread, that they were denying their world "the beauty of the unmixed and wholly God-administered fatality" (p. 200).

until deliverance came from heaven. On the other hand, if the millennium could be brought about naturally, men could play a role in its accomplishment. Believers who knew that God was depending on their efforts would surely act more forcefully than those who merely waited for the holocaust to solve the world's problems.[3]

The two reconstructions, we should note, arrive at different conclusions because their primary focus is on different events. By concentrating on the Last Judgment, the first model assumes that naturalistic theories left believers uneasy and anxious, their whole system threatened by a loss of the moral purpose so much a part of the final day. By concentrating on the millennium, the second model assumes that naturalistic theories had the opposite effect, producing an active optimism unhampered by the need for supernatural intervention. The first hypothesis ends with a vision of catastrophe without meaning; the second, a vision of meaning without catastrophe.

The claims of both theories, however much they differ, suggest that the next logical step in our inquiry ought to be a closer investigation of the boundaries which interpreters drew between the natural and supernatural aspects of the history of redemption—not so much because one hypothesis needs to be proved right and the other wrong, but because both address the central problem of this study: discovery of the motivations and logic behind New Englanders' interest in the prophecies.

A CLARIFICATION OF DISTINCTIONS

Despite the wealth of supernatural imagery in the Revelation, expositors did not interpret much of it literally. Most

---

3. This is one line of reasoning pursued in the theories discussed above, chap. 1. See especially Heimert, *Religion and the American Mind*, chap. 2; and Tuveson, *Redeemer Nation*, chap. 2.

agreed with Mede that the visions of the seven seals and many of the trumpets had already been fulfilled; and that placed a natural check on the wholesale use of the miraculous. If the seals, for instance, referred to events surrounding the fall of the Roman Empire, then interpreters would be hard pressed to talk of literal rivers of blood or an actual cascade of stars, when records made no mention of them.[4] In addition, men like Mede were aware enough of scientific developments to know that stars could not possibly fall to earth, not because God would hesitate to work miracles, but simply because the description outlined a physical impossibility. Stars were "either as big, or many times bigger than the globe of the earth," and hence there was no possible way for them to "fall" to the earth, even miraculously.[5]

Furthermore, Mede's astute scholarship showed that biblical writers themselves intended much of their supernatural imagery to be interpreted metaphorically. Comparisons with Chaldean paraphrases written about the same time as the Scriptures indicated that

> When the Prophets frequently speak of the *Sun's being darkened in its going forth, the Moon not giving her light,* and elsewhere *of the Stars falling from Heaven upon the Earth* (a phrase not to be understood *Literally*) the Targum renders these and the like Prophetic strains in words that signifie the *diminution of the Glory and Felicity* of the State, and the *Downfall of the Grandees and Chiefs* therein. . . .[6]

Thus, expositors agreed that the literal meaning of a passage could be dropped in favor of a metaphorical one, provided there was sufficient justification. But as usual the question of

4. See, e.g., Goodwin, *Works*, 3: 45–46, and generally any of the English commentaries, where rivers of blood are interpreted to mean natural events, such as Elizabeth's persecution of Roman Catholics.

5. Mede, *Works*, p. 615.

6. John Worthington, general preface, in Mede, *Works*.

what constituted sufficient justification remained hazy. Nearly everybody agreed that the resurrection of the witnesses ought to be interpreted metaphorically, whereas opinions about the "first resurrection" of the millennium differed greatly.

One apparent conclusion which might be drawn is that interpreters with a literalistic, unyielding cast of mind tended to prefer supernatural readings of the prophecies, whereas those souls more inclined to the metaphorical opted for natural solutions. This was not always the case, however, as the scientific theories of Thomas Burnet and William Whiston demonstrate. Both men wrote treatises purporting to explain the processes involved in the creation, flood, and final dissolution of the world; and while their interpretation of Scripture was markedly literal, they hardly equated "literal" with "supernatural."

Burnet's imagination was first-rate, as was his prose. *The Sacred Theory of the Earth*, issued in 1681, seemed to have an ingenious explanation for everything. The lush paradise of Eden could be accounted for easily enough by assuming that the earth's original axis had not tilted toward the sun, thus assuring a perpetual spring. On the other hand, the increased heat of that same paradisiacal sun would bake the earth's thin crust until finally the breaking shell would release the floods of Noah's deluge. If a final conflagration seemed impossible because the oceans and polar regions would halt any far-reaching fire, that could be remedied by forecasting a series of droughts to produce a world where everything was tinder dry, and oceans and lakes greatly reduced, if not evaporated completely.[7] The state of the earth could hardly be more cheerless, and Burnet described it in suitable rhetoric:

7. Thomas Burnet, *Sacred Theory of the Earth*, 6th ed. (London, 1726), 2: 73–91. The sixth edition is used here because it contains Burnet's rejoinders to his critics.

The Countenance of the Heavens will be dark and gloomy; and a Veil drawn over the Face of the Sun. The Earth in a Disposition everywhere to break into open Flames. The Tops of the Mountains smoaking; the Rivers dry, Earthquakes in several Places, the Sea sunk and retir'd into its deepest Channel, and roaring, as against some mighty Storm. These things will make the Day dead and melancholy. . . .[8]

But when the fires finally cracked the crust and Christ appeared, the earth would not remain a mere charred wreck, since the molten remains would cool—just as they had at the original creation. The result would be a millennial paradise free from pain or want, thanks again to an untilted axis of the earth.[9]

Whiston's theories were even more unorthodox. As a student, he had been quite taken with Burnet's hypothesis and even defended it as part of the traditional exercises for his bachelor's degree. But further study of "Mechanical Philosophy," and Newton's work in particular, convinced him that Burnet had not contrived a scientific enough method of getting the earth's axis tilted properly. His own initial solution was to have a comet passing near enough to the earth "and in a certain trajectory, [that] it might [sufficiently] alter the Position of the Earth's Axis."[10] Subsequent calculations scotched that idea, but Whiston remained undaunted. His final intricate theory worked everything out by bringing in a

8. Ibid., p. 147.

9. Perry Miller inexplicably omitted any mention of Burnet's millennium, making Whiston's supposed introduction of it an "incisive dramatization of what happened to the mind of western man at the end of the seventeenth century." *Errand into the Wilderness*, p. 232.

10. William Whiston, *A Vindication of the New Theory of the Earth* . . . (London, 1698), preface. Whiston provides here an interesting history of his work on the *Theory*.

comet every time he needed to get his scenario over a rough spot.

In the first place, Whiston proposed that the creation story in Genesis referred merely to the origin of the earth, not the entire universe; and that the chaos from which the world evolved was none other than the mixed atmosphere of a comet whose dust slowly began to settle and congeal. For a man who prided himself on his literal interpretation of the Scripture, this view presented a distinct problem: Genesis explicitly said that the stars, sun, and moon were created along with the earth. Whiston found his way out of the problem by supposing that since "the Prophets and Holy Penmen" were "seldom or never Philosophers," and the Hebrew people ill-prepared to understand scientific truth, God had revealed the origin in ways that would have made sense to them. The stars would *seem* as if they were newly created, when actually they had been there all along, visible now for the first time because the comet's atmospheric clouds had dispersed.[11] As for the Flood, it could be taken care of by assuming that the cool tail of another comet would set off torrential downpours when it intersected the earth's orbit on the way to the center of the solar system. And thousands of years later, if the earth was again bathed by a tail—this one already heated by its pass around the sun—then surely a huge conflagration would ensue. Conceivably, once Christ completed the final judgment, the earth itself might become a comet and for the rest of eternity roam the far reaches of the universe.[12]

Significantly, while both men's reading of the Scriptures was more naturalistic than traditional interpretations, it was also more literal. Burnet realized that the prophecies of "the Obscuration of the Sun and Moon, Earthquakes, Roarings of the troubled Sea" were meant, according to many Interpreters,

11. William Whiston, *A New Theory of the Earth* (London, 1696), pp. 27, 20.
12. Ibid., pp. 126, 368, 378.

"to be understood only in a moral Sense." But he predicted that these things would be fulfilled literally through the natural processes leading to the conflagration. As the earth's axis tilted back to its original position, the motion of the globe would produce the illusion of the stars jarring and dancing about the heavens, something which seemed to Burnet very much like falling. In addition, the smoke and vapor from the volcanoes throughout the parched world would obscure the light of the sun and moon.[13] Whiston's theory assumed that the air would be "oppressed" with meteors (which looked like falling stars) as well as steam and exhalations, since the "Air must be clog'd and burthen'd" by the comet's vaporous tail.[14] All these phenomena were quite within the bounds of nature and clearly indicate that a literal reading of the Scriptures hardly needed to be a supernatural one.

And that was one of the things which bothered Burnet's and Whiston's readers: the new explanations seemed to rely too much on natural causes. John Keill, a mathematician and supporter of Isaac Newton, tried to disprove Burnet's hypothesis by showing "the impossibility of all *Natural* and *Mechanical* explications of the deluge whatsoever." He concluded that "tho' our holy Faith stands so well confirmed by real miracles, that we are neither to make nor admit of any false ones, yet certainly we are not to detract from the value of the true ones, by pretending to deduce them from Natural and Mechanical causes."[15] And Erasmus Warren, another opponent, accused Burnet of divesting natural catastrophes of their significance as divine judgments. According to the *Sacred Theory*, the Flood was produced by a chain of causes which operated regardless of human behavior. But, asked Warren,

13. Burnet, *Sacred Theory of the Earth*, 2: 131–40.
14. Whiston, *New Theory of the Earth*, pp. 209, 372.
15. John Keill, *An Examination of Dr. Burnet's Treatise of the Earth* (Oxford, 1698), p. 33.

what if Adam had not fallen? His descendants would have suffered the consequences of the Deluge even though they had remained sinless. Catastrophic providences had thus been robbed of their meaning.[16]

Whiston too came under attack. One critic ridiculed the idea that Moses wrote Genesis for "the capacity of the Block-ish *Brick-makers* that were newly come out of Egypt, and scarcely understood Common Sense, and therefore any Story of a Cock and a Bull would serve them." But once again a greater flaw was the "rash folly to expect *Mathematical Con-gruity* in every Production, and to look for *Mechanick Laws* in the erecting of the Universe." Such theories gave aid and comfort to atheists.[17] Whiston also acknowledged that one of the objections which had been made to him privately was "That my Mechanical Account of the Deluge implies it was no divine Judgment for the World's Wickedness; but from the Necessity of the Motion of the Comet and Earth, must have happen'd whether Men had repented or not; and so induces a rigid fatality."[18]

But Whiston and Burnet had foreseen these objections and provided their own defenses. These followed three main lines of argument. In the first place, both men pointed out that their theories, however much they emphasized natural explanations, by no means excluded the miraculous. Burnet defended his use of mechanistic laws by arguing that a clock-maker was better esteemed if he made his clocks strike with-out having to do it himself every time; but at the same time, he admitted that to deny miracles "would be a Limitation of the divine Power and Will so to be bound up in second Causes."

16. Erasmus Warren, *Geologia, or a Discourse Concerning the Earth before the Deluge* (London, 1690), chap. 6.

17. John Edwards, *Brief Remarks upon Mr. Whiston's New Theory of the Earth* (London, 1697), pp. 1–2, 17.

18. Whiston, *Vindication*, p. 30.

Thus, although the desiccation of the world might come about naturally, Burnet saw no harm in having supernatural help for the conflagration itself. If Nature was "not sufficient to work her own Destruction, let us allow Destroying Angels to interest themselves in the Work," he said, adding that no one could properly complain that God's providence was diminished by his having subalterns carry out the orders: " 'Tis the true Rule and Method of it"! And of course, Christ's coming would be "wholly out of the way of natural Causes."[19] Similarly, Whiston freely granted that his theory could account for events such as the creation of Adam and Eve only by granting the immediate influence of God.[20]

Secondly, Burnet and Whiston both denied that natural events would be deprived of their moral significance merely because they obeyed mechanistic laws. To Burnet, speculation about whether the Flood would have served any purpose even if Adam had never fallen seemed only a short step away from blasphemy. If this train of thought were allowed, what was to stop men from wondering if *Christ* would be of any use under the same circumstances? More to the point, it was "a Weakness . . . to think, that when a Train is laid in Nature, and Methods concerted, for the execution of a Divine Judgment, therefore it is not *providential*." God knew quite well the "Futuritions" of both the natural and the moral world, "and hath so dispos'd the one, as to serve him in his just Judgments upon the other."[21] Whiston referred his own readers to Burnet's reply, and strenuously denied the presence of any "*rigid Fatality*" in his theory. "I believe the same" he said, "as to the Success of Prayer, the Interest of the Divine Providence, and the Deluge's being a proper effect thereof, as any other Christian does." Obviously, God in his prescience had

19. Burnet, *Sacred Theory of the Earth*, 1: 144–45; 2: 98–103.
20. Whiston, *A New Theory of the Earth*, pp. 222 ff.
21. Burnet, *Sacred Theory of the Earth*, 2: 419–20.

foreseen "the Sins, and therefore Originally dispos'd the Comet's Course for the Punishment."[22]

Thirdly, both men realized that the line between the natural and supernatural aspects of God's plan was sometimes difficult to draw. Obviously, Christ's literal descent could only be accomplished miraculously. But the description of other providences sometimes remained hazy. One of Burnet's critics objected that the process of the earth's cooling described in the *Sacred Theory* would inevitably take much longer than the six days the Bible allotted for creation. That was certainly true, Burnet admitted, if God used an ordinary providence to do the job. But "if according to an extraordinary, [then] you may suppose it made in six Minutes, if you please. 'Twas plain Work, and a simple Process, according to the Theory; consisting only of such and such Separations, and a Concretion: and either of these might be accelerated, and despatch'd in a longer or shorter Time, as Providence thought fit."[23] Burnet had not scrapped his natural processes in favor of divine fiat; he merely called on a little miraculous help to speed them up. In the same way, although the Flood had been caused naturally, Burnet assumed that the voyagers in the ark never could have survived the perils of the raging waters "if there had not been a miraculous Hand of Providence to take care of them. But 'tis hard to separate and distinguish an ordinary and extraordinary Providence in all Cases, and to mark just how far one goes, and where the other begins." The proper balance, he thought, was "a constant ordinary Providence, and an occasional extraordinary."[24]

Whiston made the connection even closer. He admitted, like Burnet, that "indeed, 'tis difficult enough, in several instances, to determine what is the effect of a natural and

22. Whiston, *Vindication*, pp. 30, 31.
23. Burnet, *Sacred Theory of the Earth*, 2: 404-05.
24. Ibid., 1: 144-45.

ordinary, and what of a supernatural and extraordinary Providence." But he used Newton's latest discoveries to prove his point.

> 'Tis now evident, That *Gravity*, the most mechanical affection of Bodies, and which seems most natural, depends entirely on the constant and efficacious, and if you will, the supernatural and miraculous Influence of Almighty God. And I do not know whether the falling of a Stone to the Earth ought not more truly to be esteem'd a *supernatural Effect*, or a *Miracle*, than what we with the greatest surprize should so stile, its remaining pendulous in the open Air; since the former requires an *active Influence* in the first Cause, while the latter supposes *Non-annihilation* only.[25]

From this point of view, almost anything that happened could be classified as miraculous, as John Edwards pointed out. Although a miracle could be defined in part as an event which surpassed finite power, Edwards argued that it also possessed the qualities of rarity and wonder.[26] Yet if not all divines were willing to agree with Whiston's definition of miracle, few would have quarreled with his conclusion that, where secondary causes had been used, God linked their natural and moral effects with infinite precision, ordering "the whole System with every individual Branch of it, as to Time, Place, Proportion, and all other Circumstances."[27]

The explanations and refinements of the two *Theories of the Earth* may not have won over Burnet's and Whiston's critics, but they at least provide us with information that helps to refine our own initial hypotheses about millennial logic.

25. Whiston, *A New Theory of the Earth*, p. 218.
26. Edwards, *Brief Remarks upon Mr. Whiston's New Theory*, pp. 41–42.
27. Whiston, *A New Theory of the Earth*, p. 219.

For one, they indicate that some critics did fear that a mechanical explanation of the deluge and conflagration might rob those judgments of their moral significance. That would seem to support our first hypothesis. But what a critic thinks his opponent ought logically to believe is not always what the opponent ends up believing. Arminians have often argued that the doctrine of predestination would encourage Calvinists to indulge in fatalistic hedonism; Cotton Mather feared that a belief in a distant conflagration would lull Christians into a sleepy complacency; and nineteenth-century postmillennialists argued that those who waited for Christ's personal coming would do nothing to spread the Gospel. Each of these "logical" conclusions landed wide of the mark because men who reject a particular doctrine are always willing to draw out of it consequences which its adherents never wished to embrace. Whiston and Burnet rightly denied that their theories encouraged fatalism, and they effectively used traditional arguments to back up their position. Like their more orthodox opponents, they believed that God's moral judgments were reflected in natural as well as supernatural events.

Whiston's and Burnet's treatises also suggest that the boundary between the ordinary and the extraordinary is not a line which can be easily used to distinguish different millennial psychologies. As Burnet said, where one kind of providence began and the other left off was hard to determine. Furthermore, the two *Theories* demonstrate that the essential element in the logic which predicts a passive eschatology is the catastrophic, not the supernatural. The reason that believers might be discouraged by a miraculous beginning to the millennium was that it made the establishment of God's kingdom depend on actions beyond the control of the faithful. But people had as little control over certain kinds of ordinary providences as they did over extraordinary ones. The natural flames produced by Whiston's comet, for instance, would be as sufficiently discouraging as a conflagration direct from the hand of God. In that case, the original focus of our inquiry has proved too narrow. Instead of concentrating exclusively on the boundary between natural and supernatural, we ought to give more attention to how men's efforts related to all providences—both ordinary and extraordinary—whose immediate source was God. To rephrase the original question, did some students of the prophecies prefer to use catastrophes to explain unfulfilled predictions? And did others prefer to rely on humanly instigated solutions?

One way to answer these questions would be to search once again the apocalyptic commentaries. The results, however, would likely prove ambiguous. Expositors remembered the central interpretational premise that prophecies would remain obscure until fulfilled by the event, and thus they often hedged their predictions.[28] Furthermore, few New Englanders had the time to spend computing the orbits of comets, speculating on the effects of an untilted axis, or devoting a lifetime to writing lengthy commentaries like Mede's. Yet there may be a way to use the dictum on prophetic obscurity to advantage. Suppose we take the divines at their own word, assume that prophecies are interpreted by the event, and give them an event to work on—tempt them, like Job, with a disaster or two and see how they react. In short, try to discover the relationship between catastrophe and eschatology by watching ministers interpret events rather than prophecies.

As Providence would have it, historians have been provided with two catastrophes which allow them to do just that. In 1727 and again in 1755, New England trembled, both literally

28. See, e.g., William Allen's treatment of the "great earthquake," which he said would undoubtedly be "extraordinary" and "out of the usual road of human power," but which also seemed to mean no more than antichristian "enemies falling out among themselves." Allen, *Of the State of the Church in Future Ages*, pp. 130–51.

and figuratively, as a result of earthquakes. Each time, ministers were summoned to their pulpits, and many of the sermons they delivered eventually found their way to the press, over twenty following the first quake and close to fifteen after the second. More than half the sermons discussed the Revelation's prophecies of earthquakes in some detail; several more alluded to future events, but merely as further means of arousing sinners to reformation ("God's shaking the Earth now, may have made these future & more dreadful things, to be more Affecting").[29] The remainder treated the calamities without discussing their relation to the Apocalypse.

From one point of view, the sermons make rather monotonous reading. The ministers of New England chose their basic themes with a consistency that verges on boredom. The earthquakes could be nothing less than a terrible judgment on the prevailing sins of the land. Profane swearing, drinking, licentiousness, and the usual catalogue of lapses made their dutiful appearance; and nearly every parishioner in New England must have heard the story of the jailer in Acts who threw himself at the feet of Paul and Silas during an earthquake, crying, "Syrs, what shall I do that I may be saved?"

But if this consistency is boring by reason of repetition, it is also interesting because of the implications it has for the present inquiry. We had suspected that perhaps those men with a catastrophic view of history would take the opportunity afforded by the disasters to express one eschatological point of view, whereas those who considered superhuman providences an inconsequential part of the prophecies would express another perspective—at least implicitly—by failing to connect the earthquakes with the latter days. But the consistency of the ministers undermines this suspicion. The themes of their sermons were affected very little by the addition or

29. Stephen Mix, *Extraordinary Displays* (New London, 1728), p. 32.

omission of prophetic material. An earthquake interpreted eschatologically received essentially the same treatment as an earthquake interpreted noneschatologically.

Catastrophe, in other words, did play an important role in eschatology, but only because certain basic attitudes about providence were shared by all New Englanders and not just by one particular group of catastrophically oriented interpreters. Ministers in 1755 as well as 1727, New Light as well as Old, accepted the prevailing assumptions that earthquakes were naturally caused, that they were inescapably meant as moral judgments, and that (most important) they were compatible with other moral judgments which God accomplished by using human instruments. They saw natural disasters as one proper part of the climax to history, not because of a preference for any specific millennial chronologies (once again a wide range of opinion appeared on that subject), but because catastrophes fell under the more general category of moral judgment, which was a necessary part of ultimate deliverance.

NATURAL CATASTROPHES AND JUDGMENT

The tremors of 1727 and 1755 were relatively minor ones, but only in retrospect: no tremor of the earth is minor to anyone in the middle of it. In 1727, most people were on their way to bed at the end of an October sabbath, when "they heard first a gentle Murmur, like a small rustling Wind, and then a more noisy Rumbling, as of Thunder at some Distance," which grew louder and louder.[30] "The crashing Noise was very amazing to me," wrote Samuel Sewall. "For I was just warm in my Bed, but not asleep. The young people were quickly frighted out of the Shaking, clattering Kitchen, and fled with weeping Cryes into our Chamber, where they made

30. Thomas Foxcroft, *The Voice of the Lord from the Deep Places of the Earth* (Boston, 1727), p. 5.

a fire, and abode there till morning." Sewall maintained an
outward magisterial calm, all the while thinking to himself of
a certain "good Bishop and his Lady . . . who were buried in
their Bed in the desolating Tempest in England; but I did not
venture to tell my thoughts."[31] Almost thirty years later, the
rumbling returned at 4:15 on a frosty November morning,
sending glasses flying from shelves, seriously damaging close
to a hundred chimneys in Boston, and cracking many more.[32]

Naturally enough, the sermons which followed this phe-
nomenon rang the familiar changes on the themes of the
jeremiad that Perry Miller has described so well. But ministers
realized they had another duty, however subordinate. The
anxious parishioners who crowded into the meeting houses
the morning after looked to them for an explanation of the
more specific workings of the earthquake. As a result, preachers generally devoted parts of their sermons to explaining
current scientific theories. Virtually everyone agreed that the
recent disturbances were naturally caused, although they
added that God could, of course, produce earthquakes supernaturally. "Some Earthquakes are from GOD immediately,"
said James Allin, noting the biblical tremors at Sinai and the
universal convulsion following the Crucifixion. Yet the age of
miracles had long ago ceased, and God now preferred to use
"the agency of second Causes" to accomplish his purpose.[33]

The natural mechanisms of the earthquakes remained the
subject of speculation. Sermons sometimes mentioned the
possibility of a "Windy Exhalation imprisoned in the Bowels
of the Earth and wanting vent"; but most of them preferred
to ascribe the cause to "*Subterraneous Fires* occasion'd by
the Fermentation of Combustible Minerals in the Earth, such

31. Sewall, *Letterbook*, 2: 229.
32. Charles Chauncy, *Earthquakes a Token of the Righteous Anger of God*
(Boston, 1755), appendix; Jonathan Mayhew, *The Expected Dissolution of All
Things* (Boston, 1755), Appendix.
33. Allin, *Thunder and Earthquake* (Boston, 1727), pp. 17–18.

as Sulpher, Salt-Petre, Vitriol, &c."[34] Thomas Prince noted that Boyle's calculations had proved there was a "terrible Atmosphere over us, [of] which few are aware, that is found to press with the weight of above *Two Thousand Pounds* on every *square Foot* of the surface of the Earth." When the compressed air in subterranean caverns was allowed to escape through a newly opened crevice, other parts of the earth might cave in. "Whole Cities, and Mountains," Prince warned, had been swallowed up in this manner.[35] John Barnard used a simpler scientific metaphor to enlighten his listeners: just as tumult resulted when fire heated water or met with gunpowder and air, so the smoldering elements in underground passages were roused into action.[36]

The only published sermon which reflected any uneasiness with the idea of a naturally caused earthquake was that of Thomas Paine, who told his congregation that "An Earthquake is wrought by the immediate mighty Power of God." Although he spent a significant portion of his time warning the audience of dangers inherent in an explanation relying on secondary causes, his ultimate position differed little from that of most New Englanders. "I don't hereby affirm, that God acts immediately without any Instrument in producing an Earthquake," he explained, but only that "God's Power is immediately ingaged, either by his own Interposition, or by him delegated to some Instrument." Earthquakes, in other words, might be naturally caused; but then again, they might not. How was it possible to tell from empirical evidence one kind of tremor from the other? It was hard to say "that

34. Ibid., p. 20.

35. Thomas Prince, *Earthquakes the Works of God* (Boston, 1727), pp. 10–11.

36. John Barnard, *Two Discourses Addressed to Young Persons* (Boston, 1727), pp. 78–83. Further examples of natural explanations include Benjamin Colman, *The Judgments of Providence* (Boston, 1727), p. vi; Foxcroft, *The Voice of the Lord*, p. 22; John Rogers, *The Nature and Necessity of Repentance* (Boston, 1728), p. 44.

this was natural and that supernatural."[37] Like Burnet and Whiston, he thought the line between the ordinary and extraordinary a difficult one to draw.

So did Jonathan Mayhew. Like everyone else, he admitted that earthquakes in modern times were the product of second causes, and thus were properly studied as a part of natural philosophy. But natural philosophy was "no more than the observing of facts, their succession and order; and reducing them to a general analogy; to certain established rules ... called the laws of nature, from their steadiness and constancy." And how well, after all, did earthquakes and other unusual events fit into that framework?

> How many things are there in the natural world, which never have been, and perhaps never will be, reduced to such a general analogy ...? How many phenomena are there, which we may call the irregulars, the anomalies, and heteroclites in the grammar ... by which God speaks to us as really, as by his written oracles?

Underneath, of course, the regularity remained, even in the disposition of earthquakes. But not being able to perceive it made the event appear marvelous. And even if men knew all the applicable general laws, they could not account for the laws themselves, which (as Whiston had pointed out) were "mysterious and inexplicable." In effect, concluded Mayhew, "the whole natural world, is really nothing but one great wonder and mystery."[38]

Thus the question of whether earthquakes were naturally or supernaturally caused was irrelevant. God was responsible for all events in the world, whether directly or through medi-

37. Thomas Paine, *The Doctrine of Earthquakes* (Boston, 1728), pp. 14–16, 26–27.

38. Jonathan Mayhew, *A Discourse on Revelation XV: 3–4* (Boston, 1755), pp. 25–28.

ate causes. Samuel Phillips echoed the sentiments of all when
he claimed that it was "the most absurd and unreasonable
Thing" for anyone to "*cast off Fear, because Natural Causes
may be assigned for Earthquakes*; For does not the Great *God*,
ordinarily, make use of *Second Causes*, for the bringing on,
and executing such Judgments . . .?" Thomas Paine under-
scored the point, appropriately enough, by turning to eschatology: "What if it shall please God to set the World on Fire,
at the last Day, by using natural second Causes (as is likely
enough he will) will that at all obscure his immediate Power,
engaged in that dreadful Action?"[39] Both Phillips and Paine
thus made sure their parishioners would not miss the crucial
point: while it was quite proper to speculate about mechanical secondary causes, the earthquakes were to be understood
first and foremost as moral judgments from God. All the details of windy exhalations and sulphurous vitriol sank into in-
significance when compared with this major premise.[40]

Many ministers went even further in conflating natural and

39. Samuel Phillips, *Three Plain Practical Discourses* (Boston, 1728), pp. 110–
11; Paine, *The Doctrine of Earthquakes*, p. 21.

40. Some historians have thought that Professor John Winthrop's *Lecture on
Earthquakes* questioned the assumption that the earthquakes were moral judgments, and in effect mounted "a devastating attack on the prevailing concepts of
the relationship of God to the universe." (Clifford K. Shipton, *Sibley's Harvard
Graduates*, 14 vols. [Boston, 1873–], 9:248. See also Raymond P. Stearns,
Science in the British Colonies in America [Urbana, Ill., 1970], p. 649.) But
Winthrop admitted that the tremor's "terrible desolations" could "justly be regarded as the tokens of an incensed DEITY," and that "there is the most perfect
coincidence, at all times, between GOD's government of the *natural* and of the
moral world" (John Winthrop, *Lecture on Earthquakes* [Boston, 1755], pp. 27,
29). Although I have seen no definite evidence of it, perhaps Winthrop denied in
private the connection between God's moral and natural government. Ezra Stiles,
for one, believed the earthquake was not a moral judgment against New England,
though in later life he changed his mind. (E. S. Morgan, *The Gentle Puritan* [New
Haven, 1962], p. 170.) For a fuller discussion of the issue, see James W. Davidson, "Eschatology in New England: 1700–1763" (Ph.D. diss., Yale University,
1973), pp. 125–28, and the works cited there.

moral events. They affirmed that natural phenomena were not only moral judgments themselves, but were also often associated with judgments meted out through the use of human instrumentalities. As John Danforth said, "even when no great Desolations have been actually made" by earthquakes, they still acted as *"awful Warnings*, portenteous Signs, and *Forerunners* of great *State-quakes*, and *Church-quakes*, and *Desolations.*" Paine pointed out that this had been the case with the tremors in New England around the time of the Pequot War; although they had not caused significant harm to the Indians, they still were a sign that part of Satan's heathen kingdom was falling.[41] Benjamin Colman applied the same lesson to his own times. Britain and her dominions seemed to him to be getting the lion's share of earthquakes, and he worried that this might be an "omen" signaling trouble for the Protestant religion, or perhaps a threat to civil liberties.[42]

In 1755 there were the same fears. Gilbert Tennent noted that "surprising Phenomina in the Firmament, the Air, or Earth, have been sometimes the Preludes of publick Calamities, or national Revolutions." He thought the late earthquakes, "extraordinary in respect of number and dreadful Effects," might be pointing to "some extraordinary Revolutions to be near at Hand!" Jonathan Parsons dilated on the earthquakes, as well as "those fearful sights, and great signs that have been in the heavens . . . in the sun, and in the moon," which were "solemn warnings of some great surprising event at the door." And Jonathan Mayhew mentioned the same possibility to his own congregation.[43]

41. John Danforth, *A Sermon Occasioned by the Late Great Earthquake* (Boston, 1728), p. 2; Paine, *Doctrine of Earthquakes*, p. 65.

42. Colman, *Judgments of Providence*, p. vii.

43. Gilbert Tennent, *The Good Man's Character and Reward Represented . . . Together with Reflections on the Presage of Approaching Calamities* (Philadelphia, 1756), p. 23; Jonathan Parsons, *Good News from a Far Country* (Portsmouth, N.H., 1756), p. 168; Mayhew, *Discourse on Rev. XV:3-4*, p. 69.

It may seem like splitting hairs to distinguish between the belief that earthquakes were themselves a divine judgment and the belief that they also accompanied tumults in the political and religious world. But these hairs are particularly relevant to this investigation. Our first hypothetical reconstruction suggested that those who posited a naturally caused conflagration could conclude that the final catastrophe might not serve as a moral judgment after all. Since New Englanders saw earthquakes as naturally caused and nonetheless also as moral judgments, this hypothesis would seem unwarranted. The second reconstruction suggested that even though natural catastrophes were moral judgments, they were generally incompatible with God's preferred method of operation, which was through human instrumentalities. But this hypothesis is damaged by the prevailing assumption that natural signs and wonders often accompanied dramatic judgments that God brought about by using men as prime actors and movers. The combination was easy enough to make. For eighteenth-century New Englanders, the natural and moral spheres were so well contempered with one another that it was not at all inappropriate to have a judgment accomplished by human instrumentalities accompanied by another one levied through natural means. If, as Benjamin Colman assumed, the British nation was becoming so sinful that God needed to warn its people of their degeneracy, why not have the country shaken by earthquakes at the same time as its civil liberties were being threatened by designing men?

EARTHQUAKES AND THE VARIETIES OF ESCHATOLOGY

Watching ministers interpret events instead of prophecies has provided some preliminary evidence about the workings of providence but, thus far, little about eschatology. In what ways did ministers associate events predicted for the latter days with their own current catastrophes?

The obvious connection to be made was with the earthquakes

predicted for the time of the conflagration, the resurrection of the witnesses, and in general as signs of Christ's coming. While some of these passages had already been interpreted metaphorically by expositors, only John Barnard explicitly dissociated the current tremors from an eschatological context. He noted that, when the Revelation predicted earthquakes, they generally stood for "great Changes and Revolutions," and that "Thus also our Blessed Saviour seems to intend Metaphorical Earthquakes, when He mentions them as signs of His Coming." His conclusion was that "possibly whenever we read of Earthquakes in the Revelations, they intend Revolutions, and Changes, in the State, or in the Church."[44] But Barnard was an exception, and most ministers would have agreed with his friend Benjamin Colman that tremors acted as signs that accompanied political tumults rather than as mere metaphors of them. If there was any spot which surpassed Britain's proclivity for earthquakes, noted Colman, it was "Italy, that seat of sodomy. . . . And why may not its fall be by literal earthquakes and eruptions of *sulphureous* flames? The fiery hand of CHRIST shall effect this."[45]

Most ministers who discussed the eschatological implications of the earthquakes could agree on the basic point that literal convulsions would play some part in the latter days. But as usual, few divines were of one mind on the more specific details of how the end would come. We look in vain for a consensus that placed the conflagration before the millennium and assumed its imminence, or a disposition which allowed a violent, superhuman providence to monopolize center stage. Instead, ministers' opinions covered a broad spectrum, ranging from the belief in the imminent end of the world to the calmer judgment that the conflagration remained on the far side of the thousand-year reign.

44. Barnard, *Two Discourses*, pp. 74–77.
45. Colman, *Judgments of Providence*, p. 28.

As might be expected, the one divine who transformed his pronouncements on the earthquake into a veritable apocalyptic manifesto was the same man who hustled two sermons on the subject off to the press, one of them going through three editions in as many months. Cotton Mather had been convinced since 1716 that "all the Signs" of Christ's coming had been given, and that therefore "it becomes us to look upon every Earthquake, as a Praemonition" of the day when antichrist would be destroyed. But he added (parting company with Colman), "what a CONFLAGRATION will be joined with it!" Whiston's calculations had ended the 1,260 years of the Roman monarchy ten years earlier; for all Cotton knew, Christ's literal coming would be the next event. "I do not speak these things, as a Melancholy Visionary," he cried, but could not resist a shot at the "commonly Received Opinions" about Christ's coming, which seemed "as if on purpose" to keep the world in a profound sleep. "If I should make the Cry, FIRE, FIRE! . . . I should be as much *mocked*, and be as little minded, as Lot was in the *Morning* of the Day he went out of Sodom."[46] Mather may not have been a Melancholy Visionary, but he was the next best thing New England could get up on such short notice.

Cotton was right on at least one point: the majority of ministers could not accept his theory that the conflagration was imminent. But he did have at least one supporter whose views, though more moderate, reflected Mather's central concerns. Thomas Prince had become a firm friend of the older minister ("as Cordial and Constant . . . as any I have," wrote Cotton once) ever since the young man's return in 1721 from a stay in England.[47] The two often compared their readings of the prophecies, and although Prince did not follow Mather

46. Cotton Mather, *The Terror of the Lord* (Boston, 1727), pp. 27–28; and *Boanerges* (Boston, 1727), pp. 44, 41.

47. Mather, *Diary*, 1:337.

on every point, he shared a penchant for the dramatic.[48] In 1719 he began his publishing career with an "improvement" of the aurora borealis which he and his friends had observed while in England. For a man steeped in the theories of Whiston and Burnet, it took little imagination to see that the smoky light was "in the shape of a Broad Sword," and its color "almost like Brimstone":

> We all began to think whether the SON of GOD was next to make His Glorious & Terrible Appearance, or the Conflagration of the World was now begun. For the Elements seem'd just as if they were melting with fervent Heat, & the Aetherial Vault to be burning over us like the fierce Agitations of the Blaze in a Furnace, or at the Top of a Fiery Oven: & the Glimmering Light look'd as if it proceeded from a *more Glorious Body behind* that was approaching nearer & about to make its sudden Appearance to our Eyes.

This must have scared the hell out of them—or to use Prince's terminology, provided a providential sight designed "for a general Observation and Terrour."[49]

The same, of course, could be said of the 1727 earthquake, since Jesus had predicted earthquakes and other disasters before his second coming, and "THEY are these PARTICULAR Earthquakes that we are now considering: of which there have been great Numbers . . . in these latter Ages." Here was warning enough of the approaching final convulsion, when Christ

48. Prince voiced one of his own particular conceits in a sermon on the downfall of antichrist. Samuel Sewall noted it, and remarked that the "One Fly . . . discovered in his Ointment" was the belief "that the 1000 years Rev. 20. stood for Three Hundred and Sixty Thousand years; taking every day of the 1000. years for a year." Sewall, *Diary*, 3:282.

49. Thomas Prince, *An Account of a Strange Appearance* (Boston, 1719), pp. 3–6, 11. Prince was criticized at the time for "supposing that dreadful things will follow such [phenomena] as Famine, Sword or Sickness." See Thomas Robie, *A Letter to a Certain Gentleman* (Boston, 1719), p. 8.

would also come "to set this lower World on Fire, to refine it, and to consume the Sinners out of it."[50] Thirty years later when the tremors returned, Prince dusted off his sermon and sent it to the press along with his more recent effort, which was published separately. The latter repeated the warnings to watch for the unexpected fire ("how near we know not") and provided a description of the late earthquake's effects as edification for his readers:

> Upon the first Shock of the Earthquake, many Persons jump'd out of their Beds, and ran immediately into the Streets, while others sprung to the Windows, trembling, and seeing their Neighbours, as it were naked; *shrieked with Apprehension of its being the Day of Judgment,* and some tho't they heard the LAST TRUMP sounding, and cry'd out for Mercy.[51]

Prince's earthquake sermons did not discuss the details of his prophetic views, but these were revealed in William Torrey's *Brief Discourse Concerning Futurities*, a seventy-year old tract that Prince arranged to have published in 1757. Torrey generally culled his points out of Joseph Mede: Christ's coming would be "personal, visible and glorious"; it would precede the millennium, as would the conflagration; and the first resurrection of saints was to be a literal one, followed by paradise state where lions would actually lie down with lambs.[52]

50. Thomas Prince, *Earthquakes the Works of God* (Boston, 1727), pp. 6, 44.

51. Thomas Prince, *An Improvement of the Doctrine of Earthquakes* (Boston, 1755), pp. 14, 16.

52. William Torrey, *A Brief Discourse Concerning Futurities* (Boston, 1755), pp. 9, 23–30, 38–41, and passim. For reasons which remain unclear, Heimert calls Torrey's tract "essentially postmillennial," though he says that Prince corrected Torrey's implicitly literal reading of the earthquakes (Heimert, *Religion and the American Mind*, p. 75). In fact, though both men were in effect premillennialists, Prince never corrected Torrey on this score, and interpreted scriptural earthquakes literally, while Torrey (following Mede) explicitly said they represented "Distress

Several other earthquake sermons demonstrated that Mede's influence remained considerable even in the 1750s. John Burt and John Rogers, two Old Lights, noted that the "universal Earthquake" at Christ's second coming would be preceded by littler ones. Although neither man discussed his views at great length, Burt associated the last convulsion with the fall of antichrist, putting the conflagration and second coming before the thousand-year reign; and Rogers noted that at the time of the fire, true believers would have "a Part in the First Resurrection."[53] Mather Byles was more explicit, envisioning the righteous being caught up in the air to avoid being burned. He concluded that the day was near ("it hasteth quickly") and accordingly issued an inspirational poem the same year, entitled "The Conflagration."[54]

It would seem natural that those who followed Mede would be likely to use their earthquake sermons as a platform for matters eschatological, since he put the conflagration and its attendant concussions ahead of the thousand years. But divines like Joseph Sewall and Benjamin Colman, who both accepted a postmillennial conflagration, also discussed the eschatological overtones of the earthquakes.[55] And perhaps the most unorthodox examples of millennial opinion were to be found in the sermons of two prominent liberals, Charles Chauncy and Jonathan Mayhew.

---

of Nations" (p. 19). Another prophetic tract by an old New England worthy (Ezekiel Cheever, schoolmaster to Samuel Sewall, among others) was published the same year and reflected the same views. Perhaps Prince sponsored it, although there is no evidence of this. See Ezekiel Cheever, *Scripture Prophecies Explained* (Boston, 1757), pp. 7–11.

53. Burt's reliance on Mede's scenario can be seen from his association of Isaiah 24th: 17–19 with Revelation 16:15–19. John Burt, *Earthquakes, the Effects of God's Wrath* (Newport, R.I., 1755), pp. 4–5, 17; John Rogers, *Three Sermons* (Boston, 1756), pp. 60–61.

54. Mather Byles, *Divine Power and Anger Displayed in Earthquakes* (Boston, 1755), pp. 25–30; and *Poems. The Conflagration* (Boston, 1755), pp. 4–5.

55. Sewall's views will be discussed later in the chapter.

Chauncy's earthquake sermon included the predictable assertion that the tremor was "a lively emblem" of the approaching "*awful day of God*"; but *The Earth Delivered from the Curse*, a sermon he preached only a few months later, evidenced an interpretation of the final days that was quite unusual. The curse, of course, was the one God had uttered upon sending Adam from the Garden of Eden, and it had made the earth a much less hospitable place. Chauncy's description of the changes in the earth reflected his familiarity with Thomas Burnet's works and a similar concern with the physical consequences of the Fall. The seasons were more extreme now, the earth less fruitful, and the air less pure (which, according to Chauncy, encouraged the growth of thorns!). The removal of this curse would come, as it had for Burnet, only through the dissolution of the world by fire. But here he parted company: "Some have tho't, that these *new heavens and earth* will be formed before the *general resurrection* and *judgment*; but 'tis with me beyond all doubt, that they are herein mistaken."[56]

That statement alone indicated how far Chauncy had departed from established millennial theories. By putting the new heavens and new earth after the Last Judgment, he rejected a postmillennial eschatology; by also putting them after the general resurrection (which included judgment of the wicked) he rejected the theories of Mede and the Mathers which asserted that evil men would be condemned and sentenced to hell only after the thousand years had ended. Chauncy's reasons for this departure were scriptural. Peter's classic passage describing the conflagration as the passing away of the earth and heaven was also "spoken of by the Apostle John" in the twenty-first chapter of the Revelation, where "the first heaven and the first earth passed away." But

56. Charles Chauncy, *The Earth Delivered from the Curse* (Boston, 1756), p. 9. Chauncy cites Burnet, p. 14.

chapter twenty had already described the dead coming forth to be judged "before [John] saw the erection of a *new earth and heavens.*" Thus Chauncy concluded that the new heavens and new earth referred not to a millennial world but to the traditional heavenly paradise, and even more astonishing, that "*this world of ours . . . the very world we now live in*, thus changed and made new, is the place, where good men, after the resurrection, and judgment, shall live and reign with Christ forever and ever."[57]

If the new heavens and earth were nothing more than heaven, then where did the millennium fit in? Chauncy remained mum. For him, the 1750s were a time when a systematic re-interpretation of Scripture led him to believe in the doctrine of universal salvation. Chauncy dared not publish these heretical views until the 1780s, and even then only anonymously. What historians have failed to appreciate about the *Mystery Hid from Ages* is that, in it, Chauncy uses the millennium to distinguish his position from the universalism of Murray and Relly. The standard orthodox objection to universalism was that sinners who had no fear of future punishment would lack any motive for behaving uprightly. But Chauncy interpreted the first resurrection as literal and applicable to sinners as well as saints. During the thousand years (which he interpreted to be "a *long* time, God only knows how long") good men would "be admitted, at Christ's second coming, to dwell with him in his *kingdom of glory* . . . while [sinful rebels] shall be banished [from] his presence, to dwell in unspeakable torment till they are wrought upon to see their folly." The

---

57. Ibid., pp. 14–15. In this conclusion he was influenced by an English Non-conformist, Joseph Hallet, who had pointed out that, contrary to popular belief, the Bible used the word *heaven* to refer only to where God had his throne, not to where good men would live after the resurrection. Hallet, *A Free Impartial Study . . . Being Notes on Some Peculiar Texts*, 3 vols. (London, 1726–36), 1:198; quoted in Chauncy, *Earth delivered*, p. 15 n.

millennium thus became the crucial period necessary for the correction of the wicked, so that *all* men might ultimately be saved without endangering the ethics of the present world.[58]

Jonathan Mayhew, too, was unorthodox in his eschatology. In a sermon delivered five days after the earthquake, he explained to his audience that the conflagration would come when fires inside the earth grew in strength and burst out upon the land. But Mayhew was unwilling to limit the destruction to the earth alone, because "for anything we know to the contrary, or have reason to think, there may be more wicked Worlds than one, which shall, at this period, undergo the same fiery doom and dissolution." In fact, Scripture hinted that the whole solar system rather than the earth alone might be destroyed: how else could the predictions of the moon's darkening and sun's not giving light be taken? And Peter had said that the faithful should look for new heavens as well as a new earth.[59] All this was contrary to the common opinion formulated by Mede, who had distinguished between three linguistic uses of the word *heaven*, concluding that in the case of the conflagration, only the "sublunary" atmosphere had been meant.[60]

But when was the cataclysm coming? Mayhew claimed no "human arithmetic" could divine the final hour, but Scriptures had said the fire would coincide with Christ's literal descent, which would be ushered in by some "astonishing tokens." The thirteenth chapter of Mark had described them, but ministers disagreed on their interpretation, Mayhew

58. Chauncy, *Mystery Hid from Ages and Generations, Made Manifest by the Gospel Revelation* (London, 1784), pp. 199, 224, and 203–24, as well as the appendix, which deals specifically with the text of the Revelation. Conrad Wright, *The Beginnings of Unitarianism in America* (Boston, 1955), chap. 8, is good on the origins of Chauncy's universalism.

59. Jonathan Mayhew, *Expected Dissolution of All Things* (Boston, 1755), pp. 33, 19–20.

60. Mede, *Works*, pp. 614–15.

noted. Earthquakes had been mentioned there, but since they were "common at other times, and in all ages," they could not be considered a reliable sign. And then there was the question of which coming was meant. Mayhew knew that "some interpret what is said in this chapter [i.e. Mark 13] concerning the coming of our Lord, of a figurative, and less proper coming, viz. as he came to destroy Jerusalem, with the whole Jewish polity." But Mayhew could not agree. "It has evidently a farther view," he concluded, looking forward to the time when Christ "shall literally descend from heaven" to pass the final judgment sentence.[61]

Mayhew made one more significant conjecture. Scripture indicated "not only that the future conflagration and last judgment will be contemporary" but also—clean contrary to Charles Chauncy's hopes—that the earth would be "thus reserved unto fire, partly, at least, for the place and scene of that punishment and perdition, which awaits the wicked." Joseph Hallet's arguments about the meaning of heaven evidently did not move him, for he envisioned one "far above the stars" which would become the final residence of the saints, "to which no flames can ascend."[62] Mayhew's deductions also led him to disagree with Chauncy on chronology. Since the Last Judgment came at the same time as the fire, and that same fire was to continue on earth as the "everlasting" flames of hell, the millennium on earth had to occur before the final catastrophe.

Mayhew was quite diffident about fixing a date for his

61. Historians have sometimes read this passage as a rejection of the postmillennial notion that Christ came to inaugurate the thousand years only figuratively. In fact, Mayhew never rejected the figurative coming but only argued that Mark 13 referred to the literal one, at the general resurrection: "indeed, there are some things in this discourse, which cannot possibly be referred to that figurative coming of Christ before mentioned; but only to the time of his coming to judge the quick and the dead." *Expected Dissolution*, p. 30.

62. Ibid., pp. 24, 32.

holocaust, but since he thought that at least a thousand years of bliss would intervene, he was naturally inclined to think the dissolution was "still very remote in futurity."[63] In a second sermon improving the earthquake, he noted the "chief articles" yet to be accomplished. Babylon would have to be "utterly destroyed; which surely, will be a great work, whenever it is accomplished"; the Jews would be converted and gathered from their wide dispersions; and the heathen Gentiles would finally see the light, uniting the whole world as disciples of Christ.[64] Of course, Jesus had warned that his second coming would be like a thief in the night, and Mayhew hastened to say that he might be mistaken in his opinion. Yet he insisted that the certainty of that coming rather than its nearness was what believers ought to remember most. In what may well have been a jab at Thomas Prince's less cautious rhetoric, he concluded that it would be "impious pretence" to "designedly impose upon and terrify men, by representing the time when [the dissolution] shall come to pass, as being either certainly, or even probably, very near at hand."[65]

Thus the prophetic opinions found in earthquake sermons ranged all the way from Cotton Mather's and Thomas Prince's dramatic use of Mede to Jonathan Mayhew's restrained postponements of the conflagration. The ministers who used eschatology to improve catastrophe were not limited to one particular version of the last days, let alone a belief in the imminence of the dissolution. Yet for all the specific disagreements, several general themes characterized the prophetic discussions—themes which are at first confusing because they appear to contradict each other.

One of these was the gloomy conclusion that, even if the

---

63. Ibid., p. 39.
64. Mayhew, *A Discourse on Rev. XV:3–4*, p. 20.
65. Mayhew, *Expected Dissolution*, p. 37. For a further examination of Mayhew's eschatology, see below, chap. 5.

conflagration was not imminent, the world was steadily declining, both physically and morally. The earthquakes, of
course, were the symbol of the natural decay; as Prince had
pointed out, their increasing frequency in recent years com-
ported with the biblical predictions of the latter days. In
1727, other divines agreed with Prince. John Fox peppered
his congregation at Woburn with a series of questions calculated to make his own feelings plain: "Have there not been
many *Earthquakes* in these latter Times? whereby these Predictions seem to be fulfilling apace?" And what about all the
volcanic eruptions—did they not "Presage, and Forebode the
near Approach, of that Universal Conflagration, which shall
bring on its Final Dissolution? Oh, have we not reason to conclude the habitable World in which we dwell is hastning on
amain to its Dissolution?" Fox did realize that the Revelation's
mention of the earthquake dividing Babylon was surely meant
metaphorically, but he could not resist adding "(and that perhaps) not only metaphorically, but literally."[66] Similarly,
John Cotton (grandson of his famous namesake) described a
"carnally secure and stupid" world which was meant to serve
as a sign reminding watchful believers that Christ might any
day "personally and visibly descend with a glorious retinue of
Holy Angels."[67] And Nathaniel Morrill, of Rye, New Hampshire, began his sermon by pointing out the supposed rash of
recent earthquakes as undoubted "forerunners of doleful and
calamitous Days" which preceded the destruction of the
wicked.[68]

Similar conclusions were reached in 1755. Thomas Foxcroft
noted that earthquakes were generally "a rare thing" when
compared with some of God's other natural judgments; but

---

66. John Fox, *God by His Power Causes the Earth and Its Inhabitants to Tremble* (Boston, 1728), pp. 10–11, 25.
67. John Cotton, *A Holy Fear of God* (Boston, 1727), pp. v–vi.
68. Nathaniel Morrill, *The Lord's Voice* (Boston, 1728), p. 2.

Scripture suggested they would perhaps "become more and more common in this last Age of the World." Foxcroft biblically observed that the earth waxed old as doth a garment, "and an old Garment easily admits of Rents." But he also measured the earth's age in a moral sense: "As the World grows *old in Sin*, and the final Dissolution approaches nearer, we may reasonably expect a greater Frequency of this Divine Judgment."[69] Thomas Prentice used the traditional rhetorical question to make the same point: when earthquakes become "in a Manner universal, they are to be regarded as Prognosticks and Forerunners of the Destruction of the whole World. And have not these Judgments of Earthquakes, desolating Storms, Inundations, &c. been unusually prevalent in the World, of later Times?" Like Foxcroft, he saw earthquakes as symbolic of the world's decay both "in a moral and natural Sense; and of its drawing towards its Dissolution."[70]

These sentiments seem to indicate what we might have expected all along: that the catastrophic interpretation encouraged by earthquakes led to the pessimistic belief that the world was marching steadily downhill toward its violent and sinful end. Yet a second search through the sermons would reveal a different set of opinions. Hopes for a spreading and universal revival sometimes stood side by side with the more pessimistic prognostics.

Thomas Prentice, for instance, thought that the last great earthquake would tear Babylon apart, but he hardly assumed that the world, or even the Roman Catholic part of it, was necessarily condemned to a catastrophic finish. He hoped God would bring on "a glorious Reformation in that most corrupt, most idolatrous, most cruel, and bloody Church."

69. Thomas Foxcroft, *The Earthquake, a Divine Visitation* (Boston, 1756), pp. 32, 41-42.

70. Thomas Prentice, *Observations Moral and Religious, on the late terrible Night of the Earthquake* (Boston, 1756), p. 11.

Prentice never specifically equated this far-reaching reformation with the millennium (it might have been, as with Whiston and Burnet, an indication of the witnesses' resurrection); but his version of the dissolution seemed to favor a postmillennial conflagration.[71] Mather Byles would have disagreed on this last point; but even so, his hopes apparently outran his logic. "How happy would it be," he exclaimed, "if this awful Providence should be blessed by God to the producing a universal Reformation and a Revival of Religion among us!"[72]

The same unusual combinations were present in the 1727 sermons. Joseph Sewall noted, as many had, that the earthquakes were signs of Christ's coming and that since no one could be sure of the hour, everyone should have their lamps trimmed and ready. But he also used imagery reminiscent of Samuel Willard's prophetic tract. There was a day near, he predicted, when Christ the Fountain would be

> opened in the extensive Preaching of the Gospel, and the abundant Effusions of the Spirit of Grace, so that many Nations shall be sprinkled, yea washed from their Sins, when *all Israel shall be saved;* and the receiving of them shall be Life from the Dead to the Gentiles!

After all, if the prophecies promised widespread conversions among the Jews, why might not New England hope for a similar dispensation?[73]

71. Ibid., pp. 21–23. He assumed that the damned would be judged at the time of the conflagration, putting the millennium before it.

72. Byles, *Divine Power*, p. 22. Note also that Foxcroft, despite all his sentiments about the decaying moral world, still hoped that God would pour out his spirit on New England in order that " 'Glory [might] dwell in our Land.' " Foxcroft, *The Earthquake*, p. 50.

73. Joseph Sewall, *The Duty of a People* (Boston, 1727), p. 22; *Repentance— The Sure Way to Escape Destruction* (Boston, 1727), pp. 30, 40. Sewall, it will be remembered, opposed Cotton Mather's excited pronouncements of 1716 (see

At Haverhill, Massachusetts, John Brown was beginning to think the dispensation might well be on its way. In the month after the earthquake he had admitted 154 persons into the church, 87 of them to the Lord's Supper. "It has looked in short, as if we were going into a New World," he wrote to a friend; "which things have occasion'd in me various thoughts—and been as surprising as the EARTHQUAKES." Brown compared recent conversions with those recorded in past years, and discovered a dramatic upsurge. "I need not make any reflections to you, on these things," he concluded; "I want very much to hear what awful effects the awful visitation has had near, and about you, and what are the thoughts of the most Judicious about the *Signs of the Times.*"[74] Brown's hopeful conjectures were published by his friend John Cotton—the same John Cotton who warned in his own earthquake sermon of a "carnally secure and stupid" world that would be awaiting Christ when he made his descent "personally and visibly . . . with a glorious retinue of Holy Angels."[75]

This contradictory evidence makes it more difficult to assess the role that catastrophe played in prophetic thought. It would be easy enough to explain the pessimism of a world hastening on amain toward its dissolution, or simple enough to account for the optimism of a world gradually reforming itself into a land of milk and honey. But how do we explain a world that seems to be doing its best to go in both directions at the same time?

---

above, chap. 2); and that attitude apparently persisted. Mather at one time considered inviting him to the sessions he had with Thomas Prince on the prophecies, but noted that Sewall might have "a Less Degree of Relish for those things, not easy to be accounted for" (Mather, *Diary*, 2:685). Sewall's earthquake sermon likewise remained quite moderate in rhetoric when compared with Mather's or even Prince's productions.

74. Appendix (separately paginated), in Cotton, *A Holy Fear of God*, pp. 5–6, 7.

75. Cotton, *A Holy Fear of God*, pp. v–vi.

SALVATION AS JUDGMENT

One possible answer might be that New Englanders retained their optimism in an attempt to make the best of a difficult situation; and in one sense that is quite correct. The Revelation itself was in effect an attempt of that sort, written to account for the afflictive catastrophes that God had sent in the guise of Roman emperors. Early Christians were faced with the simple but distressing fact that Christ had not come and that Romans were hounding them wherever they went. God must have permitted these evil things; ergo John's comforting explanation that the suffering was part of the divine plan and God's ordained way of bringing about deliverance.

For similar reasons, the ministers who sought the meaning of history in 1727 and 1755 could not ignore the earthquakes. As long as God's moral government included the natural sphere, catastrophes perforce had to be—and were—interpreted as significant parts of the overall plan. Even Jonathan Edwards (whom some historians have seen as the model postmillennialist) drew no hard line between natural and supernatural or noncatastrophic and catastrophic means of fulfilling God's plan. The British triumph at Cape Breton, brought about in part by a violent storm, seemed to him "almost miraculous"; recent providences came, "perhaps, the nearest to a parallel, with God's wonderful works of old, in Moses, Joshua's, and Hezekiah's time." Similarly, he regarded the earthquake at Lima as part of God's pouring of the vials on antichrist.[76] And when he composed a list of current events pointing to the fulfillment of the sixth vial, natural calamities were easily mixed in with humanly instigated setbacks: French sailers had started a mutiny in Toulouse; a famine around Bordeaux killed 10,000; the English took Pondi-

76. *Works* (Dwight ed.), 1:230-31.

cherry, Nantes was desolated by a violent hurricane.[77] And so on. How else could one interpret such disasters?

Yet this does not put the point strongly enough. It merely assumes that, given the presupposition of an all-powerful God who superintended the moral and natural government of the world, theologians were presented with a fait accompli by the earthquakes of 1727 and 1755. Or that, in crude terms, their moral system was threatened unless they read the earthquakes as threats from an angry God: Believe or else. Certainly this element was present in many sermons. At such times, "God stands at the door," said Eliphalet Williams:

> The Clouds gather, and thicken, look black, and lowring, seem charged with Thunder, or big with Storm and Tempest; GOD hangs out (as it were) His red, His bloody Flag, brandishes his flaming Sword in the Skies, or ariseth out of His Place, and shakes terribly the Earth, and loudly Warns a degenerate World of impending Evils.[78]

But this hardly tells all the story: calamity was not merely appropriated to the Apocalypse by the exigencies of an often violent world. A more subtle theodicy yoked misfortune with salvation not as mere necessity but as virtue. God, after all, used catastrophes for two purposes. Most obviously, they could be instruments of chastisement which led to destruction. But calamities also served "to Reclaim sinful People, and bring them to Repentance."[79] Mather expressed the notion with his usual extravagance: "O Wonderful! O Wonderful! Our GOD, instead of sending *Earthquakes* to destroy us as He justly might, He sends them to fetch us home into Himself, and to do us the greatest Good in the World!" In that

77. Stein, "*Notes*," 2:321–79.

78. Eliphalet Williams, *The Duty of a People under Dark Providences* (New London, Conn., 1756), p. 14.

79. Ibid.

sense, the afflictions were actually an example of God's kindness, and proof that "Many (very many) of the divine Judgments may justly be called Mercies."[80]

Thus the earthquake sermons reflected the same combination of gloom and hope found in apocalyptic literature. While divine anger was a terrible thing, Thomas Paine pointed out that, as with all other judgments, the tremors were "sanctified to the Elect, and made the Instruments of their spiritual Good."[81] Joseph Sewall and Charles Chauncy both used the common analogy of gold purified by fire to explain how calamities worked to the benefit of sinful saints.[82] Others noted that God made sure he combined events of judgment with those of mercy, and the 1727 sermons repeated a litany of these combinations: King George was dead, but his son reigned, great sickness had threatened, but general health prevailed; Indians almost went to war, but peace remained; great heat and drought had marred the summer weather, but New England still reaped a good harvest; thunder, lightning, and earthquakes had shocked the land, yet no lives were lost.[83] With this perspective in mind, Prince could easily explain to his listeners that a biblical text illustrating God's wrath was not at all inappropriate for a Thanksgiving sermon, since "it becomes us to sing of both Judgment and Mercy, to rejoice with Trembling."[84]

Superhuman catastrophes were thus an important part of the prophetic outlook; but it would be misleading to argue

---

80. Cotton Mather, *Boanerges*, p. 38; John Rogers, *Three Sermons*, p. 53.

81. Paine, *Doctrine of Earthquakes*, p. 38. See also Nathaniel Gookin, *Day of Trouble Near* (Boston, 1728), p. 47; and Joseph Sewall, *Repentance*, p. 26.

82. Chauncy, *Earth Delivered from the Curse*, p. 28; Joseph Sewall, *Repentance*, p. 36.

83. Samuel Phillips, *Three Plain Practical Discourses* (Boston, 1728), pp. 51–54. The same list can be found in Joseph Sewall, *Repentance*, p. 26, and William Williams, *Divine Warnings* (Boston, 1728), pp. 31–34.

84. Prince, *Earthquakes the Works of God*, p. 20.

that by removing them from the apocalyptic scenario, we could successfully purge the prophetic viewpoint of its darker components. The concept of judgment, not catastrophe, governed the use of afflictions as an essential part of the latter days. So long as New Englanders regarded judgment as an inseparable part of salvation, they would continue to combine hopeful rhetoric with the gloom of both natural and moral calamities. The earthquakes did nothing to discourage them from adopting this viewpoint; and neither did the Revelations's long description of sufferings which the saints were forced to undergo before the final deliverance.

Yet, after all this, it might be argued that we have unfairly weighted the argument by using earthquake sermons as evidence in our experiment of watching ministers interpret events instead of prophecies. Between the rumblings of 1727 and 1755 lay a much larger spiritual tremor: the Great Awakening. The historical optimism which historians have painted as arising out of this "anticipation of the latter-day glory" stands in marked contrast with the gloom-tinged hopes which the last two chapters have insisted was an integral part of the apocalyptic view of history. Jonathan Edwards optimistically believed that the witnesses of the Revelation had already been slain; how can this be reconciled with the pronouncements of 1727 and 1755? When the shocks of the earthquakes were still firm in everyone's memories, Joseph Sewall had put the situation in historical perspective by noting that "the Church flourished like the *Palm*-tree, under her pressures, of which it is observed, 'the more it is press'd down, the more it grows.' "[85] What happened when the pressures of declension, deadness, and calamity ceased? Did the enthusiasm of the Awakening promote a drift away from the traditional apocalyptic outlook, or did it only confirm the almost paradoxical model of historical progress through affliction?

85. Joseph Sewall, *Repentance*, p. 36.

4

Conversion

For any historian whose province is maintaining the New England trails running from 1700 to 1800, the Great Awakening is somewhat of an embarrassment: a giant boulder unceremoniously dropped in the middle of historical pathways that would be much more comfortably traveled had there been no boulder at all. But for better or worse, the boulder is there. The only question is, how do we traverse it?

At first glance, the most obvious approach for anyone interested in millennial thought would seem to be an emphasis on the "Great" side of the Great Awakening. For awakenings themselves were not new to New England. The earlier revivals of Solomon Stoddard in Northampton are the best known, but other towns had received similar tokens of God's favor.[1] The Great Awakening could be styled Great because it was amazingly widespread. God's spirit seemed to be breaking out not merely in isolated communities, but all across New England, the American colonies, even England and Scotland. It was this magnitude that prompted participants to draw parallels between the revival and the biblical promises of "the spirit poured out on all flesh" in the latter days of the world.

From the very beginning, promoters of the work on both sides of the Atlantic were hopeful about the revival's potential. Isaac Watts and John Guyse of London both eagerly received news of Edwards's initial successes of 1735 (though they discreetly inquired for more information on the character of this

1. Edwin S. Gaustad, *The Great Awakening In New England* (New York, 1957), chap. 2.

frontier minister).[2] Their preface to his *Faithful Narrative* called for prayers encouraging the accomplishment of biblical prophecies "concerning the large extent of this salvation in the latter days of the world." At the same time, Edwards impressed upon his congregation the international import of their own spiritual travails. "When I first heard of the notice the Rev. Dr. Watts and Dr. Guyse took of God's mercies to us," he wrote, "I took occasion to inform our congregation of it in a discourse from these words, 'A city that is set upon a hill cannot be hid'. . . . The congregation were very sensibly moved and affected."[3] When the flood began in earnest, William Cooper of Boston thought accounts like the *Faithful Narrative* would help spread the revivals. Accordingly, his preface to Edwards's newest work, *Distinguishing Marks of a Work of the Spirit of God*, asked ministers to send reports of their own revivals to Edwards for publication. Edwards liked the idea but suggested that the compilation could best be handled by one of the ministers at Boston, where news was more readily obtainable and the presses right at hand.[4]

The task fell, at least nominally, to Thomas Prince, Jr., who undoubtedly had the benefit of his father's watchful eye. *The Christian History* began publication in 1743, and was issued weekly for the next two years. Although it concentrated on accounts of the New England revivals, it borrowed a good deal of material from similar papers published in Britain. In London, there was the *Weekly History of the Progress of the Gospel* as well as less frequently issued pamphlets like *An Account of the most remarkable Particulars relating to the present Progress of the Gospel*. Glasgow had its own *Weekly His-*

---

2. C. C. Goen, ed., *The Great Awakening*, vol. 4 of *The Works of Jonathan Edwards*, Perry Miller and John Smith, gen. eds., 4 vols. (New Haven, 1958–   ), pp. 39–40 (hereafter cited as Yale *Works*).

3. Ibid., pp. 137, 210.

4. Ibid., pp. 224, 259.

tory. All of these publications emphasized and promoted the widespread nature of the Awakening, haphazard as their editing jobs may have been. The isolated minister, writing of the good news in his own country parish, would see next to his own account the similarly enthusiastic reports of others. It is here in *The Christian History*—where the Awakenings were made Great—that we would expect to find the larger millennial vision informing the spirit of the revivals.

To some extent, we do find it. It appears most often as a fitting rhetorical close to letters bringing news of the Gospel's further success. Often, writers would borrow the ecstatic conclusion from the Revelation itself, proclaiming the revivals as "only an Earnest of much greater blessings to his Church" and praying for their fulfillment: "Even so come LORD JESUS, come quickly!" John Cotton, at Halifax, hoped that God would "yet again revive his Work among us. . . . May he go on conquering and to conquer, till he has subdued the land."[5] From Georgia, William Grant expressed the same sentiments in Matherian cadences ("Oh! that all the Kingdoms of the Earth may be come the Kingdoms of our LORD JESUS CHRIST!"). John Willison of Dundee, who wrote a preface to the Scottish edition of Edwards's *Distinguishing Marks*, called on God to "hasten the Glory of the latter Days, when *the Jews shall be brought in with the Fulness of the Gentiles.*" There were Gospel successes in Rotterdam, glowing reports from far-flung missionaries; Prince Jr. passed them all along to New Englanders, with the hope that the spirit would spread to "the Aboriginals at Bengal, Cormandel, Malabar, and the Islands of Ceylon, and Batavia in the East Indies" until "the REDEEMER's conquest becomes compleat."[6]

The temptation, of course, was to identify the late spiritual

5. Thomas Prince, Jr., ed., *The Christian History*, 2 vols. (Boston, 1744-45), 2:310; 1:268, 365.
6. Ibid., 1:365, 85, 287; 2:28-29.

outbursts with the beginning of the final descent of the Holy Spirit. "What shall be the Issue of so great and glorious Appearance one may not be safe in determining," cautioned John Syms in England. But his ardor overruled his own advice: "surely it has much of the Appearance of the Glory of the latter Days, when it is said, the Glory of the LORD shall cover the earth as the Waters the Sea. . . . Even so come LORD JESUS, come quickly, Amen, Halleluia!"[7] Most people were more cautious and referred to the awakenings as "Earnests" or "Foretastes" of even greater effusions. Edwards, for one, appreciated the need for prudence, since he had already found himself "slanderously" accused of claiming that the millennium had begun in Northampton. The accusation was of course false, but he did believe that the revivals were "forerunners of those glorious times so often prophesied of in the Scriptures."[8] And that was the official position adopted by the ministers who gathered at Boston in 1743 to support the Awakening. The "Testimony and Advice" of the divines contained the usual talk of "Earnests" and the usual concluding litany: "AMEN! Even so come LORD JESUS; come Quickly!"[9]

No doubt, then, the impact of the widespread revivals fostered a hopeful and expectant view of the future. Yet the letters and histories in Prince's magazine suggest—both by what they contain and what they do not—that supporters of the Awakening retained much of the paradoxical rhetoric of affliction found in earlier versions of New England eschatology.

To begin with, there were the ambiguous statements centered on Christ's second coming. As usual, historians have the difficult job of deciding whether to take these discussions literally. The ministers of Fairfield, Connecticut, for instance,

7. Ibid., 2:102.
8. Letter, March 5, 1744, in *Works* (Dwight ed.), 1:213.
9. Prince Jr., ed., *Christian History*, 1:158, 162.

believed that maintaining the revivals "would give an hopeful Prospect of the LORD's Return, and so of the Revival of Religion from its present declining State."[10] Did they mean that Christ must literally arrive before any real improvement in religion could take place? (Even with the revivals, religion seemed to be in a "declining state.") Or did they mean that Christ's coming was a metaphorical entering into his kingdom ("and so" nothing more than a further "Revival of Religion from its present declining State")? Both interpretations were viable ones held by respected New Englanders before the Awakening.

To make matters even more confusing, some writers spoke optimistically while still using imagery associated with Christ's sudden coming to a world asleep in sin. *The Christian History* printed a letter from one J——n O——n, a country minister in England, who rhapsodized in the usual way about the spread of holy knowledge in the latter days. At the same time, the two metaphors he chose were images with a different import. The first was Christ's parable of the sower, where the recent gospel successes were likened to the seed sown in rocky ground, which sprang up quickly but soon withered. What followed was the seed sown among thorns. "Indeed this appears to be Satan's Hour, and the Power of Darkness; he seems to have got the Church like Peter, into the Sieve of Temptation." Only after all that would the seed take root in good ground. The second image was drawn from the parable of the slumbering virgins who were found unprepared at the coming of the bridegroom. This was the sort of rhetoric that Cotton Mather delighted in using to warn the world of Christ's unexpected arrival. Yet the image here was used in a confusing way, the conclusion being that the "Night of [the virgins'] Slumber is far spent, and the Day is at Hand."[11]

10. Ibid., 2:312.
11. Ibid., pp. 47–51.

The experiences William Shurtleff reported at Portsmouth, New Hampshire, appear even less consonant with the optimism of the awakenings. Shurtleff noted that the outcries of afflicted sinners in his congregation were so great that others there were reminded of the scene at Christ's coming. This thought led him to mention another recent instance when a chimney catching fire had made everyone think of the same event, "Which being believ'd by a great many, some that were not before so much affected as others, were put into deepest Distress, and great Numbers had their Convictions hereby strengthened and confirmed." Shurtleff knew what kind of reception his story was likely to have from "a great many of the Humourists of the Age," and suggested that they would do better to think a little more seriously about the day of judgment coming.[12] For him, at least, the optimism of a spreading revival was not inconsistent with thought about the approaching conflagration.

The inclusion of such letters in *The Christian History* makes it difficult to assess the role of millennial thought in the Awakening; but even more puzzling is the material not inserted in the compendium. Although letters were full of general rhetoric about the hopes of the latter days, virtually no one bothered to provide interested Christians with more specific discussions about how many vials had been poured out and how much time remained before the fall of antichrist. The one letter which examined the prophecies in any detail came from a Scottish minister, William McCulloch, who had been corresponding with Edwards on the subject. McCulloch thought the prophecies predicted that the latter-day Gospel would spread from west to east, rather than the other way around, and that his interpretation received striking confirmation in the movement of the revivals from New England in 1735 and 1740-42 to Scotland in 1742-43. Although he

12. Ibid., 1:384.

agreed that "something vastly greater" was likely to follow (as Edwards had suggested in *Thoughts on the Revival*), he felt constrained to demur on one point: "I'm afraid (which is a Thing you do not hint at) that before these glorious Times, *some dreadful Stroke* or *Trial* may be yet abiding us. May the LORD prepare us for it. But as to this, I cannot and *dare not peremptorily determine.*"[13]

Aside from this gloomy forecast, *The Christian History* is strangely devoid of prophetical speculations. If any were anxious, as John Brown had been after the 1727 earthquake, to learn "what are the thoughts of the most Judicious about the *Signs of the Times*," they seem not to have applied to Prince for the answer.[14] And if the widespread successes of the Awakening convinced many to change their opinion of when the conflagration was coming, or whether the witnesses had yet been slain, they apparently did not consider the magazine an appropriate place to announce their change of heart.

Perhaps, then, we ought to conclude that *The Christian History* failed in its attempt to make the Awakening Great; failed, at least, to make explicit and well-defined connections between the revivals and the larger work of redemption described in the Revelation. Instead (perhaps because of weak editorial direction) the magazine was left with the details of the inevitably provincial accounts sent in by excited ministers scattered throughout the country. It printed descriptions of individual conversions, featured tales of pastors deluged by requests for counseling, provided narratives of what other divines had done when people in their congregations had burst out groaning under conviction. Despite the prophetic trimmings, most of the letters to *The Christian History* dealt, in effect, not with the Great Awakening but with the personal struggles of individuals' small awakenings. And if

13. Ibid., p. 363.
14. Cotton, *A Holy Fear of God*, appendix.

that is the case, perhaps we would be better off to leave behind the daily minutiae of *The Christian History* and search elsewhere for more explicitly prophetic discussions of the Awakening.

But I would like to suggest another approach. If the Princes did not succeed in articulately connecting the Great Awakening with the small, in integrating the revivals with the larger work of redemption, it was not for lack of good intentions. For them, as for all New Lights, each individual conversion formed an integral part of the larger Awakening. The pattern behind the grand history of the Revelation, when examined more closely, was in fact the same pattern which shaped the new birth of every believer. As we have already seen, the close relationship between the larger and smaller works of redemption was partly reflected in the sometimes ambiguous definition of the coming kingdom. Edwards pointed out that, although the millennium was "the principle time" of the kingdom of heaven, it also had been "in a degree set up soon after Christ's resurrection, and . . . the Christian church in all ages of it is called the *kingdom of heaven*."[15]

If the individual's advance toward salvation was indeed of a piece with the larger progress toward the world's redemption, then we may be able to gain some insight into the substance, style, and psychology of the larger work by looking at the smaller replica.

CONVERSION AND THE AFFLICTIVE MODEL OF PROGRESS

One inevitable consequence of the revival was a practical one: ministers who welcomed it into their parishes had little free time for detailed study of the prophecies. A seemingly endless number of townspeople called on them for advice about their "soul troubles." With so many earnest requests for spiritual guidance, we can well sympathize with Thomas

15. Edwards, *History of Redemption*, in *Works*, 1:491.

Prince's joyful—and yet somewhat bewildered—recounting of the flood.

> And now was such a Time as we never knew. The Rev. Mr. Cooper was won't to say, that more came to him in one Week in deep Concern about their Souls, than in the whole twenty-four Years of his preceeding Ministry. I can also say the same as to the Numbers who repaired to me. By Mr. Cooper's Letter to his Friend in Scotland, it appears, he has had about six Hundred different Persons in three Months Time: and Mr. Webb informs me he has had in the same Space above a Thousand.[16]

From all over came similar reports. Jonathan Dickinson thought that at the height of his awakening, more came to him in one day than had before in half a year's time. And John White, who tended a parish in the fishing town of Gloucester, Maine, aptly remarked that, before, he had "not ordinarily fished for souls with a net, but with an angling rod."[17]

The scores of parishioners may have surprised their ministers, but they did not catch them unprepared. New Englanders were no strangers to soul troubles, and their Puritan predecessors had long before provided detailed guides to the appropriate paths a soul traveled from darkness into light. Authorities differed on details (some broke the process into as many as ten steps) but everyone agreed about the basic points.[18] The traditional state of a "civil," unconverted man was a numb sleepiness. No matter how regularly he attended church or how superficially pious he appeared, underneath lay a spiritual pride, a secret conviction that his good works were

16. Prince Jr., ed., *Christian History*, 2:391.
17. Shipton, *Sibley's Harvard Graduates*, 4:422.
18. For a more detailed description of this morphology, see Edmund S. Morgan, *Visible Saints* (Ithaca, N.Y., 1963), pp. 66–73. Goen discusses its application to the Awakening in Yale *Works*, 4:25–32.

acceptable to God. Thus, a man's first step toward salvation was an awareness of his total sinfulness. He had to realize that the moral law which demanded perfection convicted him in the eyes of the divine Judge. God swept away every excuse and prop he had hoped would gain him eternal life. Finally, from out of this ultimate despair came the new birth: the faith that God, through his love and mercy, had granted salvation. This grace acted as a new "inward principle" of the soul, first reordering a man's relation to God, and then transforming his relations with others in the world.

It would be difficult to overestimate the importance of the conversion experience. For New Englanders, the process itself was perhaps more important than the theology. Every child knew the theology—almost as soon as he was able to under-apprehension of the Gospel, since even devils possessed this "historical faith." In effect, unconverted men were no better off than devils unless they had experienced God's truths through the proper emotional and spiritual pilgrimage. And the pivotal point in this pilgrimage was the state of conviction. Salvation came not through gradual enlightenment or a discipline that progressively eliminated sin (there would be time enough for that as the confirmed saint grew in holiness). It came through judgment; and with judgment came self-absement. Up to a certain key point on the road to eternal life, things got better and better only insofar as they got worse and worse.

This pattern of progress through affliction, of redemption through judgment, was embedded in the Christian and, for that matter, the Hebrew tradition. The Old Testament prophets continually called for a "return to the Lord; for he has torn, that he may heal us; he has stricken, and he will bind us up."[19] And at the center of the New Testament, the Crucifixion stood as the greatest example of life through death and

19. Hosea 6:1.

victory through self-abasement. The pivotal point in Edwards's *History of Redemption* was Christ's incarnation into a life of suffering and humiliation. Step by step Edwards took his listeners along the bitter path to that last evening of betrayal:

> And here was his greatest humiliation and suffering. . . . First, his life was sold by one of his own disciples for thirty pieces of silver, which was the price of the life of a servant, as you may see in Exod. xxi.32. Then he was in that dreadful agony in the garden. There came such a dismal gloom upon his soul, that he began to be sorrowful and very heavy. . . . So violent was the agony of his soul, as to force the blood through the pores of his skin; so that while his soul was overwhelmed with amazing sorrow, his body was all clotted with blood. . . . The officers and soldiers apprehend and bind him; his disciples forsake him and flee; his own best friends do not stand by him to comfort him, in this time of his distress. . . . At length, being come to Mount Calvary, they execute the sentence which Pilate had so unrighteously pronounced. They nail him to his cross, by his hands and feet, then raise it erect, and fix one end in the ground, he being still suspended on it by the nails which pierced his hands and feet. And now Christ's sufferings are come to the extremity: now the cup which he so earnestly prayed that it might pass from him, is come, and he must, he does drink it.[20]

So it was that Christ purchased salvation, and so it was that believers followed him to make that salvation their own. His death and resurrection freed them from the bondage of the law, but it did not free them from the spiritual pilgrimage itself. Without God's grace, no one could be saved; but that grace came only through a process of humiliation and suffering which—however weakly—paralleled Christ's own.

20. Edwards, *History of Redemption*, in *Works*, 1:414–15.

This tradition had been present, of course, throughout Christian history. But the Puritan emphasis on the morphology of conversion, itself a miniature *imitatio Christi*, gave the pattern a renewed strength. And now those who had been awakened spoke of a "new birth," possible only through the symbolical death of the old, carnal man. In stressing this experience, the New Lights were only highlighting an old tradition; but they did it with such zeal that many ministers thought things had gone too far.

Old and New Lights did not fight about the necessity of conviction itself: everyone admitted the need for that. Charles Chauncy acknowledged that any convert had to pass through a stage where he was "driven out of his former Ease, and fill'd with Anxiety and Distress." And although he attacked the mannerisms of New Light converts, he cautioned that in doing so, he did not mean "to express a dislike of that *Fear*, excited by a *just Sense of Sin*, which in Respect of *adult* Persons, is *ordinarily* previous to their Conversion." What Chauncy abhorred was the emotional, often dramatic style of preaching meant to encourage a deep sense of conviction, and the equally emotional outbursts of those laboring under it. "The Passion of *Fear* may be excited not only from a just Representation of Truth to the Mind by the SPIRIT of GOD, but from the *natural Influence* of *awful Words* and *frightful Gestures*."[21]

New Lights thought Chauncy made too much of the Awakening's aberrations and underestimated the importance of thorough conviction. They were initially surprised by the spontaneous outbursts of distressed church-goers, but found it harder to claim that this deep agony was necessarily fraudulent and improper. When one woman cried out in the middle of John Cotton's service, he pleaded with her "to

21. Charles Chauncy, *Seasonable Thoughts on the State of Religion in New England* (Boston, 1743), pp. 5, 79, 80.

endeavor to compose her self, so that she might join with us in the Worship of GOD." But he could not help observing that the "Scene was *very affecting* to the Congregation; and some that were under great concern before, and were as full as they could hold, could not now help manifesting themselves."[22]

It was only a small step to the conclusion that these outcries were a positive help in trying to arouse convictions in others. James Robe, a Scottish divine, argued that if God struck "secure Sinners with the Terrors of his Wrath, whereby they are made, from a felt sense of their perishing Condition, to cry out. . . . Why must these Trophies of Victory be removed out of the Assembly?" Arousing the agony of conviction was an indispensable part of taking trophies of victory, and Robe could write with straight-faced relish of the "Noise of the Distress'd" in his own services. "It was pleasant to hear those who were in a state of Enmity with God. [All about were] Despisers of Jesus Christ, and Satan's contented slaves, some of them crying out for mercy, some that they were lost and undone."[23]

Respectable supporters of the Awakening tried to disassociate themselves from the type of preaching which relied merely on the terror of "*awful Words* and *frightful Gestures.*" But they did it in a way that by no means lessened the role of conviction. Prince made the point as strongly as he could by pointing out that, while earthquakes and storms often aroused simple terror, such fears sadly vanished soon after. "Nothing is more obvious than for people to be greatly terrified . . . and yet have *no Convictions.*" Simple fright failed because it alarmed men too little, not too much. Thus Prince thought that Gilbert Tennent's preaching was effective not so much because he laid the terrors of the Law open to them

22. Prince Jr., ed., *Christian History*, 1:261–62.
23. Ibid., pp. 36, 26.

"(for this they could pretty well bear, as long as they hoped these belonged not to them, or they could easily avoid them;)" but because he laid open to sinners "their many vain and secret *Shifts* and *Refuges, counterfeit Resemblances* of Grace, *delusive* and *damning Hopes.*"[24]

There were limits to this approach; limits made painfully clear by the melancholic suicide of Joseph Hawley, one of Edwards's parishioners. It was a grim reminder that the pattern could go wrong, and Edwards noted with unease the number of people who "had it urged upon 'em, as if somebody had spoke to 'em, 'Cut your own throat, now is a good opportunity: *now*, NOW!'"[25] Such events warned ministers not to push despair to the breaking point, but they dared not retreat too far in the opposite direction. Edwards, who penetrated the psychology of conviction with as much sensitivity as anyone, brilliantly described the tightrope that ministers were forced to walk in their spiritual counseling. On the one hand, they had to insist that God was under no obligation to show mercy to the unconverted:

> If I had taught those that came to me under trouble any other doctrine, I should have taken a most direct course utterly to have undone them; I should have directly crossed what was plainly the drift of the Spirit of God in his influences upon them. . . . And yet those that have been under awakenings have oftentimes plainly stood in need of being encouraged, by being told of the infinite and all-sufficient mercy of God in Christ; and that 'tis God's manner to succeed diligence and to bless his own means, that so awakenings and encouragements, fear and hope may be duly mixed and proportioned to preserve their minds in a just medium between the two extremes

24. Ibid., 2:388–90.
25. *A Faithful Narrative*, in Yale *Works*, 4:206–07.

of self-flattery and despondence, both which tend to slackness and negligence, and in the end to security.[26]

And so the tension inevitably remained: between hope and despair, between mercy and judgment. Salvation through conviction was too much a part of the New England heritage to have it any other way. The death and resurrection at the heart of Christianity exemplified it; the Puritan morphology of conversion expounded it; and the new birth of the Awakening heightened it.

The same perspective that informed conversion—the smallest awakening—also pervaded thinking about Greater Awakenings and the Work of Redemption as a whole. God redeemed history the same way he redeemed individuals. (Or to put the proposition Teutonically, just as ontogeny recapitulates phylogeny, so *Seelenheil* recapitulates *Heilsgeschichte*!) Thus the idea of salvation through trial and conviction could be applied at any number of levels as the basic pattern God used to bring deliverance. On a relatively small scale, the revival of a single congregation was often pictured as occurring only after a time of spiritual declension and deadness. But the same pattern could be used to understand the awakenings of whole towns, provinces, and countries. God brought his showers of grace only after humbling his people and demonstrating to them their impotence.

In an even larger sense, these social applications of the conversion model were incorporated into interpretations of the prophecies, past and future. The history of the church fell into periods that were each cast as a time when help from the Lord came only after the faithful were reduced to the direst of straits. And the entire work of redemption recapitulated the smaller repetitions of the pattern with its final struggle at Armageddon against the massed forces of antichrist, and even

26. Ibid., pp. 167–68. Edwards provides a superb description of the morphology of conversion through this section (pp. 159–91).

beyond that, the ultimate battle against Gog and Magog, when the church had stumbled at the end of the millennium. In short, if we wish to construct a "model of progress" which adequately reflects the thinking of millennial theologians, the morphology of conversion provides an excellent starting point.

One example of the way the conviction-conversion pattern was applied to a social rather than personal situation can be seen in the case of Peter Thacher. Thacher found himself, at the end of a long career, preaching to an audience which remained steadfastly unmoved while neighboring towns were joining the revival. He became increasingly discouraged about his effectiveness and was on the verge of resigning when Gilbert Tennent arrived in town and straightaway preached a rousing, successful sermon. This was humbling enough; but Tennent unwittingly made matters worse when he asserted that by *his* standards, the sermon had been a failure, and "that he never was so shut up but once." This was too much for poor Thacher, who confessed to the visiting minister all his "Discouragements in the Ministry." Tennent seemed "tenderly affected," and "on parting had such a Word as this, oft'times 'tis darkest a little before Day, the rising Sun will bring Light."[27]

The response was entirely traditional, and quite appropriate. Edwards used the same image to describe an individual's conviction ("it looks as black as midnight to them a little before the day dawns in their souls");[28] and Tennent was only applying to one particular congregation the pattern that God had used in accomplishing the Great Awakening itself. When Thomas Foxcroft defended the revival, he scolded those who failed to recognize how plainly recent events were following the pattern set down by Scripture. That the late effusions had come in times of trouble was "a marvellous fulfilling of

27. Prince Jr., ed., *Christian History*, 2:88.
28. Yale *Works*, 4:162.

that Scripture, *When the Enemy cometh in like a Flood, the Spirit of the LORD shall lift up a Standard*." The flourishing revival stood in stark contrast to the previous state of religion: "Ah! what a melancholy Prospect we had not long since. . . . But how has the cloudy Face of Things, even on a sudden, very much chang'd."[29]

This was applying the model in its simplest form, and if that had been the only way it was used, it would support nicely the traditional view of the Awakening as a watershed for millennial thought. Before the revivals, New England stood in the darkness of conviction; with them, it entered upon the upward and gradual task of perseverance on the road to perfect sanctification. But we have already seen that the psychology of conviction was more complex. A soul laboring under awakenings had to maintain the proper spiritual balance between hope and despair. On a personal level, ministers were responsible for regulating that delicate balance through the proper application of comfort and affliction, the external correlates of hope and despair. On the grander level of the work of redemption, the ultimate management of the church's spiritual estate fell to God. His task was to bring in the kingdom by maintaining in the world the proper balance of providential judgments and mercies. Remaining true to the pattern of conversion, the millennial view of history proclaimed that the salvation of the church would come as the tempo of both reward *and* affliction increased, until a dramatic resolution was achieved in the millennial state.

Now if this reading of prophetic thought is correct, then New Englanders' conceptions of eschatology cannot be explained merely by contrasting a pessimistic catastrophism with an optimistic progressivism. Instead we find ministers repeating two seemingly contradictory statements. The first

29. Preface to Jonathan Dickinson, *The True Scripture-Doctrine* (Boston, 1741), pp. i–ii.

was that the state of the world was getting better and better, and would continue to do so. The second was that Satan, seeing his kingdom effectively threatened, would make more and more trouble. Millennialists resolved the contradiction (or never noticed it in the first place) because they assumed that evil, instead of diminishing as goodness spread, would become more persistent in its opposition. Hence the common adage that the more Satan was vanquished, the more he raged; and conversely, that the more the church was oppressed, the more it flourished.

An understanding of this pattern helps to explain the paradoxical contradictions we have already discovered in early eighteenth-century millennial thought. Viewed in this light, Samuel Willard's *Checkered State of the Gospel Church* has a more coherent rationale for being checkered. He could declare that the millennium might begin before men were aware of it (and thus "have its gradual increase"), yet at the same time assert that darkness was a sign that the times were hastening on (for it is always darkest before the day). The two opinions were compatible because bringing "the Church into a more dark and dismal state than it is at the present . . . is designed in his Counsel, to make way for her deliverance."[30] For the same reasons, Samuel Sewall could note that "God many times *sets one thing against another*: and we may hope that *Unparallel'd Severity* will be succeeded by superabundant BENIGNITY." This pattern made it comprehensible to talk of a darkness which was yet "irradiated" by a "concomitant Rainbow," and to conclude that "tho' the Storm increase and grow never so Violent; yet this Angel persists with Courage and Constancy to proclaim the certain approach of a Fair Day."[31]

30. Samuel Willard, *Checkered State of the Gospel Church* (Boston, 1701), pp. 53, 63, 30.
31. Sewall, *Phenomena*, preface; also *Proposals Touching the Accomplishment of Prophecies* (Boston, 1713), pp. 5-6.

It was this pattern in the millennial outlook which united New Englanders' apparently disparate interpretations of the Revelation, and not any consistent agreement on chronology. Sewall's and Willard's sentiments were of a piece with those of Benjamin Colman and Nicholas Noyes. Even the Mathers viewed the last days with the same combination of gloom and hope. Their differences sprang from temperaments that increased the frenetic tempo of conflicting good and evil beyond the boundaries most ministers were willing to set. Cotton could not be satisfied with a simple triumph of the church; the hints of revolutions abroad were always "amazing" and "wonderful." Joel's prediction of the Holy Spirit poured on all flesh assumed virtually ecstatic proportions (*"They are coming! They are coming! They are coming!"*), while the prospect of the conflagration found him relishing the violent punishment of a sleepy, corrupt world. Cotton dreamed dreams of ecstasy and nightmares of blackness like no one else in New England, but the pattern shaping those dreams was still the same. God mingled light and darkness to bring history to its consummation.

This theory of history certainly worked well in times of declension. When God's providences seemed afflictive, and spiritual deadness or physical earthquakes were the order of the day, the rhetoric of conversion became a theodicy of comfort: reassurance that God's chastisements were not merely obstacles to be got around, but judgments which sanctified the elect.

The optimism of the Awakening did not alter the basic perspective. This can be seen, first, by an examination of the prophetic interpretations themselves. Newer expositions by Daniel Whitby and Moses Lowman did not provide any fundamentally new approaches to salvation history. Further, supporters of the Awakening had no qualms about citing older prophetic tracts. And Edwards's new ideas about the slaying of the witnesses were based on assumptions common to the traditional eschatological framework. Secondly, the Awakening itself, with all its attendant controversies and excesses, created an emotional climate of debate and controversy which elicited the usual rhetoric of progress through struggle and affliction. In effect, the gloom and hope of the conversion model not only governed New Lights' evaluation of their historical position; it also actually worked to bend social realities toward the patterns it expected and predicted.

Prophetic Expositions and the Awakening

Daniel Whitby, a liberal divine in the Church of England, joined the ranks of English expositors in 1703 with his own thoughts about the Revelation of John. This treatise, along with his larger *Paraphrase and Commentary on the New Testament*, enjoyed a publishing history which extended well into the nineteenth century. It was reprinted in America as late as 1848, when it formed part of a larger four-volume Scripture commentary by several eminent biblical scholars. By that time, the notions of pre- and postmillennial theologies had been explicitly worked out, and Henry Dana Ward could point to Whitby's work as the first example of a postmillennial formulation.[32] From Ward's point of view, the claim made good sense: the title of the tract was enough to demonstrate it. *A Treatise of the True Millennium*, Whitby had called it, appending the usual long subtitle, *Shewing that it is not a Reign of Persons Raised from the Dead, but of the Church Flourishing gloriously for a Thousand Years after the Conversion of the Jews, and the Flowing in of all Nations to them Thus Converted to the Christian Faith*. But Whitby's reasons for contesting Mede's interpretation were not Henry

---

32. Henry Ward, *History and Doctrine of the Millennium* (Boston, 1840), quoted in Tuveson, *Redeemer Nation*, p. 40.

Ward's.[33] His objections, as usual, sprang not from any grand new philosophical viewpoint, but from a peculiar textual reading of Scripture.

Whitby was particularly interested in the Jews, a group of people whom all good millennialists kept their eyes on. Having "employ'd some Thoughts upon the Mystery of the Conversion of the Jewish nation," Whitby concluded that Paul's promise of the Jews' salvation in Romans 11 referred to the same time as the Revelation's thousand-year reign. "The *New Heavens* and *New Earth*, were the very Things promised to the Jews," he reasoned, concluding that "the true *Millennium* is only a Reign of Converted Jews, and of the Gentiles flowing into them."[34] This meant that Gentile Christians played a comparatively minor part in the final drama; but Whitby thought the Scriptures justified his interpretation. After all, the Jews were God's first chosen people; and Christ's personal ministry had been "only among them, whence he is stiled *The Minister of the Circumcision*." How natural, then, that the now dead Jewish community would revive and "become a most famous Church again."[35]

Whitby was not proposing anything radically new simply by including converted Jews in the millennial reign. Virtually everyone accepted that point. But by pushing Israel to the center of the stage, as the nation principally intended by the millennial prophecies, he raised some embarrassing questions—and slighted Gentile sensibilities to boot. If Jews were to be the principal benefactors of the thousand years, how had the first resurrection come to be associated with "*Christian Martyrs beheaded for the Name of Christ*, or to be ful-

33. Ward said that his contemporaries generally preferred the prospect of a spiritual millennium, with no supernatural occurrences or times of sore affliction intervening. Ibid.

34. The *Treatise* can be found in Daniel Whitby, *A Paraphrase and Commentary of the New Testament* (London, 1727), introduction, p. 9.

35. Ibid., p. 10; other proofs, pp. 11–15.

filled in the Resurrection of them only who are chiefly Christians, not of the *Jews* but of the *Gentiles*?" Jews certainly had not been slain for the true faith, and hence if Whitby was right in his interpretation, the only conclusion left was that the first resurrection of "martyrs" was a spiritual one, referring to the revival of the Jewish church.[36]

To bolster this argument, Whitby claimed that a millennial reign of supernaturally raised martyrs was full of inconsistencies anyway. Ironically, opponents of his position had leveled the same charge against a metaphorical first resurrection; but now Whitby used their own strategy against them.[37] What, he asked, was so consistent about an earthly paradise peopled by unearthly saints? The shoe just did not fit.

> Can a spiritual body, free from grossness and ponderosity, from needing rest, sleep, clothing, sustenance, receive advantage from that universal plenty . . . or need those goods of fortune that external felicity, that temporal happiness, he hath provided it for upon earth? . . . Can the Devil, when loosed, be so foolish, as to summon up his Armies to fight against, and kill them who are immortal, and can die no more? Can Gog and Magog, with all their numerous Host, hope to prevail against them, or even dare to assault such shining radiant Bodies as they then will have? In a word, can such bodies need or receive any farther Exaltation to fit them for heaven, or for their elevation into the Clouds, to be forever with the Lord? If not, why should they live a thousand Years after God had thus fitted and prepared them for their Habitation in the highest Heavens?[38]

To Whitby, these inconsistencies belied a misunderstanding

36. Ibid., p. 15.
37. See above, chap. 2, for Increase Mather's views on this subject.
38. Whitby, *Treatise*, p. 25.

of the "true Genius of the *Christian Faith*." They displayed an unhealthy preoccupation with earthly pleasures. Christians were supposed to be "intirely dead to the World, and to the things of the World"; hence it would be incongruous for God to hold up the vision of an earthly paradise as a goal worth striving for. Jesus had told his disciples to lay up treasures in heaven, not on earth; and if that eternal paradise was the proper reward for suffering martyrs, there was "just reason to conclude our *Lord*, and his *Apostles*, knew nothing of this Reign on Earth, or thought it no great matter of [the martyrs'] Consolation."[39]

We should be wrong to view these sentiments as part of a more general world-denying asceticism. Despite the reproofs, Whitby maintained his own thousand years of outward peace and prosperity. What is more important to understand is how the vision of a millennium, and the prophecies in general, were used in this theology. Those scriptures, like many other parts of the bible, were "Gospel-Promises"—promises designed especially for Christians who needed "Consolation and Encouragement, under the Troubles of this present World." John had originally written the Revelation to comfort believers and raise their morale in difficult times. Whitby, like those before him, assumed that the prophecies were to be used in this same way. "In a word," he concluded, "to foretel Times of Peace and Plenty to succeeding Ages, to raise the Expectation of a People whose backs are bowed down, and have been long enslaved and afflicted, is very suitable to this divine Œconomy"; but to promise material rewards in return for "piety and patience" was "too mean, too much beneath the sublime Spirit of Christianity."[40]

The *Treatise* was not meant to be a full-scale commentary on the Revelation; it attempted only to prove its specific case

39. Ibid., pp. 27–28.
40. Ibid.

for a millennium consisting primarily of the spiritual revival of the Jewish church. Although Whitby had written amply on the rest of the New Testament canon, he left the last book of the Bible alone, claiming he had neither "sufficient reading nor judgment to discern the intendment of the prophecies contained in that book."[41] One man who was less modest about his own abilities was Moses Lowman, an English Nonconformist. Most of Lowman's years were spent as a minister at Clapham, where his preaching showed much diligence and apparently little else. His strong point was hermeneutics, not homiletics. In 1738 he issued a *Paraphrase and Notes upon the Revelation of St. John*, which nicely complemented Whitby's other commentaries. Later editors recognized this fact and published both men's expositions in one volume.

Lowman agreed with most of the specific arguments in Whitby's *Treatise*, and more important, with its traditional conception of the prophecies as comforting promises. John's visions portrayed the church as continually subjected to "a melancholy state of long and prevailing corruption." It certainly would have been nicer to have a more pleasant tale, but the function of prophecy was "to foretell things as they shall really be, how afflictive soever." When actual events confirmed these dismal predictions, Christians were provided with assurance of a rather backhanded but nonetheless comforting sort. Precisely because things looked so bad in the world, the church had the greatest grounds for hope: all was going according to God's plan. Prophecy was most helpful

> when we might be tempted to forsake true religion, by the power of prevailing error and reigning corruption; or when we might be greatly dejected, and despair of success,

41. Quoted in Moses Lowman, *A Paraphrase on the Revelation of St. John*, in Simon Patrick, et al., *A Critical Commentary and Paraphrase on the Old and New Testament* (Philadelphia, 1848), 4:1012.

> where opposition to true religion is so powerful and vio-
> lent, as hardly to leave a reasonable prospect of bearing
> up against it. In such a state of things, which has often
> happened, it has been the use of prophecy, to keep up
> the hearts of good men with lively and affecting rep-
> resentations of the majesty, the power and goodness of
> God. . . .[42]

Lowman proceeded to apply this general motif to his own specific interpretations of the prophecies. Mede had been wrong, he thought, in using synchronisms to conflate various sections of the Revelation. John's book foretold three distinct periods of history, and none of the visions describing them overlapped. Hence, the sounding of the trumpets followed chronologically the opening of the seals; and after both came the prophecies in the "little book" about the temple, the slain witnesses, and the seven vials. Lowman explained that each period was actually a miniature replica of the larger pattern of salvation he had already described. Within each time span, there was a "state of danger, opposition and trouble" for the church, whose worsening affliction was remarkably removed to introduce a state of "peace, safety and happiness." It was the afflictive model of progress at work: things getting better only as they got worse.

Thus, although the first period began with some gospel successes, the church's harassment by Rome increased as it drew to a close. Just before Constantine appeared for the church's deliverance, "severe persecutions were almost perpetually renewed," and "seemed to threaten the utter destruction" of those who would not renounce their faith. Nor did the brief respite under Constantine last long. The trumpets marked a time when a whole swarm of idolatrous nations endangered the gains that had been made. Mahomet, in particular, was so

42. Ibid., pp. 1012–14.

successful that he seemed to "threaten the ruin of the Christian name and religion in the east." But Charles Martel in 734 saved the day by preserving the western parts of the empire.[43] One suspects Martel had this greatness thrust upon him not so much because of his stunning efforts on behalf of the faith but because Lowman's adoption of a nonsynchronal time-scheme meant that he had to hurry things along in order to have enough room for his third and greatest period.

That began in 756, when Pepin helped the Pope to wrest the papal state free of the influence of the Lombards, thus signaling the start of more trouble for the church. At the same time, Lowman had to get right to work pouring his vials, since he had calculated that each one took about two hundred years to complete. But because he began them at a time when antichrist was everywhere triumphing, his angels seemed to be pouring with rather indiscriminate aim. The popes deceived multitudes, the priesthood hunted down true believers, and the Crusades spilled just about everybody's blood.[44] The fifth vial, poured at the time of the Reformation, did better at hitting the mark, and Lowman predicted even greater judgments against Rome under the sixth and seventh vials. But since these remained in the future, one could only make tentative guesses. Perhaps the Turks would invade the papal dominions sometime between 1700 and 1900; and as for the last battle at Armageddon, "we can only guess at the historical events." But the specifics did not really matter; the mere knowledge that God would triumph was sufficient "to encourage patience and faithfulness, from hope in God's promises of protection and deliverance."[45]

In short, although Lowman agreed with Whitby's interpretation of the first resurrection (and referred readers to argu-

43. Ibid., pp. 1016–17.
44. Ibid., p. 1087.
45. Ibid., pp. 1082–83.

ments in the *Treatise* for "full satisfaction" on the point),
that event hardly dominated his conception of the apocalypse.
It would likely not occur until the year 2016, and until that
time, the prophecies would perform their usual function of
encouraging patience, faith, and hope. And these virtues were
not designed to foster an activist theology. Lowman went out
of his way to answer the objection that the study of the Revelation had "dangerous consequences" that would encourage
"great disorders." Actually, the prophecies preached the contrary: "Here are no directions, or the least encouragements
given to the church, or Christians, *as saints*, but to patience
and perseverance . . . no encouragement of sedition or mutiny, of violence and injustice, no not to their greatest enemies
or in their greatest dangers." The faithful were instructed to
"wait the time God has appointed for their deliverance; hoping that God will, by his own hand of providence, execute his
designs."[46] If anything, Lowman's interpretation of the Revelation emphasized more than most, prophecy's essential
task of providing comfort under trials.

Whitby, Lowman, and other expositors thus added variety
to the growing corpus of prophetic interpretations while still
underscoring the prevalent social applications of the prophecies.[47] In similar fashion, supporters of the Awakening saw
little new about their own attitudes concerning the redemption of history.[48] When opponents pressed them to defend

46. Ibid., p. 1019.

47. Other expositors included Charles Daubuz, a Huguenot exile whose thou-
sand-page commentary reasserted the necessity of a literal first resurrection and
strongly opposed Whitby's notion of an expanded role for the Jews during the
millennium. Lowman, of course, disagreed with Daubuz's views but used the
volume to buttress certain of his own textual readings. See Charles Daubuz, *A
Perpetual Commentary on the Revelation of St. John* (London, 1720), pp. 39–40,
46–47, 869, 908–09, 929. (Daubuz's title may at first appear to claim too much
for his work, but anyone who tries to plow through the volume will have to admit that reading it certainly *feels* like a perpetual labor.)

48. Variety in specific interpretations persisted. Thomas Prince apparently con-

their positions, they naturally cited older prophetic sermons as proof of their legitimacy.

Thomas Prince took on this task in *The Christian History*. New England had experienced smaller revivals, and by providing the magazine with accounts of them Prince hoped to demonstrate that the present Awakening was merely a grander form of what had before been accepted as a work of God. More important for our purposes, Prince's excerpts indicate that New Englanders were not doing anything new in interpreting revivals as foretastes of the millennial period. In 1721, Eliphalet Adams celebrated the rash of conversions at Windham, Connecticut, with the same hopeful rhetoric present in the Awakening. "Who can tell," he cried, "but that as he hath begun to pour out his good Spirit, so he may please to perfect the good Work and cause the good Savour of his Knowledge to spread far and wide?" Certainly the times were "*drawing nearer*" when the "*whole Earth may be filled with the Knowledge of the Glory of the Lord.*"[49] Fifteen years earlier Samuel Danforth had expressed similar thoughts after a revival in his own parish at Taunton. He believed that quite possibly "the *Time* of the *pouring out of the SPIRIT upon all Flesh* may be at the Door."[50]

Danforth's choice of Scripture is interesting, since Joel's prophecy was also one of Cotton Mather's favorites. Mather may have sometimes thought the conflagration imminent,

---

tinued to uphold the Mathers' views. James Davenport, at the height of his enthusiasm, suggested that the world would shortly "be involved in devouring flames." (*Boston Weekly Newsletter*, July 4, 1742). Gilbert Tennent also seems to have believed in a premillennial conflagration. (The evidence, however, is not entirely conclusive; for a discussion of it, see Davidson, "Eschatology in New England," pp. 189-90.) But men like Joseph Sewall, we must assume, continued to believe in a metaphorical resurrection of the martyrs, as, of course, did Jonathan Edwards.

49. Prince Jr., ed., *Christian History*, 1:132-34. Originally published in Eliphalet Adams, *A Sermon preached at Windham* (New London, Conn., 1721), pp. vi, 40.

50. Prince Jr., ed., *Christian History*, 1:111.

but he also waxed ecstatic in the belief that angels of the
Holy Spirit were coming to spread the Gospel across the land.
Thus, when Thomas Foxcroft began casting around for an
appropriate source to quote in a discussion of the "signs of
the times" during the Awakening, he lit on a passage out of
Mather's *Theopolis Americana*. Cotton had not found it at all
inconsistent to talk hopefully of a coming "holy City in
AMERICA" while still worrying about the sinful, sleepy state
of New England; and Foxcroft did not find it at all inconsistent to borrow from such theology.[51]

One man who apparently did was Jonathan Edwards. The
only significant piece of eschatological reinterpretation to
come out of the Awakening was his *Humble Attempt to Promote Explicit Agreement and Visible Union of God's People
in Extraordinary Prayer . . . Pursuant to Scripture Promises
and Prophecies Concerning the Last Times*. Edwards here ad-
vocated the spread of a practice begun by ministers in Scotland: weekly and quarterly prayer meetings designed to seek
God's aid in reviving the flagging spirit of the Awakening.
The prophecies were the principal source of encouragement
to the faithful, since they predicted a spread of the Holy
Spirit in the latter days. But Edwards foresaw one major
problem. Many prophetic expositors had argued that the slaying of the faithful witnesses in Revelation 11 was yet to be
accomplished. If that were true, then the Scriptures predicted
a desolate time ahead.[52] Obviously, Edwards reasoned, those
who agreed with that interpretation would find it "a great
damp to their hope, courage and activity," since they would
never see the dawning of the millennium: only the "dismal
time that shall precede it." Why would anyone want to pray

51. Foxcroft, preface, in Dickinson, *True Scripture-Doctrine*, pp. ii–iii. Foxcroft
is quoting from Cotton Mather, *Theopolis Americana* (Boston, 1710), p. 42.

52. Rev. 11:7–12. Readers should remember not to confuse this resurrection
with the first and second resurrections associated more immediately with the
millennium.

to hasten on a time when religion would be almost totally extinguished?[53] So Edwards concluded that interpreters had misread the Revelation, and that the witnesses had already been slain. Men could join the concert of prayer without fearing terrible times ahead.

All this certainly seems to substantiate the belief that Edwards reinterpreted the chronology of last events in order to purge millennial thought of its darker features, and in so doing, provided a new, more optimistic model of redemption history. What makes the case especially strong is not the shift in chronology per se (Cotton Mather, among others, believed that the witnesses had already been slain), but Edwards's open and explicit declaration that the prospect of black times ahead for the church would contribute to a detrimental psychological attitude on the part of believers. Edwards's interpretation did differ from those of his predecessors. But when the specific arguments in the *Humble Attempt* are set in the overall context of the treatise and the larger framework of Edwards's eschatology, what seems at first a momentous change becomes more properly a shift in emphasis. The afflictive model of progress remained central to his understanding of history.

Edwards, as we have seen, was no newcomer to prophetic speculation. He had already formed his own opinions on the major points of interpretation when he began his apocalyptic notebook in 1723. In general, his reconstruction of the latter days had more in common with the ideas of Willard and Colman than with those of the Mathers or Thomas Prince. The notebook's early entries accepted Mede's traditional opinion that only two vials had been poured—one by Wycliff and Hus, and the other by the coming of the Reformation. At that rate, it would take a good deal of time to get all seven

53. Edwards, *A Humble Attempt*, in *Works*, 3:472.

finished off, and Edwards placed the fifth as late as 1866. That nicely coincided with the termination of the church's forty-two months (or 1,260 days) in the wilderness. Satan's final overthrow would be complete by about the year 2000, in time to begin the seventh millennium of the world's existence. The fitness of that scheme was obvious: "The first six thousand years are six days of labor, and the seventh is a sabbath of rest."[54]

Edwards thought, as had many before him, that this millennial sabbath would not involve a literal resurrection of the martyrs. When the Revelation spoke of a resurrection, this meant only that the Christian spirit which had been reflected in the devotion of former persecuted saints would then rise to prominence in their successors, the saints of the millennial period. The connection between the two groups lay in the essential act of regeneration common to all Christians. The new birth in the individual had a double fulfillment, first in the spiritual change achieved in this life, and secondly in the final glorification after death. And this process was repeated on a larger scale: "As there is a spiritual resurrection, a first resurrection, of particular believers, so there is a coming spiritual resurrection of the world in general."[55] On the other hand, the resurrection at the end of the millennium was literal, summoning all saints to the glorification that followed the final triumph over Gog, Magog, and Satan.

This was the general position Edwards had formulated at the beginning of his career. His active mind hardly let the matter rest, however, and the notebook charts the changes in his eschatology over the years. And there certainly were changes. But Edwards spent an inordinate amount of time—from our point of view—polishing up the same kind of miscellaneous conjectures which prophetic expositors typically

54. Stein, "Notes," 1:68.
55. Ibid., p. 100; also p. 135.

relished. Like Samuel Sewall, he wondered how geography would influence the choice of a millennial capital. His candidate was Canaan, whose pivotal location between three continents made it "the most advantageously posited" site.[56] Or, like Daniel Whitby, he debated whether the Jewish nation would recapture its homeland and, if so, whether Gentiles could live within the borders. (The Jews would and the Gentiles could.) Edwards also spent time wrestling with larger issues, but the changes in his position had few practical consequences.

The influence of Moses Lowman's *Exposition* illustrates this point well. Edwards began to read the *Exposition* sometime after 1738, and Lowman's judicious handling of the rise of the papacy persuaded him to drop his old interpretation in favor of the hypothesis (proved "beyond all contradiction") that five vials had already been poured.[57] But since Lowman had started his vials earlier, and made them take longer, the net result was about the same in terms of Edwards's overall timetable. The sabbatic millennium, originally scheduled to begin around the year 2000, was only sixteen years later according to the revised computations. Furthermore, Edwards did not swallow the *Exposition* whole. Lowman's refusal to use synchronisms seemed particularly contrary to "the method of almost all the prophecies of Scripture"; and it confounded "the order of the prophecies of [the Revelation] more than former interpretations, especially in the eleventh chapter."[58]

That eleventh chapter described the plight of the witnesses, who were to be slain after their 1,260 days of prophesying.

56. Ibid., pp. 76–77. Edwards did not call this spot the New Jerusalem as Sewall had, because of a different interpretation of Rev. 21–22. But both men were referring to the central locus of the millennial reign.
57. Ibid., p. 404.
58. Ibid., 2:316–18.

Edwards accepted Lowman's beginning the 1,260 days at 756 (hence the arrival of the millennium in 2016); but he could not believe that the witnesses would be slain so close to the coming thousand years, since then the battle of the witnesses would have to be equated with the final conflict at Armageddon. Surely that was impossible, because the saints were to triumph at Armageddon, whereas the witnesses were not only slain but were said to be left unburied in the streets as a sign of their degradation.[59] Edwards could in no way imagine that the church would again be subject to such total debasement. Could anyone possibly expect, he asked,

> that Satan will ever find means to bring things to pass, that after all the increase of light that has been made in the world, since the Reformation, there shall be a return of more dark time than in the depth of the darkness of Popery, before the Reformation, when the church of God shall be nearer total extinction, and have less visibility, all true religion and light be blotted out of the memories of mankind, Satan's kingdom of darkness be more firmly established, all monuments of true religion be more abolished, and that the state of the world should be such, that it should appear further from any hope of a revival of true religion than it has ever done; is this conceivable. . . ?[60]

Thus Edwards's whole-hearted acceptance of only half of Lowman's theories led to greater and greater tangles, and the Northampton minister looked hard for a way out.

Characteristically, his active mind found several. Since God often provided for a double fulfillment of prophecies, the first being a weaker anticipation of the greater, the rising of

59. Letter, March 5, 1744, in *Works*, (Dwight ed.), 1:214–15.
60. Ibid., p. 214. The same argument appears in the notebook and also in the *Humble Attempt*, in *Works*, 3:473.

the witnesses might be fulfilled in several steps. God might, "out of great compassion to his church, . . . anticipate the appointed great deliverance that shall be at the end of these days." After all, he had done just that with the Reformation. If that argument lacked force, Edwards was willing to suggest that Lowman had perhaps started the 1,260 years a bit too late. The *Humble Attempt* modestly suggested a few alternate possibilities that brought the end of the period back into the eighteenth century.[61] And finally, Edwards pointed out that the original text describing the witnesses' death could be interpreted as occurring throughout the 1,260 years instead of after it.[62]

Lowman's commentary probably would have forced Edwards to deal with these problems regardless of the circumstances around him. But Professor Stephen Stein's careful dating of the entries in the apocalyptic notebook indicates that Edwards first began seriously considering the problem of the witnesses sometime in 1740, as the Awakening was spreading across New England.[63] We may reasonably suppose that the increasing showers of grace strengthened his conviction that the church would never wholly sink into darkness, and that God indeed might be shortening the time of the 1,260 days. Certainly his intensive study of the problem provided a firmer theoretical base than most ministers had for their hopes that the revival was "the dawning, or at least, a prelude, of that glorious work of God, so often foretold in Scripture." And when the Awakening seemed to falter, the *Humble Attempt* showed that Edwards's hope still lay in a gradual fulfillment of the prophecies through a revival of prayer. The union resulting from it "will gradually spread

61. Stein, "Notes," 2:236; Edwards, *Works*, 3:482 ff.

62. *A Humble Attempt*, in *Works*, 3:481. Here he followed Lowman, who in turn depended on Daubuz.

63. Stein, "Notes," p. *132.*

more and more, and increase to greater degrees, with which at length will gradually be introduced a revival of religion," until finally "the awakening reaches those that are in the *highest stations*, and until whole nations be awakened."[64]

Edwards even offered (with great diffidence) a more detailed scenario of this gradual fall. The sixth vial, he suggested, was meant to dry up the income and supplies of the papal state; and that was proceeding apace.[65] Meanwhile, even if God did not greatly shorten the time, much remained to be done. Suppose one allowed half a century to get the Protestant world peaceably united, and another fifty years to win over the Catholics. Add to that another century to take care of the Mohammedans and Jews, and the last hundred to enlighten the heathen and stamp out vice and recalcitrant enemies. Even if that were not the exact order of accomplishment, the enormity of the task indicated that it could hardly be finished "at one stroke." The great event undoubtedly would be brought about "by a gradual progress of religion."[66]

Without a doubt, then, Edwards thought that things were gradually getting better and better. Yet another reading of the same documents can provide enough cautious and gloomy prognostics to make historians skeptical about Edwards's optimistic predictions. When William McCulloch criticized him for not mentioning "more general and formidable trials" yet to come, Edwards denied that he had ever meant to say the church would be free of troubles. It was his opinion, he said, that "there would probably be many sore conflicts and terrible convulsions, and many changes, revivings and intermissions, and returns of dark clouds, and threatening appearances" before the final victory. The battle of

64. *Thoughts on the Revival*, in Yale *Works*, 4:353; *A Humble Attempt*, in *Works*, 3:432–33.

65. Edwards kept a list of events in his notebook pointing to such an accomplishment; Stein, "Notes," 2:321–79.

66. *A Humble Attempt*, in *Works*, 3:493.

Armageddon might not result in defeat for the church, but there would still be "a great and mighty struggle between the kingdom of Christ and the kingdom of Satan, attended with the greatest and most extensive convulsions and commotion, that ever were upon the face of the earth, wherein doubtless many particular christians will suffer, and perhaps some parts of the Church."[67] The *Humble Attempt* repeated the litany that the last battle would be "the most violent struggle of Satan," the "most general commotion that ever was in the world," and the "greatest conflict" ever. For it seemed obvious to Edwards that the whole history of redemption led up to this last climactic act. To accomplish it, the whole world was "groaning and travailing in pain," like a woman in labor. Thus the Scriptures painted "the last struggles and changes that shall immediately precede this event, as being the greatest of all; as the last pangs of a woman in travail are the most violent."[68]

The obvious conclusion to be drawn from all of this is that Edwards was the master of a quick-working and voluble tongue; able to paint with glowing optimism the coming millennium while still reassuring his more pessimistic colleagues that plenty enough trouble remained to suit them. Obvious, except that we know this combination of gloom and hope was central to the entire millennial rhetoric; that things might be getting better and better, but the whole creation was groaning and travailing in the process; that God reclaimed his people the way he reclaimed individuals, through the process of sanctification through humiliation. Edwards was conscious that his new theories about the witnesses might be interpreted as a threat to that truism, and acknowledged the specific parallel. It might be objected, he wrote in his notebook, that generally before God delivered his people in any remarkable

67. Letter, March 5, 1744, in *Works* (Dwight ed.), 1:213.
68. Edwards, *Works*, 3:482, 501, 450–51. See also p. 478.

way, he had them "reduced to the greatest, their distress [is] the most," just as he did "before the conversion, salvation and comfort of a particular soul. And God's dealings with his church are observably parallel with his dealings with particular souls." Similarly, Christ's most extreme sufferings were the last ones, just before his resurrection.[69]

Edwards had three answers to this objection, and each deserves careful consideration. The first admitted that God commonly brought deliverance to a people when they were at "the height of their calamity." But Edwards suggested that after this had happened there was often a space which intervened before the final salvation, just as there was with individual believers. "Most commonly the first comforts, given at the very time of a sinner's conversion, are not so great as follow afterwards. And often great conflicts and troubles intervene." So it was throughout salvation history. Jesus, although at his lowest during the Crucifixion, was not totally delivered at the Resurrection, but had to wait for the Ascension to achieve complete glory. The persecutions before Constantine's times were the greatest, but they abated about ten years before the Christian emperor took the throne.[70] Edwards's tack here was to accept the model of conversion, to emphasize the ups and downs which were part of the perserverance following a believer's initial deliverance, and in that way to align the model more closely with his own emphases.

That reply indicated some change in perspective, but Edwards's second response made it clear that the change was hardly radical. The Revelation predicted that the witnesses would be slain by antichrist, something which would not happen at Armageddon. But that did not mean that the church of God would not "suffer extreme oppression and be brought very low" just before the last battle—only that the distress

69. Stein, "Notes," 2:240.
70. Ibid., pp. 241, 245–47.

would come "not directly by the power of Antichrist, but in some other way; yet in general by the things of the same tendency, and all by Satan." As proof of this, Edwards noted that the Reformation had come after the witnesses' death, and yet the church was "now reduced very low, and to great extremity, through the prevalance of deism, atheism, heresy and profaneness."[71] This argument was not a denial of afflictions ahead; merely a question of who would inflict them.

That was because all Edwards's hopes could not erode his underlying belief that affliction—and more importantly its internal correlate, conviction—was an inseparable part of salvation. Edwards recognized that the crucial factor in the process was the internal psychological state, and not the external stimulus. If those proper feelings of abasement and awe, of dependence on God, of guilt under the law, could be achieved in some other way, then the textual question of the witnesses could be solved without endangering the fundamental process of redemption. It was a brilliant insight, but the final argument came out sounding as though Edwards were attempting to have his cake and eat it.

> 'Tis manifest that immediately before that glorious event, the popish powers will collect all their strength. . . . They shall join hand in hand; the combination will be exceeding strong; their schemes shall be laid very deep; their preparations shall be immense. The devil will assist them to his utmost; all the powers of hell shall be awakened and engaged. Satan will engage other parts of his kingdom of darkness in the world, to engage in the help of the Romish power; strong leagues and alliances shall be entered into. The ends of the earth, as it were, shall be stirred; emissaries shall be most busily and successfully employed in order to the most formidable and vast

71. Ibid., pp. 247–48.

preparations. They shall be like Pharoah with all the strength of Egypt and his mighty host of chariots and horsemen, all ready for the battle, and in their own imagination sure of success, vaunting in themselves, in their greatly exceeding the people of God in external pomp and power, so that they shall seem as nothing to 'em. They, greatly irritated and enraged, shall come with whetted resolutions of the most merciless cruelties. The appearances will be such as strongly to impress the minds of God's people with a sense of their enemies' power and their own comparative weakness, and the greatness of the sufferings intended them, and lively apprehensions of their danger.

And this show of force, with enemies at first beginning "to prevail and exercise their cruelties," would induce the proper feelings of humility and abasement in the faithful, and thus be "as good a preparation for the glorious deliverance" as if Satan's forces had actually triumphed.[72]

It apparently never occurred to Edwards that by letting this heretofore well-kept divine secret out of the bag, he would be thwarting God's purpose by raising up a generation of hopeful Christians who knew their triumph at Armageddon was inevitable. That puts the issue facetiously, but the point underneath remains. Edwards was not sensitive to the irony in his rationalizations because he viewed the process of redemption in the same paradoxical manner as his contemporaries. And for their part, they showed no signs of rushing to embrace Edwards's new specific interpretation.[73]

72. Ibid., pp. 248–49. Edwards also discussed the conversion parallel in a letter to McCulloch, May 12, 1743 in *Works* (Dwight ed.), 1:197.

73. The only definite agreement I have been able to locate is a letter from John Willison in Scotland, who wrote that he agreed "that Antichrist's fall will be gradual, in the way you explain it" (*Works* [Dwight ed.], 1:272). McCulloch, as we have seen, did not agree with Edwards. Nor did Aaron Burr, Jonathan Parsons, or

But perhaps the most vivid illustration of the traditional afflictive model of progress can be found in the only other detailed analysis of the prophecies published at the time of the Awakening. Robert Fleming's *The Fulfillment of the Scriptures* was a volume Edwards himself found useful, even though it had been first published in 1671.[74] Thomas Foxcroft called the Scotsman's treatise a "celebrated Piece" in his preface to the first American edition (1742), and other New Lights agreed with him.[75] In some ways, Fleming's volume seems an unlikely choice for publication in a time of hopes buoyed by unprecedented revivals. Fleming was writing in what he thought was "a dark time." Everywhere, the church was "suffering and afflicted, whilst the whole earth besides seemeth to be at ease." Sinful men were running rampant "whilst the *good man doth* (alas!) *perish*." Thus his view of prophecy mirrored Lowman's: Scripture predictions were "precious promises" which took the Christian "safe thorow this labyrinth of the world." Only when the millennium itself came would there be "no more need for a Christian to go to a promise and adventure upon it; we shall then no more watch, with the watchman in a dark and stormy night, and hope for the breaking of the day."[76]

Despite the dark and stormy nights, Fleming held out the promise of progress for the church. God, after all, accom-

---

even Samuel Hopkins. See Aaron Burr, *A Sermon Preached before the Synod of New York* (New York, 1756), pp. 21-26; Jonathan Parsons, *Sixty Sermons on Various Subjects* (Newburyport, Mass., 1779), 1:408; Samuel Hopkins, *A Treatise on the Millennium* (Boston, 1793), pp. 150-53.

74. Robert Fleming, *The Fulfilling of the Scriptures* (Boston, 1742). See Edwards's citations in *Thoughts on the Revival*, Yale *Works*, 4:307-10, 529.

75. Fleming, *Fulfilling of the Scriptures*, preface. That same year, Samuel Finley recommended it as "very serviceable to the present Age," in *Christ Triumphing* (Boston, 1742), preface; see also Jonathan Parson's use of it in *Sixty Sermons*, 1:368.

76. Fleming, *Fulfilling of the Scriptures*, pp. xiii, 6.

plished his prophecies one at a time; redemption was a process, "not perfected at once, but . . . still gradually carrying on." God's clear promises and the beginnings already made showed men that the work could not halt until the final perfect day. In short, Fleming managed to combine the gloomy and the hopeful in the usual way. "It may seem strange," he admitted, "how the Church's trouble and strait is oft seen to increase, with the first stirrings of her deliverance"; but that was "indeed a piece of the Lord's way with his Church." Luther had triumphed, and was immediately beset by Anabaptists; Edward VI hardly had time to purify his church before Mary Tudor succeeded him. And the Bible was replete with similar examples.[77] The whole treatise, in fact, was written from this "it-may-seem-strange" perspective. That "overclouding and darkness" should appear right after spiritual blessings "would seem a strange piece of providence." That "shakings and commotions" usually attended the coming of the Gospel might "also seem strange, yea, are ready to make many stumble." But what was rhetorically represented as strange to believers was actually the traditional formula of sanctification through affliction. The Saints' complaint had always been "the Lord's wounding them with the wound of a *cruel one*."[78]

The upshot of this logic was Fleming's belief that things were getting better because events had taken a turn for the worse! Did the forces of antichrist seem to be causing more trouble than ever? This was good news. "For when this party seems now to get up, and begins to move a war, we have sure ground to believe his further falling thereby." Was the church in a declining and woeful state? This might be unfortunate news if it was just *one* church on the decline—then there was a chance that that particular church might perish. "But since

77. Ibid., pp. 6, 173, 155–57.
78. Ibid., pp. 158, 167–68.

this seems to be a *consumption over the whole earth*, a matter of lamentation and spreading complaint, through the whole reformed Church, we may look on it as a very promising ground." The modern reader cannot suppress an indulgent smile and the speculation that if Fleming had ever lived to see the thousand years of peace and prosperity, he might have denounced it as the worst setback in the history of the church. The smile vanishes as Fleming almost rises to meet the challenge: Scripture shows, he says, that the church needs to be "thus tossed . . . a long calm being no less her hazard, than a sharp storm. . . . Oh how oft hath the Church lost more by a few years peace, than a long continued war!"[79]

No, that is pushing Fleming too far. He was no opponent of the millennium, and we may safely resume our smiles. But of all the available treatises on scriptural prophecies, why on earth did Thomas Foxcroft have to pick this one to support the Awakening?

A RHETORIC OF POLARIZATION

We can answer that in part from what we already know about the temper of previous prophetic expositions. The Puritan apocalyptic tradition saw redemption, whether on an individual or social level, as a process of judgment as well as mercy, a pilgrimage through the valley of the shadow as well as a sojourn in the millennial heights. That theological tradition lay at the heart of New England theology, and it would have taken an extremely glorious set of providences to purge the church of that point of view. The Awakenings were indeed glorious; no doubt they inspired in men like Edwards a vision of the beauty of union between God and his people. But the revivals were also the most divisive and controversial disturbances New England had seen. Responsible supporters of the Awakening had to deal both with the men who flatly

79. Ibid., pp. 176, 183, 178.

denied that the revivals were a work of God and with the zealots who seemed bent on proving that the opposers were right.

And here was where Fleming was so relevant: he recognized
that a period of progress for the Gospel was inevitably accompanied by both opposition and excesses. The pattern Fleming
described made it easier to understand that there were two
kinds of works going on in the Awakening, one by "the Holy
Ghost, in convincing, humbling, and converting Souls; and as
evidently, a Work of the Devil, in promoting what tends to
blast and ruin that Work."[80] Those who had steeped themselves in Fleming's it-may-seem-strange rhetoric knew that
"shakings and commotions" were a part of the Spirit's progress. Thus "this complex State of Things" seemed to Foxcroft
a "notable Discovery of the Fulfilling of the Scriptures."
Fleming's treatment of affliction and blessings was sure to ad-
minister "much Light" in explaining such a "Coincidence of
Facts" as were presented by the commotions of the Awakening.[81]

Foxcroft was merely commending a truism which many
New Lights were already using: the more Satan was chained,
the more he raged. That was comforting news indeed for
those ministers who found their colleagues attacking them
for supporting what seemed obviously a work of God. From
Scotland, James Robe wrote New Englanders he was persuaded that "*the further Progress this blessed Work should
make, the greater Opposition would be made to it*; and *the
more* CHRIST *should triumph, the more Satan would rage*,"
which I now see come to pass." George Whitefield was so well
prepared to meet with Satan's efforts that he was surprised
when the devil did not oblige him. "I wonder we have no
more adversaries," he remarked after preaching to a crowd of

80. Foxcroft in ibid., p. xi. Foxcroft is here quoting another minister of the
same opinion.
81. Ibid.

thousands in Philadelphia. "By and by, I expect Satan and his emissaries to rage horribly. I endeavored to warn my hearers of it."[82] When Satan's emissaries did raise objections, William Cooper was ready with his own similar warning. "That some entertain prejudices against this work, and others revile and reproach it," did not make it any less a work of God; in fact, "it would else want one mark of its being so; for the spirit of this world, and the Spirit which is of God, are contrary the one to the other. I don't wonder, that Satan rages, and shews his rage in some that are under his influence, when his kingdom is so shaken."[83]

The logic of this argument made it a two-edged sword. Satan had a double strategy of encouraging both opposers and extreme zealots. The faithful were, of course, comforted to know that opposition was only another proof of the revival's validity. And they felt that perhaps even opponents might be won over if they could only be made to see how the devil was setting up the extremists in order to conceal the Awakening's true value. When Chauncy objected that some apparent conversions were actually delusions, supporters could point to Fleming's observation that "*when there is some remarkable work of God on foot in a land . . . Satan setteth up some usual counterfeit there of . . .* with a very strange *resemblance* of the same." "Who can wonder," asked New Lights in their official "Testimony and Advice," "if at such a time as this, Satan should intermingle himself . . . ?"[84]

By the time the "Testimony and Advice" had been signed, the Awakening was already beginning to recede from its spiritual heights. And with the decline came a corresponding

82. Prince Jr., ed., *Christian History*, 1:51. See also 2:59. *George Whitefield's Journals* (reprint of the 1905 ed.; Gainesville, Fla., 1969), p. 356.

83. Introduction to Edwards, *Distinguishing Marks*, in Yale *Works*, 4:222.

84. Fleming, *Fulfilling of the Scripture*, p. 164; Prince Jr., ed., *Christian History*, 1:162.

reemphasis on the church as a threatened small band waiting for deliverance from its chastened state. At the beginning of the revivals, Thomas Foxcroft had contrasted the period before as a time when the enemy had come in like a flood; and now Edwards, writing McCulloch in March 1744, spoke of the present "very melancholy" times in the same terms: "the Enemy has come in like a flood, in various respects, until the deluge has overwhelmed the whole land." It was a day of Satan's triumph—but of course, fortunately, one of "God's People's Humiliation, which will be better to them in the end than their elevations and raptures."[85] Declension had once again set in.

We should remember that the *Humble Attempt* was written in this "destitute" and "very low" time (1747); consequently, it had much of the old jeremiad in it.

> How lamentable is the moral and religious state of these American colonies; of New England in particular! How much is that kind of religion that was professed and much experienced and practised, in the first, and apparently the best times of New England, grown and growing out of credit! What fierce and violent contentions have been of late among ministers and people, about things of a religious nature! How much is the gospel ministry grown into contempt! And the work of the ministry, in many respects, laid under uncommon difficulties, and even in danger of sinking amongst us! How many of our congregations and churches rending in pieces! Church discipline weakened, and ordinances less and less regarded!

The key remedy was prayer—particularly prayer "from the dust of Zion." When Scripture talked of a world in travail it meant, at least in part, a "wrestling and agonizing" on the part of faithful petitioners. Christ longed to deliver his

85. *Works* (Dwight ed.), 1:212.

church, but he did so only after he heard its cries from "the clefts of the rock, in the secret places of the stairs; in a low and obscure state, driven into secret corners."[86]

In focusing on prayer as a central means for enlarging the kingdom, Edwards placed himself in the center of New England's apocalyptic tradition. "These happy Times [of the millennium] are to be ushered in by Prayer," Samuel Willard had argued, and Increase Mather concurred.[87] Cotton Mather recommended a whole spectrum of prayers to help hasten the final days, including "public Supplication, to be maintained by our Churches, in a successive and repeated practice thereof."[88] For that reason, he had been quite receptive to a proposal that came to him from London in 1712, similar to the one Edwards was to receive from Scotland thirty-five years later. Cotton's correspondents had agreed to spend an hour each week in prayer "for the Deliverance and Enlargement" of the church; they thought "Public Prayers" were perhaps more effective because of the "*Union* and *Harmony*" in them. Cotton liked the proposal, and added it to his already busy schedule of meetings and prayers to hasten the times. "It may be attended with wondrous Consequences," he noted, and proceeded to send around copies of the letter to the religious societies he had already organized—"and so, draw as many of them as may be, into the Agreement."[89]

Edwards's humble attempt and Mather's modest proposal

86. Edwards, *Works*, 3:458, 454–56.

87. Willard, *Fountain Opened*, pp. 125–26. Increase wrote a treatise entirely devoted to the point; *A Discourse Concerning Faith and Fervency in Prayer*, passim.

88. Cotton Mather, *Things for a Distressed People* (Boston, 1697), p. 29. Mather emphasized—like Edwards—the travail and importunity that true prayer required. See *A Companion for the Afflicted* (Boston, 1701).

89. The proposal is reprinted in Manierre, ed., *The Diary of Cotton Mather for the Year 1712, pp. 115–18; see also pp. 86, 101*. Edwards was apparently unaware of the precedent.

were thus both a part of the greater millennial tradition which provided rhetorics well suited to their times. The Great Awakening no less than the preceding period of declension created disturbing and ambiguous situations which prophetic thought explained well—nay, even predicted in advance. That was the beauty of the afflictive model of progress: it promised redemption of a sort which the mixed temper of the Awakening could provide. The prophecies, as Sir Isaac would have said, were interpreted by the events. But at this point our modern skepticism returns. A momentous upheaval like the Awakening would have produced contentions even if it had not been seen as part of the history of redemption; but might we not also argue that the millennial logic itself helped to foster the conditions it predicted?— that Isaac Newton might better have reversed himself and said that events were interpreted—and shaped—by the prophecies?

This happened most obviously, perhaps, when the grand vision succeeded in clothing smaller events in the raiment of larger ones. We have already seen how the prophecies helped the individual believer to place his own pilgrimage within an immensely larger and more important context. Edwards explained the relationship nicely in his *History of the Work of Redemption*—itself New England's grandest summary of the plan. The whole design was like a river whose innumerable branches met only at the end of their respective journeys to the sea. Without knowledge of the overall plan which Scripture provided, men would be unable to perceive the direction of the movement, and the different tributaries would most likely appear as a "mere jumble and confusion to us, because of the limitedness of our sight." At close range, they seemed to be running in all different directions; and even when viewed from a distance, the terrain revealed "innumerable obstacles and impediments in the way to hinder their ever uniting and coming to the ocean, as rocks, and mountains, and the like."[90] But by keeping the ultimate destiny of the rivers in mind, the bewildered believer could take comfort in the knowledge that God's plan was somehow being fulfilled.

Less able to take comfort, however, were those who ended up being cast as the rocks, mountains, and other "impediments." The same vision that united the true believer with the forces of light also tended to place the sincere opposer with the forces of darkness; and that was perhaps the greatest paradox of the millennial dream. To see opposition to the revivals as confirmation of their validity because "the more Satan was chained, the more he raged" certainly raised the hopes of uncertain believers; but it also raised the hackles of opposers. The latter suddenly found themselves fitted into a larger-than-life battle either as emissaries of Satan or, almost as bad, as the unwitting dupes he manipulated to block the progress of redemption. When millennialists raised the stakes in their battle and used eschatological rhetoric to help make an ambiguous world clearer, they also created a climate which encouraged a polarization of attitudes.

Conversion, the smallest unit in the pattern of salvation, reinforced in its own way the perspective of the larger historical vision. It heightened the commitment of the believer to his faith by forcing him to confirm it in the psychological crucible of humiliation, conviction, and the new birth. The established morphology painted the end result of conversion as a dramatic reversal in personality: the old sinner by the grace of God made new. In truth, the process might well be a gradual one, taking a long period of time; and many non-church-members were hardly "sunk in sin" before their new birth—as witness the scrupulous refusal of many to attend Communion even in Stoddardean churches. But even though the reality may well have been different from the ideal, the convert's pilgrimage had him starting the journey, not as a

90. Edwards, *Works*, 1:511.

conscientious person attempting to clarify and strengthen his faith, but as a sleepy worldling blind to the truth and numb to the spirit until the terrors of the law reached him.

If a convert was able to convince himself that his old sins had rendered him incapable of seeing the world in proper perspective, then would it be so difficult to attribute similar motives to men who disagreed with the New Light? John White, who became a supporter of the Awakening and who had long feared the threat of Arminianism, showed how the logic might be used. "You may be confident that your Opinions are right," he told Arminians, "as the Jews were, that Christ was an Impostor. . . . Yet 'tis with you as it was with them." White could be so sure of himself because he too had once been in that sleepy state: "I am able to say, as one said when disputing with *Quakers*, I was a *Quaker* before I was a *Christian*: so I was an *Arminian* before I was a *Christian*. But God of his infinite Mercy has brought me off from that unsafe and false way." Thus a "thorow Work of Conversion" was "the most effectual Security against corrupt Principles and Practices," because such a work would remove the scales from a man's eyes. A sinner might think his beliefs were based on sincere convictions; but in truth, "'tis Pride that prompts thereto."[91]

The polarizing effects of the conversion model appear most clearly, of course, in the extremists of the movement. It is easy enough to see the effects James Davenport would create by telling all who disagreed with him that they were still slaves of Satan, or the impression David Brainerd would produce by announcing that Chauncy Whittelsey had no more grace than a chair. Similarly, Whitefield's ability to alienate clergy with his injudicious remarks is well known. Any political, religious, of social movement is likely to have its radicals who are ready to assign designing and sinful motives

91. John White, *New England's Lamentations* (Boston, 1734), pp. 26-29.

to people who oppose them. What is more interesting is the tendency of the rhetoric of conversion and the larger work of redemption to push moderates toward antagonistic positions.

Men like Foxcroft, Prince, and Edwards were quite aware of the divisiveness created by a censorious spirit, and they tried to guard against it. When Foxcroft introduced Jonathan Dickinson's discussion of true Scripture doctrine, he noted that, although it condemned Arminianism, men with a true "Christian Temper" would realize there were "*many* good Men of the *Arminian* Persuasion."[92] Prince inserted a timely injunction in *The Christian History* on the dangers of Phariseeism, warning both sides in the disputes that "those that most object it to others may be most deeply infected with it themselves." Edwards spoke frankly to Whitefield about the pitfalls of judging others' eternal states too freely, and his works contain many warnings to the "zealous friends of this glorious work of God" to refrain from "managing the controversy with opposers with too much heat and appearance of an angry zeal."[93] Yet for all the good intentions, an unconscious abrasiveness remained; and it can be best seen in the two principal defenses of the revival written by Edwards himself: the *Distinguishing Marks of a Work of the Spirit of God* and *Some Thoughts on the Revival of Religion*.

Distinguishing Marks purported to explain to those who had doubts about the revival what exactly constituted such a valid work—how, in effect, errors and excesses could creep in and still not blemish the work as a whole. But doubters were not likely to be encouraged by William Cooper's prefatory comments about Satan's opposition to the revival through "some that are under his influence." Cooper thought that the

---

92. Dickinson, *True Scripture-Doctrine*, pp. v–vi. He was immediately attacked by Andrew Croswell for saying this; see the *Boston Weekly Post Boy*, April 26, 1742; also April 12 and April 19.

93. Prince Jr., ed., *Christian History*, 1:136; Yale *Works*, 4:287.

"malignity" of some of the objectors approached "the unpardonable sin"; and he suggested that if anyone remained unconvinced after reading Edwards's arguments, the least they could do was remain silent, "and stop their oppositions, lest haply they should be found even to fight against God."

For it was God's plan of redemption that was being opposed: Edwards made that clear. Anyone who had studied the overall design would see too many parallels to deny that. When Christ first appeared on earth, the Jews opposed him; now when he appeared in the spirit, it was "no wonder at all" that men reviled the work—"yea, it would be a wonder if it should be otherwise." Just as God was provoked by the Jews who refused to acknowledge Christ, so now was He likely to move in wrath against those who failed to acknowledge him in this work, "notwithstanding what they may plead of the great stumbling blocks that are in the way. . . . The teachers of the Jewish church found innumerable stumbling blocks, that were to them insuperable."[94]

So Charles Chauncy and his ilk found themselves labeled as Pharisees of the worst sort: men who would not even recognize Christ. Even "silent ministers" who thought it best not to commit themselves either way actually stood "in the way of the work." And what added insult to injury was the conversion psychology: the Jews "were assured that they had just cause for their scruples," just as present-day opposers were. But the discerning of the truth depended on having the right spiritual principles within. That was precisely why God allowed so many stumbling blocks in his whole design. "'Tis with Christ's works as it was with his parables: things that are difficult to men's dark minds are ordered of purpose, for the trial of persons' dispositions and spiritual sense, and that persons of corrupt minds, and of an unbelieving, perverse, cavil-

94. *Distinguishing Marks*, in Yale *Works*, 4:222–24; 271–72.

ing spirit, seeing might see and not understand." The eschatological consequence was clear: many who had ostensibly
prayed for "that glorious reformation spoken of in Scripture"
knew no more of what they wished for than the Jews did
when they prayed for the coming of Christ.[95]

The same rhetoric accompanied the *Thoughts on the Revival.* The essay's entire middle section was devoted to demonstrating the obligation of supporting the work, and "the
Danger of the Contrary." And Edwards made it clear, just as
John had in his advice to the church of Laodicea (Rev. 3),
that at a time like the present "there is no such thing as being
neuters; there is a necessity of being either for or against the
king that then gloriously appears." The grand vision of
redemption was once again escalating the consequences of
the whole debate, and it was used quite consciously for that
purpose. The section, often quoted by historians, about
Edwards's hopes for America as the site for the dawning glorious work, stands right in the middle of this plea to opposers.
"I have thus long insisted on this point," Edwards explained,
"because if these things are so, it greatly manifests how much
it behooves us to encourage and promote this work, and how
dangerous it will be to forbear to do so."[96]

Edwards then proceeded to show how dangerous it would
be for anyone in New England—"rulers, ministers and people,
high and low, rich and poor, old and young"—to oppose the
work. The technique of exhortation for each group was similar, and was illustrated nicely in his warning to authors who
publicly discussed the revivals. Scripture provided the ground
for the warning: in this case the maxim in Judges, that "they
that handle the pen of the writer" would come to the help of
the Lord. Edwards's next step was to use typology and escha-

95. Ibid., pp. 273–74.
96. *Thoughts on the Revival*, in Yale *Works*, 4:349, 358; see pp. 353–58 for
the speculations about America.

tology to apply that Scripture to his own times in a way that magnified the consequences of everyday actions. Since these words in Scripture

> were indited by a Spirit that had a perfect view of all events to the end of the world, and had a special eye on this song, to that great event of the deliverance of God's church in the latter days, of which this deliverance of Israel was a type, 'tis not unlikely that they have respect to authors, those that should fight against the kingdom of Satan with their pens.

The final step in the process was to apply the passage to those who opposed the revivals, which Edwards did in a rather ominous way:

> Those therefore that publish pamphlets to the disadvantage of this work, and tending either directly or indirectly to bring it under suspicion and to discourage or hinder it, would do well thoroughly to consider whether this be not indeed the work of God; and whether if it be, it is not likely that God will go forth as fire, to consume all that stands in his way, and so burn up those pamphlets; and whether there be not danger that the fire that is kindled in them, will scorch the authors.[97]

Edwards certainly meant well in all of this. He wanted only to promote a more perfect harmony and union among believers. If doubters would just stop printing objections, the millennial world everyone longed for might come more quickly. But doubters did not stop doubting, and part of the reason was the unconscious offensiveness of such rhetoric. People did not like being told, however charitably, that they were opposing Christ's work because "it touches them, in something that is dear to their carnal minds; and because they see

97. Ibid., pp. 370-79, 380-81.

the tendency of it is to cross their pride, and deprive them of the object of their lusts."[98] Ironically, the humble attempts at union failed in part because they could too easily become subtle but nonetheless disruptive exercises in spiritual pride.

The millennial dream, then, both made and unmade the hopes of those who welcomed the Awakening. Made the hopes, not only because the revivals seemed like foretastes of the glorious promises, but also because the afflictive model of progress explained the divisive aspects of the religious turmoil as an inevitable, and in some ways beneficial, part of the road to salvation. It told believers—as the Revelation had been telling them for many centuries—that God sanctified his saints by such oppositions; that deliverance came for the church as it came for individual believers: out of a struggle with the forces of darkness. In the midst of that struggle, Scripture promises helped to explain where the many streams were flowing, where the great work was tending—especially when the events themselves did not always give sufficient signs.

And here was where the hopes were unmade. For the very act of incorporating small skirmishes into the grand drama created divisions even as it predicted them, irritated opposers even as it reassured the faithful. The conversion rhetoric which assumed that true believers could discern the signs of the times also assumed that it was carnal pride which prompted opposition. Unfortunately, Robert Fleming may have judged human nature correctly when he remarked that the church had lost more ground "by a few years peace, than [by] a long continued war." But even more unfortunately, the millennial rhetoric discouraged an emotional climate where his proposition could be tested.

98. Ibid., p. 381.

PART 2: Applying the Logic

5

History and Theodicy

We began our investigation by admitting that for modern readers the construction of a millennial logic presented a difficult challenge, given the strangeness and obscurity both of the prophecies and the expositions of them. The first half of this book has used the first half of the eighteenth century to explore several hypotheses designed to explain the way in which eschatology shaped the social perspectives of those who concerned themselves with it. Not all of the theories proved viable, but it is at least clear that expositors did express a number of consistent themes which, taken together, constitute a coherent eschatological outlook.

Central to this outlook was the notion of eschatology as theodicy. The Revelation explained God's ways with man—why the faithful were chastised and why harsh judgments were a necessary prelude to any final peace. The prophecies' social function was to support "the faith and constancy of the church, in every state of affliction."[1] Thus eighteenth-century divines measured progress toward the millennium in terms of the judgments necessary for redemption, and their sermons reflected the litany which combined pessimism with optimism and the gloomy with the hopeful. God used his afflictions as a goldsmith did his hammer: "Knock, knock, knock; knock, knock, knock, to finish the plate: It was to perfect them, not to punish them."[2]

1. Lowman, *Paraphrase on the Revelation*, in Patrick, *Critical Commentary*, 4:1013.
2. Ezekiel Cheever made the comment to Samuel Sewall. Sewall, *Diary*, 2:230.

The 1750s and early 1760s provide two striking examples of how the afflictive model of salvation functioned socially: both as a theodicy used to support traditional theological arguments defending God's honor, and as a comforting history which put into perspective New England's trying times. In the first instance, it was the New Lights who capitalized on the history of redemption to defend their heightened conception of God's omnipotence and his wisdom in the permission of sin. In the second case, both the Calvinists and the more liberal theologians seized on the prophetic patterns of salvation to explain the threats posed by the French and Indian War.

HISTORY AS THEODICY

The supporters of the Great Awakening have been more commonly associated with millennial ideologies than have their opponents, the theological liberals, and for several good reasons. The most conspicuous one is that they wrote more on the subject. Edwards, of course, composed the most outstanding attempt to place the prophecies in historical perspective: the *History of the Work of Redemption*. And his two lieutenants, Bellamy and Hopkins, published their own speculations on the Revelation. In contrast, leading liberals gave less explicit attention to the subject. Although Mayhew and Chauncy sometimes discussed eschatology in their sermons, neither offered the press a separate treatise on the subject. Samuel Langdon, a moderate with liberal leanings, did have plans for publishing an extensive commentary on John's visions, but his proposals for the volume elicited few subscriptions, and the project languished until 1791.[3]

3. Langdon's interest in the Revelation can be seen in his sermon, *A Rational Explication of St. John's Vision of the Two Beasts* (Portsmouth, N.H., 1774). The proposals for the larger volume are in the Advertisement at the front. The longer commentary is *Observations on the Revelation of St. John* (Worcester, Mass., 1791). Langdon considered himself a moderate Calvinist, but he had been

New Lights were attracted to the millennial outlook because it had a natural affinity for the larger concerns of Awakening theology. Most obviously, the hope engendered by the successful revivals led to thoughts of the coming kingdom. Equally important was the ability of the afflictive model of redemption to explain the fierce opposition to the revivals as yet another example of Satan raging even as he was being chained. The preceding chapter suggested that New Lights readily accepted this version of history partly because it was a grander elaboration of the new birth at the heart of the revivals. But the history of redemption reinforced another central thrust of Awakening theology: the reassertion of God's sovereignty.

In one sense, the stress on conversion was itself a part of this reassertion. A thorough conviction came only when a sinner perceived his own unrighteousness in relation to the overwhelming power and justice of God. Salvation was possible only when the sinner realized that human ability counted for naught in the process. God demanded faith, but only He had the power to provide it. When Arminians argued that a person could act as a free moral agent in choosing whether or not to believe the Gospel, New Lights accused them of robbing God of his sovereign power, leaving him dependent on the actions of men. Liberals retorted that Calvinists were the ones who insulted the Deity, by exalting omnipotence at the expense of goodness. If human actions were so totally dependent on the divine will, then was not God directly responsible for all the moral evil loose in the world? That, at least, was what liberals saw as the logical extension of the argument; and to answer the charge, New Lights turned to the prophe-

affected by the theology of men like Charles Chauncy and John Taylor more than he might have admitted—as his good friend Ezra Stiles knew. See Shipton, *Sibley's Harvard Graduates*, 10:508–28; Ezra Stiles, *Literary Diary*, ed. Henry M. Dexter (New York, 1901), 2:190–92.

cies as well as to the more traditional philosophical arguments.

Before examining the Calvinist position more closely, we should eliminate one possible confusion. Although Old and New Lights debated the extent of God's responsibility for evil, both sides agreed that the misfortunes arising out of *natural* disasters were properly attributed to the divine will. Thus Jonathan Mayhew began his sermon on the Boston fire of 1760 by quoting the prophet Amos: "Shall there be evil in a city, and the Lord hath not done it?" God was undoubtedly the architect of all events in the world, "the denial of which must terminate, not merely in the denial of a universal superintending providence, but of one or other of God's attributes; either his omniscience, or his omnipotence, if not of both." But Mayhew was quick to point out that Amos was not talking about "moral evil, or sin; but only natural, viz. pain, affliction and calamity." To conceive of God's "over-ruling providence, as to make him the author, or approver, of men's sinful actions" would be going too far: "blaspheming God, under the shew and appearance of doing honor to him." Mayhew suggested that there were some ministers "who could not perhaps easily acquit themselves of this charge."[4]

It was the question of moral evil, then, on which Calvinists and liberals parted; and by the time Mayhew delivered his sermon in 1760, the debate had raged long enough to insure that the public understood his allusions. The polemical controversy opened in 1757, when Samuel Webster published an imaginary *Winter Evening's Conversation* between a minister and several parishioners on the subject of Original Sin.[5]

4. Jonathan Mayhew, *God's Hand and Providence to Be Religiously Acknowledged* ... (Boston, 1760), pp. 7–11.

5. Samuel Webster, *A Winter Evening's Conversation*, 2d ed. (New Haven, 1757). The second edition has an appendix added by a Connecticut sympathizer. Webster later cautioned that this did not necessarily reflect his own views. The debate over Original Sin had been going on for some time already in England, with some rumblings in New England as well. But Webster's tract was the first

Webster denied that anyone was liable to damnation simply because he had sinned in Adam's fall, and pled his case by painting the lurid consequences of the doctrine for infants who had died at birth. Obviously, mere babes were incapable of repentance and were thus doomed to hell on account of Adam's imputed sins. "How can you reconcile it to the goodness, the holiness or the justice of God," asked Webster's minister,

> to make them heirs of hell, and send them into the world only to breathe and die, and then take them away to hell, or even send them to hell from their mother's womb before even they have seen the light of life? What! make them first to open their eyes in torments, and all this for a sin which certainly they had no hand in . . . ?

That sort of doctrine naturally led people "into very dishonorable thoughts of God." In effect, some Christians were "guilty of holding what even *heathen* would blush at, and all the world, have ever accounted the highest blasphemy, namely, that *God is the author of sin.*"[6]

Webster's arguments showed that his differences with the Calvinists extended beyond the question of Original Sin. He assumed that if infants were not to be sent to hell, it followed that they remained sinless until they became "moral agents," free to determine their own actions. Similarly, he argued that it made no sense to say that all men were guilty because they were "in" Adam when he sinned. Even supposing that "we were in the *loins* of our father *Adam, soul* and *body* at that

---

frontal attack issued in the colonies. For more details, see H. Shelton Smith, *Changing Conceptions of Original Sin* (New York, 1955); and Joseph Haroutunian, *Piety Versus Moralism* (New York, 1932).

6. Webster, *Winter Evening's Conversation*, pp. 5-6, 24. Calvinist Peter Clark attacked Webster's position in *The Scripture Doctrine of Original Sin, Stated and Defended, in a Summer Morning's Conversation* (Boston, 1758). Webster replied in *The Winter Evening's Conversation Vindicated* (Boston, 1759).

time; I would ask whether any would venture to say we were *moral agents* at that time, so as to be accountable for our actions. Few, I believe will be so absurd as to assert it."[7] Webster assumed that God could hold people accountable only for sins they had committed as free moral agents.

But that meant Adam's original sin was merely the tip of the iceberg. Below lay the countless other transgressions which men had perpetrated regardless of what they inherited from Adam. God could be cleared of all responsibility for these if it was assumed that men possessed self-determining wills unconstrained by any prior necessary causes. Under this scheme, a person was properly responsible for his own sins; it was the imputed ones that were difficult to justify. But Calvinists assumed, as Edwards reiterated in his *Enquiry into the Freedom of the Will*, that it was nonsense to talk of a self-determining will. God had foreknowledge of men's decisions, and he had that foreknowledge because he knew the causes which necessarily led men to choose as they did. Edwards thus asserted that free will was not incompatible with necessity. To liberals, this only compounded the problem. Now it seemed that Calvinists had made God the author of *all* the sins of the world, not just those imputed by Adam's fall.

Thus, while the specific debate over Original Sin continued,[8] Joseph Bellamy and Samuel Hopkins both moved to deal with the larger issues at stake. Bellamy issued a substantial collection of sermons written on the general theme of "the Wisdom of God in the Permission of Sin"; he also included a sermon on the divinity of Christ, and another—because he

7. Webster, *Winter Evening's Conversation*, pp. 6, 9.

8. Edwards's treatise on the subject, though not written for the controversy, appeared in 1757; Charles Chauncy also entered the lists with a short discussion. Jonathan Edwards, *The Great Christian Doctrine of Original Sin*, Yale *Works*, vol. 3; Charles Chauncy, *The Opinion of One That Has Perused the Summer Morning's Conversation* (Boston 1759). Clyde Holbrook discusses the controversy at greater length in his introduction to Edwards's *Original Sin*, Yale *Works*, vol. 3.

considered it relevant to the general topic—on the millennium. Hopkins followed suit the next year with *Sin, Thro Divine Interposition, An Advantage to the Universe.*[9] Both men were disturbed to hear many people making the assumption that "'If God foreordained whatsoever comes to pass, then he foreordained Sin.' As though," continued Bellamy, "it were evidently the greatest Absurdity in Nature, to suppose, that God really thought it best in the whole, that Sin should ever exist in the World he had made." But he and Hopkins knew there was ample evidence to prove that all the sin and misery in the universe was "for the general Good of the Whole" and would "answer some good End that shall much more than counter-balance the Evil."[10] The evidence could be found by anyone who took the trouble to study the history of redemption.

That, of course, is the phrase Edwards chose to describe his own study of the prophecies, and perhaps it was not entirely a coincidence that he hoped to spend more time on the subject in 1757 and 1758, when "the prevailing errors of the present day" were at such a height.[11] Edwards's project, had he ever completed it, would undoubtedly have been less polemical than either Bellamy's or Hopkins's tracts of 1758–59, but he shared with his two disciples the same broad perspective which united eschatology, the history of the end of the world, with the long history that preceded it. Edwards thus considered his proposed project to be "a body of divinity in an entire new method," and not simply another exposition of the prophecies. New, because it was

9. Joseph Bellamy, *Sermons upon the Following Subjects* (Boston, 1758). This was issued separately from his more specific attack on Webster's tract published the same year, *A Letter to the Rev. Author of the Winter Evening's Conversation* (Boston, 1758). Samuel Hopkins, *Sin, Thro Divine Interposition* (Boston, 1759).
10. Bellamy, *Sermons upon the Following Subjects*, p. 111; Hopkins, *Sin*, p. i.
11. Letter of October 19, 1757, in *Works* (Dwight ed.), 1:569.

thrown into the form of a history; considering the affair
of Christian Theology, as the whole of it, in each part,
stands in reference to the great work of redemption by
Jesus Christ;... beginning from eternity, and descending from thence to the great work and successive dispensations of the infinitely wise God, in time, considering
the chief events coming to pass in the church of God, and
revolutions in the world of mankind, affecting the state
of the church and the affair of redemption, which we
have an account of in history or prophecy; till at last, we
come to the general resurrection, last judgment, and
consummation of all things;... This history will be carried on with regard to all three worlds, heaven, earth, and
hell; considering the connected, successive events and
alterations in each, so far as the scriptures give any light;
introducing all parts of divinity in that order which
is most scriptural and most natural; a method which
appears to me the most beautiful and entertaining, wherein every divine doctrine will appear to the greatest advantage, in the brightest light, in the most striking manner,
shewing the admirable contexture and harmony of the
whole.[12]

Bellamy and Hopkins, too, saw the bringing of good out of
evil as the recurring pattern exhibited in that "harmony of
the whole," and in that way used the history of redemption
as a theodicy which demonstrated how admirably evil had
been incorporated into the divine plan. The Bible contained
"an authentick History of the Conduct of the Deity, for a
long Series of many hundred Years," said Bellamy (echoing
Edwards), "and by prophetic Representations, opens to our
View Things yet to come to pass, as far down as to the End
of the World." Furthermore, since the whole plan of salvation

12. Ibid., pp. 569–70.

was "harmonious and consistent," understanding one part of
the drama would make it easier to fathom the entire design.
"So that if we can see the Wisdom of God in the Permission
of Sin in some instances," he reasoned, "we may justly argue
to his Wisdom in his whole grand Scheme." Hopkins agreed.
If Scripture had shown that God had overruled evil in some
instances, "why may he not, yea, why *will* he not, *in every
instance*?"[13]

Thus Bellamy and Hopkins recited Scripture history precisely because it provided examples of the pattern of light
out of dark that was so much a part of eschatological rhetoric.
God permitted soldiers to slay Israel's first-born males in
order that the Hebrews would be weaned from the idols and
pleasures of Egypt; he permitted Pharoah to tyrannize the
Chosen People, in order that they would be forced to cross
the wilderness to the land of Canaan. The relevant moral for
readers living in the present "exceeding gloomy and dark"
days[14] was that the faithful should bear up in difficult times,
for "if these Dispensations of divine Providence . . . appeared
[to Moses] so full of Divine Beauty, Wisdom and Glory; how
know we that God's whole Plan of Government, how Dark
soever it may appear to a revolted World, under God's displeasure, may to Saints and Angels . . . appear perfect in
Wisdom."[15] The pattern of redemption was uniform, so the
contemporary church would be delivered from the mystical
Babylon just as surely as Israel had been freed from the original one.[16]

Jonathan Parsons, another New Light, expressed the same
unified view of history in a sermon which may well have
been delivered around the time Hopkins and Bellamy were

13. Bellamy, *Sermons*, pp. 122, 104; Hopkins, *Sin*, p. 8.
14. Bellamy, *Sermons*, p. vi.
15. Ibid., pp. 78–79, 85.
16. Ibid., p. 104.

writing their own theodicies.[17] The Scriptures advised the faithful to respect the divine government of the world, Parsons noted; "but when we view it, there appears such a mixture of light and darkness, that we are non-plus'd, and know not what to say or what to conclude." The answer, as usual, could be found in the Bible stories which demonstrated that when God promised his people something, events often seemed to take a step backward—precisely the opposite of what the faithful might hope. Parsons pointed out (quite rightly) that Robert Fleming had made the same connection between light and darkness in his expositions of the prophecies that had been reissued in New England during the Awakening.[18]

If the pattern of light rising out of darkness was a consistent one in the Bible, then the confusing signs of the present were easily enough explained. Satan was indeed stirring, and would "probably, soon assemble a great army to mar the prosperity of the church for a short time." But this was in many ways hopeful, since the greatest deliverance in history would come the way the others had. "When the enemies of the church have got to the height, the year of the redeemed will come. When the church is in a forsaken condition, and begins to say her wound is incurable, then God says . . . *I will*

17. Jonathan Parsons, "God's dispensations, at times, unsearchable," in *Sixty Sermons on Various Subjects*, 2 vols. (Newburyport, Mass., 1779), 1:358-408. Since these sermons are in a collection that was published posthumously, it is impossible to determine when this one was preached. However, internal evidence suggests that the late 1750s may have been the time. In another set of sermons, published in 1756, Parsons warned that a great event was "nigh at hand"; that "terrible things in righteousness" would precede it; and that, indeed, there had already been some signs (*Good News from a Far Country* [Portsmouth, 1756], p. 168). In the sermon on God's dispensations, he also said there were "evident presages of a dreadful storm coming upon church and state" (p. 380). In any case, his concerns were quite similar to those of Hopkins and Bellamy.

18. Parsons, *Sixty Sermons*, pp. 360-68. Fleming's work is discussed above, chap. 4.

restore health unto thee." This may have been cheer of a dubious sort, but it was the best Parsons could offer. He refused to say whether "the present clouds that are spread over church and state, are not to rise from one degree of darkness to another, until it is most terrible and universal darkness" or whether the present darkness would "vanish away, and the light break in with great glory, before the darkest day"; but either alternative would be consistent with God's grand plan.[19]

It is against this backdrop of God's wisdom in the permission of sin that we must view Joseph Bellamy's sermon on the millennium. Bellamy had read some of the major English expositions of the prophecies, but his ideas on the subject were not original, nor did he take much time to elaborate on them. A footnote and a few pages of text in the sermon indicate that he followed Edwards in relying on Moses Lowman.[20] His prime concern, however, was neither the nature of the millennium nor the details of its arrival, but rather the way in which the thousand years served as a comforting vision of ultimate good brought out of many preceding woes.

The opening of the sermon made that clear. Bellamy explained that the Bible was called "the good man's book" because it was designed to help the saint understand the situation he was always finding himself in. That situation (as we have learned from our acquaintance with prophetic rhetoric) could be most succinctly characterized as Down and Out.[21] Consequently, the Bible was "widely adapted to ease the

19. Parsons, *Sixty Sermons*, pp. 379–80, 407–08, 388. For another sermon that develops these same patterns, although not in an eschatological context, see no. 46, "God's antient dispensations towards his people designed for future improvement of his Church," pp. 488 ff.

20. Bellamy, *Sermons*, p. 52 n. He also consulted and quoted Charles Daubuz, however, who interpreted the first resurrection literally.

21. Ibid., pp. 44–45. Bellamy's description of the situation was of course more expansive, but it amounted to the same thing.

good Man's pained Heart, and afford consolation in this most
interesting and important point; as it gives the strongest As-
surances that the Cause of Vertue shall finally prevail." God
had comforted his embattled church throughout history with
promises of deliverance, and the millennium was simply the
last and greatest of these. Just as the Jews would have been
grief-stricken in Babylon had it not been for God's promises
to them, "how insupportable" would have been the sadness
of the church

> thro' the long, dark, cruel reign of mystical Babylon,
> while they beheld Error and Wickedness universally pre-
> vail, Satan getting his Will in almost every Thing, and to
> Appearance no signs of better Times, but all Things wear-
> ing a dreadful Aspect before their Eyes; how great their
> Grief; how sinking their Discouragements, how almost
> insuperable their Temptations to apostatize, and forsake
> a Cause that Heaven seemed to forsake, had not the Day
> of Deliverance been expressly foretold. . . .

And now, as the world approached the end of that mystical
reign, the saints should once again trust in the divine predictions. Bellamy used one of the standard rhetorical construc-
tions of prophetic expositions to hammer home his point:

> And, what if Mankind are ever so estranged from God?
> And what if they are ever so averse to Reconciliation?
> And what if Satan reigns in the Courts of Princes, in the
> Councils of the Clergy, as well as in the Cottages of the
> Poor? And what if even the whole World in a Manner, lies
> in Wickedness? so that a general Conflagration might
> rather be expected, as it is so eminently deserved;—are
> these Things any Bar in the Way?[22]

22. Ibid., pp. 44, 45, 57. This "What if . . ."rhetoric is out of the same mold as
some of the maxims already described in chapter 4 ("the more Satan is
chained . . . ," etc.), which were standard ways of explaining the combination of

All this rhetoric—examples of which could be multiplied to the point of exhaustion—indicates how much Bellamy used the history of redemption as a theodicy of comfort. But perhaps the quaintest and most striking demonstration of that concern was the minister's brief foray into the area of millennial demographics.

Bellamy was aware of the numerous scriptural passages which suggested that only a small proportion of mankind would be saved. "Many are called but few are chosen" was one; "Strait is the gate and narrow is the way," another. Yet Bellamy thought that perhaps these sayings were meant to be applied only to the times preceding the long era of peace and prosperity. If the millennium was to be as full of saints as he hoped, then possibly the majority of mankind would be saved after all! Some ministers, Thomas Prince among them, had suggested that the thousand years mentioned in the Revelation might actually stand for 360,000 years, since the 1,260 days of the witnesses and other prophetic numbers had been calculated on the assumption that a day signified a year. In that case, the total number of saints would easily surpass the number of sinners sent to hell.[23] But even if the millennium were only to last for the shorter period, Bellamy thought he could prove that the number of inhabitants would be large enough to easily overbalance the number of damned from earlier years. It was not the sort of population study that Ben Franklin

---

light and dark in the prophecies. Compare Bellamy's questions with a similar set by Jonathan Mayhew: "What tho' you see iniquity abound, which may perhaps bring sore calamities upon us? . . . What tho' treacherous and barbarous nations are now ravaging our borders and laying waste our country? What tho' you hear of wars, of earthquakes and inundations in divers places. . . . What tho' the idolatrous corrupters of christianity, or mystical Babylon, should long triumph?" And on and on. "Still you know, that the Lord God Almighty, the King of Saints reigneth." Mayhew, *A Discourse on Rev. XV:3-4*, p. 69.

23. Bellamy does not mention Prince by name, but Samuel Sewall had noted Prince's theory. See above, chap. 3.

might undertake, but to Bellamy it had infinitely greater significance.[24]

New Englanders, as everyone knew, were doubling at the rate of once every twenty-five years, and the Hebrews had done the same at the astounding pace of once every fourteen while they were in Egypt. Thus it would be "moderate" to assume a doubling rate of once every fifty years for the inhabitants of the millennial world, particularly since pestilence, famine, and other destroying judgments would be absent. In that case, the population would double itself twenty times over the whole thousand years; for every man at the beginning of the millennium, there would be two in fifty years, four in a hundred years, and so on. Bellamy computed the results in a table, as indicated below, and discovered there would be over a million people living in the last fifty-year span for every person who had lived at the beginning—not to mention a sum total of 2,097,150 souls living over the entire thousand-year period for every one person living at the time the reign commenced.

1	2
2	4
3	8
4	16
5	32
6	64
7	128
8	256
9	512
10	1,024
11	2,048
12	4,096

24. The material in this paragraph, as well as the description of the millennial computations that follow, can be found in Bellamy, *Sermons*, pp. 62–66.

13	8,192
14	16,384
15	37,768
16	65,536
17	131,072
18	262,144
19	524,288
20	1,048,576
Sum TOTAL	2,097,150

Bellamy further supposed that the population throughout the 6,000 years before the millennium would always remain equal to the number at the beginning of that period—a generous assumption. And he estimated that the population changed completely once every fifty years. That would mean (dividing 6,000 by 50) that 120 people had lived in the previous history of the world for every one person alive at the beginning of the millennium. The rest of the figuring seemed to be simple logic:

Suppose all before the Millennium lost [i.e. damned] = 120
Suppose all in the Millennium saved = 2,097,150
Then 120 : 2,097,150 :: 1 : 17,456 – 40/120   Q.E.D.

In other words, for every soul lost before the thousand years, over seventeen thousand would be saved afterward!

The precise ratio of 1 to 17,456 and 40/120 of a soul, followed by a confident Q.E.D., make an amusing end to the string of calculations, but it should not obscure the point of Bellamy's arithmetic. He freely admitted that God had not revealed the exact proportions of saved to damned, and that his calculations were merely an indication of what was possible. What the faithful should remember was that "the holy Scriptures encourage us to look for Things exceeding great and glorious; even for such events as put a new Face on all

God's past Dispensations. (See the following Sermons on the Wisdom of God in the Permission of Sin.)"[25] When the saints could picture the proper relation between the present evil times and the final deliverance, when they could finally understand that there was a necessary connection between the two, then they would recognize and even rejoice in God's decision to let sin into the world. Hopkins summed up the Calvinist position quite clearly: "The Scripture don't represent the Work of Redemption, as what God has wrought to *mend* and *patch up*, as well as he could, a World that is spoil'd and ruin'd by Sin; as if there would have been *more Good* in the World, upon the whole, if there had been no Sin, and so no Redemption by Christ."[26]

That was the crux (the term is appropriate) of the Calvinist millennial theodicy: it was better to have the evil that brought with it Christ's redemption of the elect and the millennial triumph of the church than not to have Christ and the history of redemption at all. And that was a position which many liberals found extreme. While Webster, Chauncy, and others addressed the more specific question of Original Sin, Samuel Moody challenged the Calvinists on God's responsibility for evil.[27] Moody complained that Bellamy was too confident of the positive value of sin, and that it was not at all obvious that just because God allowed evil in the world he should also "think best there should be Sin in a State of Perfection and Holiness." And that was implicitly what Bellamy was saying by claiming that the present world was the best one God could possibly have made. The most any sensible divine could admit was "that God is holy;—hates Sin—cannot be the Author of it; and therefore the Creature must."[28]

25. Ibid., p. 66 n.

26. Hopkins, *Sin*, p. 9.

27. Samuel Moody, *An Attempt to Point Out the Fatal and Pernicious Consequences of the Rev. Mr. Joseph Bellamy's Doctrines* (Boston, 1759).

28. Ibid., pp. 7, 8 n.

Of course, if men were directly responsible for sin, it could be argued without offending the Deity that this world was not the best possible creation after all. So Moody proceeded to do what Bellamy and Hopkins would have considered unthinkable: namely, to suggest arguments "which incline me to think, it would have been most for God's Glory, and the Happiness of the Creation, had moral Evil never been introduced into this System." If Adam and Eve had never fallen, "compleat Order and Harmony" would have still remained in the universe, an alternative that was surely more desirable than the present one. Otherwise, why had God placed them in such a perfect situation in the first place? "And if it was best, they should be loyal, obedient and happy, I cannot see how it was best they should rebel and be miserable."[29] Moody followed out the corollaries of his suppositions until they led straight to Bellamy's millennial calculus. If Adam had not fallen, sin and death would be unknown and all creatures could have obeyed more perfectly the command to be fruitful and multiply. Since "Mr. *Bellamy* is so dexterous in arithmetical Calculations, he may, for his own Satisfaction, compute how many there must have been now in the World; and whether they would not have so greatly exceeded in Number as to have made the Quantity of Happiness, in the sum, superior to what it could be even on his own Hypothesis." Moody anticipated the traditions of modern scholars and saved his most waspish criticisms for a footnote, where he called the computations "so wildly absurd" that they needed no refutation. He only suggested that "those formidable Rows of Figures be reduc'd to 000's, a Coalescence of which into one great 0 . . . if of no other Advantage, will facilitate the Work of the Printer."[30]

29. Ibid., pp. 19–22.
30. Ibid., p. 23 n. Moody was not the only one who failed to buy Bellamy's math. Israel Dewey embroiled his pastor, Samuel Hopkins, in an argument over the wisdom of God in the permission of sin, and complained that Bellamy "com-

Moody's conclusion was that most of the arguments in the *Wisdom of God* were as unreasonable as the computations in the millennial calculus. But Bellamy and Hopkins were not inclined to listen to Reason. They remained steadfastly convinced that the incontrovertible history laid out in the Bible was worth infinitely more than the frail theories of rational philosophy. As a result, they continued to cling to the promises of the prophecies in difficult times and to the history of redemption as a sure proof of God's sovereign wisdom in the permission of sin.

THEODICY AS HISTORY

Old Lights did not feel the need to defend God's honor after the manner of the Calvinists, but they did have to square their conception of his overruling providence with the threatening events confronting them in the mid-1750s. Liberals and Calvinists alike found themselves at the edge of a war whose outcome would determine the ultimate master of the North American continent. Although the English had been working as aggressively as the French to gain a decisive hegemony in the backcountry, most colonists were naturally inclined to see France, that "Limb of the MOTHER OF HARLOTS," as the villain of the piece.[31] Aaron Burr's discourse on the subject in 1755 was typical in its fear of dark and deep-laid French plans. With the establishment of Fort Duquesne on the Ohio, he argued, France had managed to close the final link between the St. Lawrence and the Mississippi in her campaign of encirclement. What was to stop her now from launching a secret

---

putes like a Merchant *Profit* and *Loss* by Permission of Sin" to show "that Sin will prove 9600 millions [souls] clear *Gain* & *Profit* to the Universe." Stiles, *Literary Diary*, 1:280. Stiles noted that although the argument occurred ten years before Hopkins's dismissal, it may well have been one of the factors which began to turn his people against him.

31. John Ballantine, *The Importance of God's Presence* (Boston, 1756), p. 19.

offensive before formally declaring war? If Britain did not act quickly, the consequences would be grim: "Our Sea-port Towns sack'd, and land in Ashes!—Our Country ravaged! our Houses plunder'd! . . . Our *Wives* and *Daughters* delivered to the Lusts and Fury of a lawless Soldiery!—Our helpless Babes dashed against the Stones!"[32]

Quite a few congregations were provided with the same frightening vision of prosperous colonies reduced to ruins.[33] In many ministers' eyes, there was a good chance that England might find herself forced out of the New World, leaving the surviving colonists to the whims of an arbitrary papist government—all of which would seem a rather pessimistic assessment in light of the oft-professed belief that antichrist had been gradually falling for several centuries. But of course Satan raged as he fell, and for a while the French and Indian war proved that he could rage with considerable success.

England, as usual, managed to do everything in her power to lose the conflict before finally turning around to win it. Braddock, Shirley, and Boscawen were foiled in the opening moves of the war and the following two years brought a string of military failures. The colonies' stock just about hit bottom when Montcalm took the offensive and occupied Fort William Henry on Lake George in August 1757, threatening "a dreadful Irruption with Fire and Sword into the Bowels of our Country." As one minister later reminded his congregation, "You can't have forgotten the Surprize and Consternation of that Day. . . . We were ready to give up all for lost."[34] Only with the capture of Louisbourg in July 1758 did England begin her string of victories—Duquesne, Niagara, Crown Point, Ticonderoga—which led to the climactic reduction of Quebec

32. Aaron Burr, *A Discourse delivered at New-Ark* (New York, 1755), p. 40.

33. Such rhetoric was common in sermons of the period. See, e.g., Theodorus Freylinghuysen, *Wars and Rumors of Wars* (New York, 1755), p. 18.

34. Amos Adams, *Songs of Victory* (Boston, 1759), p. 23.

in September 1759. To many observers, it seemed as if a desperate situation had been transformed almost miraculously into a time of jubilant rejoicing.

Of course the turnabout was actually less dramatic. In retrospect, it is easy enough to see that France would have been hard put to reduce the colonies to ashes and leave in the wake of their forced entry a growing tribe of unwanted French bastards. But believers who were familiar with the prophetic patterns of history knew that the world's redemption came only through a cycle of trials for the faithful, culminating in the climactic tests of the slain witnesses and the battle of Armageddon. Undoubtedly, the present war was one of the many trials leading to ultimate victory. The question was, which one? Was it merely a preparatory struggle, like others that had come before? Or could it perhaps be the beginning of the last major rage of the beast? In the opening years of the war, the answer to that question was not at all clear.

Such a mood of uncertainty may well have sparked a renewed interest in the Signs of the Times. Whatever the reasons, more than the usual quota of prophetic tracts appeared in the second half of the 1750s, ranging from considered expositions by major figures to more obscure ramblings by men of lesser rank.

The Reverend David Imrie was among those of the latter category. Imrie tended a flock in Annandale, Scotland, and had not paid much attention to the prophecies until prodded by the hopes aroused through the Concert of Prayer. His subsequent investigations into prophetic numbers led him to make some startling conclusions in a letter to a friend, first published in Edinburgh in 1755 and a year later in the colonies. Imrie argued that the last events before Christ's coming were nearer than people suspected. The conversion of the Jews and Gentiles, the fall of antichrist, the introduction of the millennium were all to take place in the next forty years. This seemed like good news indeed, since the "dreadful days" that were "coming on the earth" would be particularly directed toward the Roman Catholic Babylon. But Imrie also noted that before the whore fell, power would be given her "to distress the *protestant churches* by wars and persecutions." And only then would the faithful understand the passage in the Revelation which spoke of martyrs made white by the blood of the Lamb: "OH! the blessed meaning contained under that expression *made white*; it means no less than that in these trying times they shall be able to stand with firmness and constancy to the cause of Christ . . . and shall be honoured to die the martyrs death."[35]

Imrie would not commit himself to a definite date for the beginning of these persecutions, but he believed it would be within seven years after the date of his letter, 1754. When the judgments began, fully two-thirds of the world would be cut off, while the remaining saints would be gathered into a "place of safety." Or at least relative safety; Imrie felt sure no "*preternatural* judgments" would be allowed to touch the faithful. They might have to put up with a few natural ones, like famine, sword, and pestilence, but these would be inflicted only insofar as the divine plan required. After all, "as by the œconomy of nature, silver cannot be brought out of ore, but by means of the furnace, so by the œconomy of providence, the day of blessedness cannot be brought about, but by the means of the preceding days of judgment."[36]

By the time Imrie's letter reached the colonies, his predictions were striking some people as being ominously close to the mark. A note accompanying the pamphlet informed the publisher that Imrie had previously discussed the earthquakes of 1750 and 1751 with friends and had suggested that even more prodigious ones were on their way. And shortly there-

35. *A Letter from the Reverend Mr. David Imrie* (Boston, 1756), pp. 5-7.
36. Ibid., pp. 8-9.

after came the disasters at Lisbon and New England! "Mr Imrie further thinks," the publisher added, that "'The *present Commotions* between *Us* and the *French* are a beginning of the Judgments spoke of in his printed Letter.'"[37] But many ministers must have remained skeptical. Imrie's predictions were uncomfortably definite and left little room for error. Jonathan Edwards commended the Scotsman's "disposition to be searching into the prophecies of Scripture," but refused wholehearted approval, remarking that events had often before humbled divines who "have been over forward to fix the times and the seasons" of accomplishment.[38]

Christopher Love and Richard Clarke provided even more precipitous timetables than Imrie. Love's forecast for the 1750s and 1760s gained added weight by virtue of his having expired on the chopping block a century earlier under the auspices of the Cromwell regime. At that time he had left his followers a list of predictions which one New England publisher evidently thought would make interesting reading in 1759. The list was short and to the point:

Great Earthquakes and Commotions by Sea and Land	1756
Great Wars in Germany and America	1757
Destruction of Popery, Babylon's Fall	1758
Anger of God Against the Wicked	1759
God will be known	1760
A great Man arises, Stars wander, Moon as blood	1761
Asia, Africa, America will tremble	1762
Great Earthquake over all the World	1763
God known by all; general reformation[39]	

37. Ibid., p. 17.

38. Letter of Edwards to William McCulloch, April 10, 1756, in *Works* (Dwight ed.), 1:553.

39. *The Strange and Wonderful Predictions of Mr. Christopher Love* (Boston, 1759), broadside. Love's predictions surfaced again later in the century, being reprinted in 1791, 1793, 1794, 1795, 1797, and 1798.

In the same year Richard Clarke took note of Love's calculations and supplied some of his own. The results were as confusing in grammar and syntax as they were in arithmetic, but it was at least clear that Clarke thought the slaying of the witnesses would begin in 1758 or 1759, followed by speedy accomplishments of other vials and plagues in the next five or six years.[40] The tract appeared in Charleston and Philadelphia as well as in Boston, and attracted enough attention to elicit an equally tortuous rebuttal entitled *From a Folio Manuscript, in the Archive of a Certain Aged Gormogon . . . Questions and Answers Are Extracted . . . with the Author (Harne Kileo) His Leave.*[41] Fortunately, Clarke never attempted to answer the Aged Gormogon.

No doubt many of the more discerning members of the public dismissed these productions as little more than extravagant diversions. But that was because the would-be prophets were too overconfident in their detailed predictions, not because they forecast strange and trying times for New England. The disasters of the war, coming as they did on the heels of the earthquake of 1755, imparted a sense of crisis to discussions of the prophecies; a note of urgency that was as much present in the sermons of respectable ministers as in the peregrinations of obscure cranks.

"Some great event is nigh at hand," warned Jonathan Parsons in 1756. The recent "great earthquakes," the "fearful sights, and great signs that have been in the heavens," as well as the current "distress of nations," were all undoubtedly

40. Richard Clarke, *The Prophetic Numbers of Daniel and John Calculated* (Boston, 1759), pp. 8, 20.

41. *From a Folio Manuscript, in the Archive of a Certain Aged Gormogon . . .* (Boston, 1759). A Gormogon (the term is pseudo-Chinese) was a member of a society imitating the Freemasons and founded early in the eighteenth century. The main thrust of Kileo's rebuttal was that Love and Clarke were too hasty in their predictions, and that events of the last days would not be fulfilled until the 1950s.

warnings of greater calamities. Timothy Harrington echoed Parson's thoughts. "The awful Shakings in the World natural, together with the present Commotions and Convulsions of the World moral, seem to portend . . . some considerable Event near opening upon us," he said.[42] The Scriptures suggested that Babylon would be "posses'd of Power and Grandeur, immediately preceding her destruction"; and in light of the circumstances, Harrington felt obliged to raise the distressing question of "whether [the whore] shall not repossess the Grandeur, which she had before the Reformation, and add *America* too? And whether the present Aspects of divine Providence are not introductory to such a dreadful Scene?" John Mellen confronted the men of Lancaster with the same possibility as they gathered for a general muster and inspection of arms. How high Babylon might rise, or "how she may yet surfeit in the blood of the saints" was not easy to tell. New England might well find herself without the true Gospel. "Our land may be given to the beast," he concluded; "the inhabitants to the sword, the righteous to the fire of martyrdom, our wives to ravishment, and our sons and our daughters to death & torture!"[43]

The manner in which the war sharpened and focused the eschatological perspective can be seen especially well in a comparison of two disquisitions on the prophecies, one by John Gill and the other by Aaron Burr. Gill was an English Baptist who had delivered a series of three sermons during the early 1750s based on a text out of Isaiah 21: "Watchman, What of the Night?" The sermons were published in the colo-

42. Jonathan Parsons, *Good News from a Far Country* (Portsmouth, N.H., 1756), p. 168; Timothy Harrington, *Prevailing Wickedness, and Distressing Judgments* (Boston, 1756), p. 26. For similar sentiments, see Gilbert Tennent, *The Good Man's Character and Reward Represented . . . Together with Reflections on the Presages of Approaching Calamities* (Philadelphia, 1756), pp. 23, 39.

43. Harrington, *Prevailing Wickedness*, p. 27; John Mellen, *The Duty of All to Be Ready for Future Impending Events* (Boston, 1756), pp. 19–20.

nies for the first time in 1756—the same year, as it happened, that President Burr delivered his own thoughts on the identical text.[44]

The setting in Isaiah was a familiar one, with a threatened and anxious people begging the prophetic watchman for an indication of when they might be delivered. The reply they received was the usual combination of darkness and light: "The Watchman said, The Morning Cometh, and also the Night." Gill explained, predictably enough, that the answer illustrated the "constant succession and revolution" of mornings and nights throughout history: the glory of primitive Christianity followed by decline; the success of Constantine followed by Mahomet and antichrist. What remained to be determined was where the church stood in the latest cycle. Gill's reading of the prophecies led him to believe that the world was heading toward the blackest of nights. "Signs of the even-tide" were manifest and would "shortly appear yet more and more." It would not be long, in fact, before the final slaying of the witnesses was accomplished. True, some expositors had suggested the punishment had already been meted out, but Gill thought these interpretations were mistaken. The slaying would have to be complete, and the Protestant religion universally rejected. As long as some "civil or worldly establishments" remained where reformed churches were "established by the laws of the countries,"

44. John Gill, *Three Sermons*, 4th ed. (Boston, 1756); Aaron Burr, *Sermon Preached before the Synod of New-York* (New York, 1756). Burr may not have read the Boston edition before he delivered his own sermon in August, but the similarity of subject matter, as well as some structural parallels, suggest that he may well have had access to one of the earlier English editions. (Compare, e.g., Gill's discussion of antichrist's fall and the woe trumpets, pp. 29–31, with Burr's discussion of the same, pp. 29–30; also the historical summaries, Gill, pp. 20–25, and Burr, pp. 13–18.) Gill's three sermons, preached December 27, 1750, January 1, 1752, and December 27, 1752, were originally published separately but went through many editions, on into the nineteenth century.

there were worse times ahead when the light of the Gospel would be "wholly withdrawn."[45]

In general outline, Burr's sermon followed Gill's exposition. He agreed that "the darkest part of Night yet remains," and that "the *glorious Times* . . . will be preceded with a Season of the sorest Calamity and Distress." Consequently (and despite Jonathan Edwards's publicly expressed hopes to the contrary), the witnesses had not been slain. The point had to be made with circumspection; Edwards, after all, was a good friend and a father-in-law to boot. But Burr's chronological calculations indicated that the 1,260 days of prophesying in sackcloth had not fully elapsed; and more important, the slaying seemed to belong at the end of the beast's reign because only in that way would it fit the accepted pattern of redemption. God's usual method was to "prepare his Church and his People for *extraordinary Favours*, by *extraordinary Trials*, and in the present corrupt State of Things, it seems highly proper that it should be so."[46]

All these points merely echoed the ones made in Gill's sermons. What differentiated the two pieces most strikingly was the sharp edge the specific events of the war gave to Burr's commentary. Gill predicted dark times but confined himself to general disparagement of theological liberals and the growing influence of popery in England. For Burr the situation was different, the danger immediate. Britain was the "last stronghold" against the antichristian powers; if France now managed to subdue her, the rest of the world would be no match for the armies of the beast. And the present state of

45. Gill, *Three Sermons*, pp. 26–29. Gill's exposition also advanced the novel idea of a double millennium, the first being a spiritual reign of Christ and the second thousand years encompassing his literal reign. See pp. 70–73; 33–34.

46. Burr, *A Sermon*, pp. 21–25. Although Burr did not have Edwards's treatise directly at hand when replying to the objections, he later reviewed it, and noted that even the scheme outlined in the *Humble Attempt* called for a "remaining mighty conflict" (p. 26 n.)

"Publick Affairs" certainly wore "a dark Aspect." The disasters in the colonies, of course, were duly enumerated; but European matters seemed equally grim. The Queen of Hungary, England's old ally, had basely joined with the enemy, and Poland was flirting with the same idea. Spain, too, was waiting in the wings ready to declare war when the opportunity afforded. The conclusion was obvious: "have we not Reason to fear, that God will purify his Churches in the Furnace, that they may come forth as *Gold tried and refined*? Can we expect, that so much *Dross* and *Corruption*, as is now found among us, will be purged off any other Way?"[47]

Burr thus joined Mellen, Harrington, and many others in assuming that the signs of the times warranted a gloomy set of prognostics—gloomier, in fact, than almost any which had been offered by New Englanders in the previous half-century. Even Cotton Mather, a man always ready to make the worst of a bad situation, had never seriously considered the possibility that the Reformed church would be run off the face of the earth. He believed the slaying of the witnesses had been accomplished and interpreted any news he received of reformations throughout Europe as "glorious anticipations" of the coming kingdom. In 1756, few students of the Revelation were willing to argue as hopefully as either Mather or Edwards had about the witnesses.

Yet if the forecast was gloomier, the way out of the dilemma remained the same, since the afflictive model of progress thrived on trouble. Ministers consoled their flocks as they always had, by holding out the millennium as a time that would offset present evils and by identifying the present sufferings, however extreme, with the perpetual trials of the church. Thus, Theodorus Frelinghuysen explained to the 1755 Crown Point expedition that, although Christ himself had listed "Wars and Rumors of Wars" as inevitable burdens of the

47. Burr, *A Sermon*, pp. 26-30.

church, the pitched battles were only one part of a greater canvas of miseries:

> While it hath been my Business to see the Visions of the Almighty, I have seen horrible Sights.—I have seen Impiety and Oppression successful; Innocence I have seen oppressed and abused. Those who feared the Lord, and eschewed Evil, I have seen agonizing under Affliction upon Affliction, while at the same time, such as had not the Fear of God before their Eyes, nor his Greatness upon their Hearts, were elevated with Prosperity.—The wicked and ungodly I have seen raised to Wealth and Honour, to Posts and Profits, while the sincere Worshipper of the Deity was as a despised Lamp, as one mocked of his Neighbour, and laughed to scorn. . . . All these things, and worse than these, mine Eyes have seen, mine Ears have heard, and myself have felt. . . .

These miseries would be insupportable were it not for the fact that God worked to bring "Light out of Darkness, and Life out of Death." Appropriately, Frelinghuysen used the illustration of the conflagration to make his point. It was frightening to think that the globe would be swept by fire; "but that it will serve to purify and renew it, makes more than ample Amends."[48] Amos Adams took up the same refrain, noting that Christ said he came not to bring peace but a sword. For that reason, Christians not only shared in calamities common to mankind, they were actually "the peculiar Object of the implacable Malice of the World"—from the first trials of early believers down through the slaying of the witnesses.[49] In such trying times, even a good man was likely to question the reason for all the suffering.

48. Frelinghuysen, *Wars and Rumors of Wars*, pp. 24, 3-4.
49. Amos Adams, *The Expediency and Utility of War* (Boston, 1759), pp. 1, 6.

> When you read and hear of the Calamities God has per-
> mitted upon the World by the Sword; when you think
> how many Thousands, I had almost said Millions, had
> been sacrificed to the Pride of Princes . . . you are ready
> to ask, 'What are the Reasons of God's Judgments; what
> ends, agreeable to divine Wisdom, are answer'd? . . .'[50]

The end above all ends (in this world at least) was the
millennial reign, which formed the basis for the "hopes we
entertain of Deliverance from the State of Woe." Even though
Adams knew the present generation would probably die "long
e'er that Day," and even though men were not able to understand perfectly the steps needed "to bring on that most perfect State of the World," the grand vision alone gave "an enlarged View . . . of the benevolent Designs of the *Father of
Mercies*!" Frelinghuysen also viewed the millennium as "one
great Comfort" in his text, since it promised a time, however
distant, when a peaceful world would not be "molested by
Wars and Rumors of Wars."[51] And Thomas Barnard, although
careful to disassociate himself from the Calvinist view of
God's wisdom in the permission of sin, still constructed a
theodicy which affirmed that corrective afflictions were the
indispensable tools needed to bring about the millennial "consummation of all Things."[52] The judgments of the present

50. Ibid., p. 15.

51. Ibid., pp. 28–30. Frelinghuysen, *Wars and Rumors of Wars*, p. 26. Frelinghuysen would not commit himself definitely, but thought it probable that the
thousand-year reign would not come until around the year 2000. He preferred
Whiston's theory of a comet setting off the final conflagration but, unlike Whiston, moved the fire to the close of the millennium (pp. 27–29).

52. Thomas Barnard, *A Sermon Preached to the Ancient and Honorable Artillery Company* (Boston, 1758), pp. 7, 17; also pp. 11–12. Barnard's sermon is
particularly notable for the care it takes to discuss some of the philosophical arguments more traditionally associated with theodicies. In doing so, Barnard dis-
credited the idea that God's wisdom was beyond the ken of men, or that the
doctrine of Original Sin could explain evil—a solution which cut the Gordian knot
rather "than untying it" (pp. 8–10).

age could be justified for their own sake, simply because they served to chastise the wicked and refine the saints. "But how glorious," he concluded, "if the present State of Things be but one Step in the progressive Scheme of Happiness for which he has designed this World, in its various Ages?" It was this larger vision which Barnard and others kept in mind when the nation found itself "surrounded with all the Horrors of War, and dejected by a Train of past ill-Successes in it."[53]

Thus the millennial theodicy helped prepare New England for the worst; it assured her, as Timothy Harrington said, that even if "God hath absolutely determined that the Besom of Destruction shall pass over [the country]; and that these Provinces shall become the Possession of our Enemies; and an Appendage of Rome; yet our Interest shall be safe." But there was always one other possibility. Perhaps God had not absolutely determined on destruction; perhaps his cup of wrath might be allowed to pass. Even as Burr told his listeners that "it seems as if Things were come to the last Extremity, and that it was time for God to appear," he prayed that last extremity had not come, and that a reformation of morals (as well as a new commander of British troops) might be sufficient to drive the French from the land.[54] And John Mellen allowed that if God willed it, a successful war might open the way for conversion of the heathen and the spread of Christianity throughout the continent. All of which "would be glorious indeed, resembling the state of the church in the latter days."[55] These sentiments perforce remained

53. Ibid., pp. 17, 5–6.

54. Harrington, *Prevailing Wickedness*, p. 31; Burr, *A Sermon*, pp. 38, 41–43. See also William Hobby's cautious hope that Babylon's fall was not very far off. William Hobby, *The Happiness of a People* (Boston, 1758), p. 22.

55. Mellen, *Duty*, pp. 21–22. Mellen stopped short of identifying this period with the millennium, although not because he thought the conflagration intervened. When the last fire came, so would the general resurrection, and the saints

little more than guarded hopes, even into the summer of 1759. But with the capture of Quebec and Montreal, the colonies were confronted with the astonishing possibility that the Harlot might soon be driven out of North America. "The American DUNKIRK and the Western BABYLON are fallen!" proclaimed Mellen.[56]

Jonathan Mayhew chose prophetic texts to celebrate both the reduction of Quebec and the victory at Montreal a year later, since it seemed evident that the late military successes helped forward "the kingdom of Christ, the extension thereof, and its establishment in its power and purity throughout the earth." The prophecies had revealed God's "unalterable purpose, in due time, tho' gradually, to consume and destroy the beast and false prophet," and judging from "some late occurrences in Europe and elsewhere" the destruction of antichrist might well be "at no very great distance from the present."[57] Mayhew was reluctant to see the victories as fulfillment of any specific passage of the Revelation, but the prophecies gave a clear, if general, outline of the remaining events to be accomplished.[58]

First of all, the surrender of France might well be only the beginning of more hopeful developments in Europe. If Spain and Portugal took proper note of the object lesson confronting them, they might soon openly break with Rome. And with knowledge and learning constantly on the increase, many of the common people in popish countries would be discovering how badly they had been treated. That might well lead to

---

would go directly to the "everlasting" heaven. John Mellen, *Fifteen Discourses upon Doctrinal, Connected Subjects* (Boston, 1765), pp. 498–500.

56. John Mellen, *A Sermon Preached at the West Parish in Lancaster* (Boston, 1760), p. 16.

57. Jonathan Mayhew, *Two Discourses Delivered October 9, 1760* (Boston, 1760), p. 9; *Two Discourses Delivered October 25, 1759* (Boston, 1759), pp. 49–50.

58. Mayhew, *Two Discourses, 1760*, p. 63.

revolutions. Secondly, the victory in the New World gave the English access to a multitude of aboriginals who had previously been under the evil influence of Roman priests. With France gone, the Indians would not be able to play off one white country against another, and so would inevitably become more "tractable and submissive," more open to receiving the Protestant truth.[59] The opening of a whole continent made it even possible to conceive of a grand, future American empire "(I do not mean an independent one)" where the people were religious, the Indians converted, and the nation prosperous. That, by Mayhew's reckoning, was still more than a century away, but New Englanders could rejoice that progress was being made toward it.[60]

Other Thanksgiving sermons were equally hopeful about the future. Samuel Langdon recalled England's long career as the Elect Nation (to use William Haller's phrase), constantly protected by "almost miraculous" providences. The latest blessings were merely "a prelude to further favors"and a token of assurance that God would "continue his care of the reformed churches, till all the prophecies of the new testament against the mystical Babylon are accomplished." Of course, the good fortune was not merely intended for Great Britain, but for the whole *"protestant interest."* And the success obtained by Prussia, combined with developments on other fronts, indicated that antichrist's fall "may be much nearer than we imagine."[61] Similarly, Samuel Haven and Nathaniel

59. Ibid., pp. 52–60.

60. Mayhew, *Two Discourses, 1759*, pp. 60–61. It is perhaps ironic, considering the case that has been made by some historians for a progressive New Light post-millennialism, that Mayhew's conception of history here comes closer to typical nineteenth-century models of progress than that of any other New England minister of the period. Similar tendencies, though less marked, are present in the theodicy of Thomas Barnard (another liberal). See Barnard, *A Sermon*, particularly p. 7, and part 2 in general.

61. Samuel Langdon, *Joy and Gratitude to God for . . . the Conquest of Quebec* (Portsmouth, N.H., 1760), pp. 17, 23–25, 42–43.

Appleton rejoiced that God was pouring out his vials of wrath on the beast, and that religion could now spread freely throughout the land.[62]

With such prospects opening up, believers could breathe a sigh of relief. The cup of wrath had indeed been allowed to pass. Thanksgiving sermons talked about judgments, but they were more often the vials being poured on the enemy, less often the trials which the witnesses were to have undergone. But while students of the prophecies understandably dispensed for the moment with the gloom of the previous years, they did not reject the pattern of history of which that gloom was a part. God had delivered his people in this war as he had in the past, by first testing them in the fire of conflict. "Thus we were disappointed and humbled from year to year," explained Samuel Langdon:

> almost everything went against us; the enemy gain'd ground, fortified and secur'd every pass into their own country, grew more and more animated. . . . But when God had thus prov'd and humbled and convinc'd us that *the race is not to the swift* . . . His Providence bro't about a change of measures at Home, the happy effects of which soon reach'd America.[63]

So everyone rejoiced, but not without tempering their joy with a remembrance of the "dark Appearances preceding our late Successes." As Thomas Foxcroft pointed out, even in a Thanksgiving sermon it was essential to "sing both of Mercy and of Judgment."[64] Mercy and judgment, deliverance and

---

62. Samuel Haven, *Joy and Salvation by Christ; His Arm Displayed in the Protestant Cause* (Portsmouth, N.H., 1763), p. 39; Nathaniel Appleton, *A Sermon Preached October 9 . . . Occasioned by the Surrender of Montreal* (Boston, 1760), pp. 5–7, 36.

63. Langdon, *Joy*, pp. 37–38. For similar characterizations of the war as typical of the whole deliverance from the depths of despair pattern, see also Appleton, *A Sermon*, p. 23; Haven, *Joy and Salvation*, pp. 19–31.

64. Thomas Foxcroft, *Grateful Reflexions* (Boston, 1760), p. 34.

affliction, the millennial reign and the slain witnesses: these contrasts were inseparably bound up in the afflictive model of progress. New Englanders would continue to hope that the final years of peace and prosperity were approaching, but until that time came, they would use the prophecies to defend an omnipotent and benevolent God in a world filled with the power and malevolence of the wicked. The millennium may have held out a future where it would be possible to attain the perfection of man; but more important, it did so in a way that provided a present where it would be possible to maintain the perfection of God.

6

Revelation and Revolution

With the "Western BABYLON" fallen and the French "Limb of the MOTHER OF HARLOTS" effectively banished from North America, the colonists felt they had good reason for optimism. Thomas Barnard reminded His Excellency Francis Bernard and the other worthies gathered for the 1763 Massachusetts elections that they had only to "call to Mind" the fears "which possessed us in the Year 1756" to realize how serious the French threat had seemed. But now, said Barnard (with the serene air of an astigmatic prophet), "Now commences the Aera of our quiet Enjoyment of those Liberties."[1] He did not know, of course, that Governor Bernard had that very week written to Charles Townshend and Richard Jackson urging a thorough administrative reform of the colonies; nor could he guess that Townshend, George Grenville, and others would take that task to heart.[2] The upshot of their determination was twenty years of arguing and fighting over what constituted a quiet enjoyment of one's liberties, and Barnard would be dead by the time a second Peace of Paris was concluded. But many other ministers were on hand to suffuse the Revolutionary victory with millennial significance.

The millennial rhetoric of 1783, in fact, is in many ways indistinguishable from that of 1763. When Jonathan Mayhew's

1. Thomas Barnard, *A Sermon Preached before His Excellency Francis Bernard, Esq. . . . May 25, 1763* (Boston, 1763), p. 44.
2. Letter to Townshend, May 18, 1763; to Jackson, May 21, 1763, in the Bernard Papers, Harvard College Library, cited in Edmund S. and Helen M. Morgan, *The Stamp Act Crisis* (New York, 1963), p. 24.

vision of a grand future American empire is separated from
its parenthetical qualification "(I do not mean an independent
one)," his descriptions of a bountiful America and a Europe
where antichrist was on the wane stand comfortably with
David Tappan's later conviction that "this immense northern
continent" would be blessed by "a greater height of perfection and glory than the world has yet seen," and that in
Europe, "every wheel of Providence seems now in motion
to hasten on the downfall of tyranny, of Popish superstition
and bigotry."[3] Barnard's view of flourishing arts and com-
merce as an accompaniment to Christ's future "Dominion
from Sea to Sea" can be supplanted in 1783 by George Duffield's visions of things to come, where the husbandman shall
"enjoy the fruits of his labour; the merchant trade, secure of
his gain; the mechanic indulge his inventive genius . . . [and]
JESUS go forth conquering and to conquer."[4] Other orators
noted that Christ's first coming was at a time when the whole
world was at peace, and hoped—much as Barnard had twenty
years before—that "the present general tranquillity, shall be
introductory to that long-wished for day."[5]

To discover that the Revolutionary War produced the same
millennial hopes and the same prophetic clichés as the French
and Indian conflict is at one and the same time tantalizing
and disquieting. Tantalizing, because it tends to confirm what
an increasing number of scholars have suspected and what
earlier chapters of the present story have suggested: that given
New Englanders' continuing interest in the history of redemp-

3. Jonathan Mayhew, *Two Discourses Delivered October 25, 1759* (Boston,
1759), pp. 49–50; 60–61. David Tappan, *A Discourse Delivered at the Third
Parish in Newbury* (Boston, 1783), pp. 11–12.

4. Barnard, *Sermon Preached*, pp. 42, 44. George Duffield, *A Sermon Preached
in the Third Presbyterian Church in the City of Philadelphia* (Boston, 1784), pp.
17–18.

5. John Lathrop, *A Discourse on the Peace* (Boston, 1784), p. 34. See also Levi
Frisbie, *An Oration, Delivered at Ipswich* (Boston, 1783), p. 18.

tion, they would naturally believe that "the American Revolution is a principal link" in the grand chain of providences "hastening on the accomplishment of the scripture-prophecies relative to the *millennial state*."[6] At the same time, the similarity of responses at twenty years' distance generates a certain amount of unease, considering the magnitude of events which separated the pronouncements. Theories of Lawrence Gipson notwithstanding, the American Revolution was more than a dress rehearsal for the French and Indian War. Britain's threat to the liberties of the colonists raised substantive political and social questions which France's earlier challenge had left undiscussed; and it is in the discussion of these issues that one might hope to trace the impact and influence of millennial aspirations on political ideology. But our initial foray into the territory reveals merely a repetition of the old clichés and the implication that prophetic speculation did not play any significant role in causing or shaping the Revolution—indeed, that religion itself had (in Bernard Bailyn's words) "no singular influence on the Revolutionary movement."[7]

Even without the weight of such an eminent scholar behind it, that opinion would be disheartening to contemplate—especially in a book which has stressed so much the importance of millennial thought. But disheartening only at first glance. A moment's reflection will indicate that our apprehensions are grounded on the old scholarly preference for research that ends with positive rather than negative conclusions. In many instances that preference is valid. If the focus of this inquiry were Revolutionary ideology per se, there would be little value in concluding that millennialism did not influence it. (A good many things, after all, have not influenced Revolutionary ideology.) But our subject is eschatology, and whether

---

6. Tappan, *A Discourse*, p. 13.

7. Bernard Bailyn, "Religion and Revolution: Three Biographical Studies," *Perspectives in American History* 4 (1970): 85–169.

or how it influenced political and social attitudes; more specifically here, whether or how it influenced Revolutionary ideology. We can avoid a negative conclusion by turning the question around and asking whether Revolutionary ideology influenced eschatology. Undeniably, Revolutionary ideology *did* influence eschatology. But the answer to the first question is just as important, even if it yields a negative response. If eschatology did not influence Revolutionary ideology, why didn't it?

That question becomes even more intriguing because, a priori, the connection between millennialism and social or political action seems a logical and easy one to make. New Englanders believed that a time was soon coming when a Christian empire of prosperity would spread throughout the land; when all men would live together in peace. They believed that, although God used natural and sometimes even supernatural providences to accomplish his designs, the actions of men were important instruments for bringing in the kingdom. How natural, then, for millennial ideology to inspire a movement which in effect brought the kingdom a step closer. Yet that did not happen, and Bailyn is right. Millennial thought and religious sermonizing may have "translated" political ideas into moral imperatives; they did not themselves provide the rationale for mounting a revolution.

The purpose of this chapter, then, is twofold. First, it seeks to determine what there was about the millennial logic of New England that made it less suitable for influencing political and social ideology than we might have imagined. Second, it attempts to answer how Revolutionary ideology did alter the contours of the traditional millennial outlook.

CONVERSION AND THE SOCIAL ORDER

The millennial perspective of New Englanders, we have seen, focused not on a utopian model of social perfection but on a history which catalogued events, past and future, leading to the final triumph of Christ's kingdom. Preoccupation was not with the millennium itself (Edwards's *History of Redemption* devoted only four pages out of 220 to the subject) but with the pattern of God's actions within history which shaped the struggle between the Lamb and the beast. And the pattern which both consciously and unconsciously gave the drama its form was that of an individual's conversion. As Edwards explained, "the carrying on the work of redemption, as it respects the elect church in general . . . is very much after the same manner as the carrying of the same work and the same light in a particular soul, from the time of its conversion, till it is perfected and crowned in glory."[8] This inseparable connection between the smaller and larger works of redemption entailed certain millennial assumptions about the political and social order, and Edwards's lucid analysis of conversion provides a good starting point for uncovering them.

What happened, asked Edwards, when a properly convicted sinner experienced regeneration? Simply this: God conferred a new spiritual "principle," or a "divine supernatural spring of life and action," which went to work reorganizing the old, natural man. Adam originally possessed both the natural and supernatural principles, but with the Fall, he forfeited the latter, leaving only the natural principles within.[9] Those natural principles were not themselves inherently evil, but so long as they lacked the guidance of the supernatural, they inevitably led men into sin. At conversion, the "spiritual principle" returned to reorder the soul. Edwards realized that this description of a "spiritual principle" was not particularly exact or "determinate," but he at least knew what he did not wish to signify: a basic change of men's existing mental faculties.

8. *History of Redemption*, in *Works*, 1:315.
9. *Religious Affections*, in Yale *Works*, 2:200.

> So this new spiritual sense is not a new faculty of under-
> standing, but it is a new foundation laid in the nature of
> the soul, for a new kind of exercises of the same faculty of
> understanding. So [also,] that new holy disposition of
> heart that attends this new sense, is not a new faculty of
> will, but a foundation laid in the nature of the soul, for a
> new kind of exercise of the same faculty of will.[10]

Conversion, in other words, was not the creation of new powers of will or understanding, only the reordering of existing
ones.

In this context, Edwards's description focused on the inner
workings of a man's soul; but the same formulas served as a
basis for his social ethics. The heart of the new spiritual principle was the quality of charity, or love. Although the first
step of reordering the soul turned a man's love toward God,
it inevitably led also to a proper attitude toward men, "because of the relation they stand in to [God] as his children or
creatures."[11] Thus Edwards's conception of how social ethics
were to be perfected paralleled his notion of how the soul itself was saved. Just as a newly regenerate man did not possess
any new faculties, so the ideal society would have no need
for new institutions to bring about peace and brotherhood.
In both cases, the inward, spiritual principle was the key force
which set aright the already existing structures. "Christian love,
or charity," explained Edwards, "tends to make all behave
suitably to their condition whatever it may be; if below others,
not to envy them, and if above others, not to be proud or
puffed up with their prosperity."[12]

Thus the structure of the conversion experience encouraged
a rather prosaic view of social reform. Edwards could consider

10. Ibid., 2:201, 206.
11. Edwards, *Charity and Its Fruits* (New York, 1851), p. 8.
12. Ibid., pp. 186–87.

the effects of the spiritual principle on the soul in grand, almost mystical terms, but he was content to leave the external trappings of the social order as they stood, confident that the regenerate spirit would breathe sufficient perfection into them. Nowhere is this more evident than in his exposition of *Charity and Its Fruits*, a series of sermons preached to his congregation over a period of six months in 1738. Each week he took a phrase from St. Paul's discussion of charity in the thirteenth chapter of 1 Corinthians and expounded on the implication of the passage. The result was a traditional set of ethics that ran in accordance with Edwards's principles.

Charity "envyeth not," said Paul; so the regenerate poor would not envy men who possessed more than they. After all, Christ was very far from envying "those that were of worldly wealth and honor, or coveting their condition. He rather chose to continue in his own low estate." And if a rich man were governed by the principle of love and did not "vaunt" himself, "this tends to reconcile others to his high circumstances, and make them satisfied that he should enjoy his high elevation." Charity was humble, and thus helped "to prevent a levelling behavior." A humble man recognized it was "best that there should be gradations in society; that some should be above others, and should be honored and submitted to as such." And charity was meek and long-suffering, so that where the principle of love had not yet reordered existing institutions, a regenerate man would be "willing to suffer much . . . for the sake of peace, rather than do what [he had] the opportunity and perhaps the right to do" to defend himself.[13] In short, charity placed men and the existing social orders in their proper arrangement.

In March of 1739, half a year after he had finished his long exposition of charity, Edwards began another series of sermons that were ultimately published as the *History of Re-*

13. Ibid., pp. 173, 186, 206, 108.

demption. The close chronological relation is appropriate since the History of Redemption was simply the Fruits of Charity writ large. Edwards formulated his vision of the perfect society merely by imagining what the present world would be like if "holiness . . . were inscribed on every thing." Monarchs would still rule the world, but instead of governing wickedly as most had in the past, they would "employ all their power, and glory and riches, for Christ, and the good of his church." Likewise, although powerful merchants would still have "great wealth and influence," they would use it properly. The traditional virtues of "meekness, forgiveness and long-suffering, gentleness" would shine as never before—although Edwards did not make entirely clear how Christians would get a chance to suffer long and forgive profusely in a land where injustice was virtually unknown![14]

Although Edwards's millennial world was a society notably traditional in its social ethics, we cannot conclude that a conversion-oriented millennial outlook naturally encouraged the preservation of the political and social status quo. The Revolution produced enough millennial patriots to scotch that hypothesis. What can be said with more assurance is that the conversionist millennium was simply apolitical in its impact. Since the bringing in of the kingdom was achieved essentially through nonpolitical avenues, any number of different social or political orders would work well in a regenerate world. Edwards himself illustrated this distinction nicely in his private "Notes on the Apocalypse." "There are many passages in Scripture," he wrote, "which do seem to intend, that as well the civil as the ecclesiastical polities of the nations, shall be overthrown, and a theocracy ensue." Taken alone, that statement seems revolutionary and in contrast with the tamer passages in the *History of Redemption.* But Edwards went on

14. *History of Redemption,* in *Works,* 1:491-94.

to explain more precisely what he meant. "Not that civil government shall in any measure be overthrown, or that the world shall be reduced to an anarchical state; but the absolute and despotic power of the kings of the earth shall be taken away, and liberty shall reign throughout the earth." There might well be "different forms of government, very many"; it was just that the men in charge would never rule "contrary to true liberty."[15]

This apolitical bent is evident also in Joseph Bellamy's only election sermon, preached in 1762. Bellamy eschewed the usual Lockean clichés of the period and instead advanced as his basic thesis the contention that "the only way for this Colony to be a Happy Community is to be a righteous People." As with Edwards, love was the key ingredient of righteousness, and also as with Edwards, Bellamy's political vision amounted to imagining "what the consequences would be, should Righteousness . . . descend on crowned Heads, and fill the Courts of Princes, and spread down through every Rank, even down to the meanest Cottager, and to the poorest Beggar."[16] What followed was a series of imaginary scenes (a homiletic device Bellamy often employed) describing the consequences of putting contemporary society through the millennial laundry.

Kings, even "the most haughty Monarchs of the Earth," would at once be "turned into other men, 'be converted and

15. Stein, "Notes," 1:82–83. Stein has established that this entry was written before June 1724 (1:83n.). It is interesting to compare Edwards's use here of the antimonarchical passages of 1 Samuel 8, and their adoption by Tom Paine in *Common Sense*. Edwards assumes that the animus of God is directed against kings who rule unwisely and approves of the authority English rulers possessed in civil matters. Paine attributes God's displeasure to the monarchical institution itself: "*i.e.*, not of any particular King, but the general manner of the Kings of the Earth." *Common Sense* (Boston, 1776), p. 10.

16. Joseph Bellamy, *A Sermon Delivered before the General Assembly* (New London, 1762), pp. 6, 13-14.

become as little Children.'" Where before they had slaughtered thousands of their subjects in aimless wars, now their humility and "self-abhorrence" would be so great that universal peace would reign. "Take your right my Brother," says one of Bellamy's happy rulers, "and let me have mine, and let us live in love and peace, and seek the true happiness of our subjects, and no longer go on sacrificing thousands of precious lives, in quarrels, which honest men might settle with the utmost ease."[17] As with royal families, so with parliaments, nobles, and the rest of the kingdom. Ministers would preach nothing but the holiest sermons; merchants would employ just weights and just measures. (They could well afford to, "while Wealth flows in upon them from every quarter"!) Even the few remaining poor would be happy, since they "are as Humble as they are Poor. They quietly submit to Providence, they are thankful for the little they have . . . and instead of envying their Neighbors, they rejoice in their prosperity."[18] Bellamy feared some listeners might think he was describing a "fictitious state of Things." But the Lord's Prayer did petition God to let his "kingdom come, on earth as it is in heaven"; and the day was drawing nigh when Satan would be "'bound a thousand years.' And then 'the Wolf shall dwell with the Lamb, and the Leopard shall lie down with the Kid.'"[19]

Edwards's grandson, Timothy Dwight, also shared an absorbing interest in the prophecies. Unlike Bellamy (who published nothing after 1770, though he lived twenty years longer), Dwight was a vocal patriot and sometime chaplain in the Revolutionary Army. In 1776, he told the "young gentlemen" of Yale's graduating class that, since the millennium would probably not begin before the year 2000, they would "scarcely live to enjoy the summit of American glory." But he added,

17. Ibid., pp. 15–16.
18. Ibid., pp. 16–20.
19. Ibid., p. 21.

"you now see the foundations of that glory laid."[20] Significantly, the foundations Dwight enumerated were not the ideological credos of the Revolutionary cause, but the benefits which would naturally accrue to the country as men grew in both natural and moral rectitude. Some of Dwight's audience would one day become doctors, he noted. Well then, "Need I remind you that it is a peculiar mark of the millennian period, that human life shall be lengthened, and that the child shall die a hundred years old?" With the science of botany advancing as it was, the medicinal worth of the many flora and fauna would soon be discovered. Other graduates would become lawyers; and as the millennium approached, fewer scoundrels and knaves would disgrace the profession. Similarly, those in legislative and government posts would be duly qualified masters of the law. The natural conclusion Dwight made was that virtuous men constituted the source of the millennial splendor: "With such Citizens, with such a Clergy, with such a Laity, as above described, in prospect, we can scarce forbear to address the enraptured hymn of Isaiah to our country, and sing Arise, shine, for thy light is come . . . !"[21]

Dwight played his millennial trumpet throughout the Revolution: a sermon rejoicing over Burgoyne's defeat as part of the prophetic scheme; the republication in 1780 of "America," a poem he had issued anonymously a decade before; and after Cornwallis's surrender, another prophetic sermon. Through them all he championed Edwards's notion that the central experience of grace was the essential means of ushering in the peaceable kingdom, although he also granted "natural" knowledge a useful preparatory role. He believed that the "human affairs" of his day were "constantly progressive towards what may be termed natural perfection. In

20. Timothy Dwight, *A Valedictory Address to the Young Gentlemen . . . July 25, 1776* (New Haven, [1776]), p. 15.
21. Ibid., pp. 19–20, 22.

this progress, they are preparing the way for the commencement of that moral perfection which is the immediate effect
of the Spirit of God." Thus Dwight spoke (in terms reminiscent of Bellamy's vision) of a day when kings might "esteem
it more desireable to tread the pleasing, beneficial walks of
science and justice, than to sacrifice thousands of lives, and
millions of treasure" for ridiculous causes. Although Dwight
also gave passing mention to the "rational ideas of civil polity"
developed by Montesquieu and Beccaria, he concentrated
more on the virtuous improvements to be had through a
"milder administration" of government and a "universal civil-
ity of deportment."[22]

Both Dwight and Bellamy reflected the major premises of a
theology inspired by the Awakening and rationalized by
Edwards. Theological liberals, of course, developed their
divinity from a different perspective. They were less inclined
to stress the process of conversion or its detailed formulations
of a reorganizing spiritual principle; consequently, their
ethics and, by implication, their own visions of a millennial
state, were not tied so closely to the conversion model. Yet
the end result of Old and New Light millennial visions was
the same. Even Charles Chauncy acknowledged that a "work
of God" most properly referred to the grace given a man,
"sometimes, called the *New-Creation*; sometimes the *New-
Birth*; sometimes the *Spirit's Renovation*; sometimes *Conversion*." And Old Lights demanded as much as Edwards that
moral virtue flow from that experience of renewal. Thus,
even Chauncy's noneschatological interpretation of Isaiah's
prophecy of the lion lying down with the lamb pointed to an
apolitical solution to the problem of conflict in society:

> when Men are effectually wrought upon by divine Grace,
> the Roughness of their Temper shall be smoothed, their

22. Dwight, *Sermon Preached at Northampton . . . Occasioned by the Capture
of the British Army* (Hartford, 1781), pp. 31–32.

Passions restrained and brought into Order, so that they shall live together in Love and Peace. . . . Such persons as were once ravenous in their Dispositions, should undergo a *Transformation,* as if a Wolf should change his Nature, and of *Savage* become Gentle so as to feed with Lambs. . . .[23]

Similarly, when Ebenezer Gay explained the prophecy in the Revelation concerning the "woman in the wilderness," he stressed the "future encrease" of the church when converts would exemplify the "beauties of holiness, purity of doctrine and worship,—of heart and manners; a well regulated temper and a well ordered conversation."[24]

Thomas Barnard's vision of a millennium, though of a markedly liberal bent, was still based on the assumption that Jesus provided "such a System of practical Religion," that "if lived up to, would establish universal Peace on Earth and Goodwill among Men." Barnard replaced the New Light emphasis on conversion with the persuasiveness of a good example, but in both cases the development of personal rectitude promoted a "public Spirit, Union in Councils, due Subordination and its Duties, Temperance, Prudence, Courage," which in turn led to peace within a nation. When other countries saw that Britain's supremacy in world affairs was based on the virtue of her people, then the peace of one nation would spread to all.[25] Barnard enthusiastically endorsed Bishop Joseph Butler's vision, "not so vast or remote," of a state where "there would be no such Thing as Faction,"

23. Charles Chauncy, *Seasonable Thoughts on the State of Religion in New England* (Boston, 1743), pp. 4–5, 17.

24. Ebenezer Gay, *St. John's Vision of the Woman Cloathed with the Sun . . . Explained and Improved* (Boston, 1766), pp. 19, 22–23. Gay indicates in his footnotes an acquaintance with the works of Drue Cressener, William Whiston, and Moses Lowman. For his own development of the importance of charity, see *A Beloved Disciple of Jesus Christ Characterized* (Boston, 1766), pp. 17–19. Both sermons were preached shortly after Jonathan Mayhew's death.

25. Thomas Barnard, *A Sermon Preached to the Ancient and Honorable Artillery Company*, p. 19, 21.

where "Public Determinations" would result from the "united Wisdom of the Community," each person contributing his own particular skills, and each enjoying the "Fruits of his own Virtue." The good Bishop's conception of how the millennium would be inaugurated was more rational and genteel than a New England Awakening, but the pattern of spreading virtue was the same:

> Add the general influence, which such a kingdom would have over the Face of the Earth, by Way of Example particularly, and the Reverence which would be paid it. It would plainly be superior to all others, and the World must gradually come under its Empire. . . .[26]

From the perspective afforded us by yet two more centuries of war, murder, and strife, these millennial aspirations seem a good deal like watered and wishful thinking. But Edwards, Bellamy, Barnard, and Butler were perceptive enough, granted their aspirations. Anyone planning on a millennium where men actually live at peace with one another had better find some way to remake human nature. Millennialists rightly saw individual regeneration as a crucial element in their plans. But what was useful, even essential, in creating a worldly paradise, was not so useful in developing an ideology of revolution in America. This chapter is not the place to detail the formation of that ideology, which has been done well by Bernard Bailyn, Pauline Maier, and others. But a comparison of the millennial and Revolutionary perspectives on a number of key points is sufficient to show how the two modes of thinking differed from each other.

The millennial vision assumed that man's nature could be renewed, and looked for God's grace to change it; Revolutionary ideology assumed that man's nature would remain de-

26. Joseph Butler, Bishop of Durham, *The Analogy of Faith*, quoted in Barnard, *Sermon Preached to the . . . Artillery Company*, pp. 20–21.

praved, and looked for ways to control it. Political order, after all, had been created to cope with man's "fallen and degenerate state." Samuel West's 1776 election sermon elaborated truisms which had been repeated many times before: "Men of unbridled lusts, were they not restrained by the power of the civil magistrate, would spread horror and desolation around them. This makes it absolutely necessary that societies should form themselves into politic bodies."[27] Yet while the creation of the state made order possible, it inevitably placed some men in positions of power, and thus gave depravity another area in which to work. Power converted "a good man in private life to a tyrant in office" and, like spiritous liquors, was "known to be intoxicating in its nature."[28] It constantly threatened to deprive subjects of the liberties that were rightfully theirs. As Joseph Warren and other Revolutionary ideologues made clear, men remained free not merely because government existed, but because a certain kind of government preserved "inviolate the constitution on which the public safety depends."[29]

Constitution was a word undergoing considerable change during this period, but undeniably it encompassed a number of institutional checks on the unwarranted power of rulers—checks which the Whigs feared were being swept aside in America. The increased jurisdiction given the Admiralty Courts, beginning with the Sugar and Stamp acts, and the refusal of the Crown to grant colonial judiciaries independence from the executive, were central bones of contention in the Revolutionary dispute. If the Admiralty Courts deprived men of the right to a trial by their peers, and judges remained in

27. Samuel West, *A Sermon Preached before the Honorable Council*, in John Wingate Thornton, *Pulpit of the American Revolution* (Boston, 1876), pp. 273–74.

28. Quoted in Barnard Bailyn, *Ideological Origins of the American Revolution* (Cambridge, Mass., 1967), p. 60.

29. Joseph Warren, *An Oration delivered March 5, 1772* (Boston, 1772), p. 6.

office only at the whim of the executive, power could too
easily encroach upon the people's liberty. As one pamphleteer noted,

> to look for strict impartiality and a pure administration
> of justice, to expect that power should be confined with-
> in its legal limits and right and justice done to the subject
> by men who are dependent, is to ridicule all laws against
> bribery and corruption, and to say that human nature is
> insensible of the love or above the lure of honor, interest
> or promotion.[30]

The millennial ideology approached the issue of the courts
from a different perspective. If the inward spirit of grace
spread throughout society, the courts would not be abused.
Not only would the machinery of justice work well, it would
hardly ever be needed! Thus, when the revivals of the Great
Awakening fostered hopes of the approaching millennium,
Thomas Prince, Jr., printed excited letters from ministers
who reported a dramatic drop in the number of cases brought
before the justices.[31] Similarly, Bellamy imagined in his election sermon a time unspoiled by litigation: "Go into Courts
of Justice, and behold, they are unfrequented! for the People
are become righteous, and live in Love." And as independence
arrived in 1776, Timothy Dwight hoped for the creation of a
millennial judiciary guaranteed by the virtue of those who sat
on it. "That meanness, that infernal knavery, which multiplies
needless litigations . . . you will shun rather than death or in-
famy," he told Yale students.[32]

The issue of standing armies provides another illustration of
the differing perspectives. In effect, the millennial rhetoric
eliminated the problem by assuming there would be no need

---

30. *A Letter To the People of Pennsylvania* (Philadelphia, 1760), p. 7.
31. Thomas Prince, Jr., *The Christian History*, 1:52-53.
32. Bellamy, *Sermon Delivered*, p. 16. Dwight, *Valedictory Address*, pp. 18-19.

for standing armies when regenerate kings put aside their dreams of aggrandizement. "So many paths to peaceful reputation may . . . be presented to the mind," explained Dwight, "that the glory of conquest and bloodshed may cease to delight ambition."[33] The ideology of the Revolution, on the other hand, refused to depend on the good graces (or Grace) of the ruler. "Who are a free people?" asked John Lovell. "Not those who do not suffer actual oppression; but those who have a *constitutional check upon the power to oppress.*" Lovell spoke to commemorate the Boston Massacre, an event which proved the validity of John Trenchard's old warnings about standing armies. Since it was Parliament and not the colonial assemblies who summoned or disbanded the troops, Lovell concluded that Americans had lost their constitutional liberty. "What check have *we* upon a *British* Army?"[34]

A third area which differentiates the two perspectives is the problem patriots faced at the close of the war: disruption and disunity from within. Traditional political theory held that factions and interest groups inevitably split large countries asunder. How would the young republic deal with the problem? Millennial logic assumed that the danger would not prove overwhelming and posited a future American kingdom of Christ united by a common heritage. Ebenezer Baldwin, a pastor from Danbury, Connecticut, noted that nations which were formed by combining several distinct cultures ultimately ended with "arbitrary and despotic Government." But the millennial "Empire forming in British America, having a different Origin, rising from the growth of a single People used to the Enjoyment of both civil and religious Liberty from its infant State," would not be destroyed by the plague of clashing interests. Dwight noted the country's unity

33. Dwight, *Sermon Preached at Northampton*, p. 32.
34. James Lovell, *An Oration Delivered April 2d, 1771* (Boston, 1771), pp. 10–11.

through "the same religion, the same manners, the same interests, the same language and the same essential forms and principles of civil government"—an auspicious combination which the world had not seen "since the building of Babel till the present time."[35]

While such a vision undoubtedly inspired patriots, it contributed little to the thinking which ultimately came to view factions or parties as a necessary part of the political state. When Madison discussed factions in his famous Tenth Federalist, he suggested that they could be dealt with either by removing their causes or by controlling their effects. The millennial impulse was to try the former, allowing grace and its subsequent influence to create a harmonious unity. (Or, to use Madison's words, to eliminate the problem "by giving to every citizen the same opinions, the same passions, and the same interests.") Yet Madison was not as hopeful as Dwight about that possibility. Man's reason remained too easily influenced by self-love; since "the latent causes of faction are thus sown in the nature of man," the only practical solution was to control their effects. And so Madison went on to elaborate his famous theory.

The issues of judicial tenure, standing armies, and quarreling factions all illustrate the marked differences between the millennial and Revolutionary approaches to the social order. Yet the two perspectives were not mutually exclusive. The millennial logic of New England was essentially apolitical in import, so it did not prevent the men who accepted it from also espousing the current Whig ideology. Patriots who did, combined the belief that a strong constitution was needed to check the evils of men corrupted by power, with the conviction that a virtuous body politic was needed if a free constitution were to remain safe. Thus, as Perry Miller has noted, sermons that elaborated the familiar Whig political theory al-

35. Ebenezer Baldwin, *The Duty of Rejoicing Under Calamities and Afflictions* (New York, 1776), pp. 38–40 n. Dwight, *Valedictory Address*, p. 10.

so contained substantial repetitions of the traditional jeremiad themes calling for personal reformation.[36] Insofar as the millennial vision heightened the perception of this need for reformation, it complemented the Revolutionary rhetoric aimed at securing a free constitution.

Nathaniel Niles illustrated this amalgamation of themes in the Massachusetts election sermon of 1774. Civil liberty, he explained, was not simply a matter of people "thinking themselves free," since they might be deluded. Nor was it merely a government which the majority of people approved, since a hundred men could tyrannize as easily as one. "Civil liberty consists, not in any inclinations of the members of the community; but in the being and due administration of such a system of laws, as effectually tends to the greatest felicity of the state." The proper government was of laws, not of men, and it insured that a "royal offender" might be brought to trial, "to procure an impartial sentence against him, and to inflict deserved punishment, as in the case of the meanest subject."[37]

Thus far, Niles saw constitutional safeguards as essential to a free government. At the same time, he argued that a constitution worked perfectly only when duly administered; and even then, it would satisfy only those citizens who already had a disposition for freedom. "Liberty is so illy calculated to give pleasure to either a tyrannical, or, licentious spirit, that it proves a galling curb to both. A free spirit,—a spirit that is consonant to a free constitution . . .—this and this only, can extract and taste all the sweets of liberty." With enough of that spirit of liberty abroad in the land, Niles could imagine a state where faction and strife would be as absent as they were in Edwards's and Bellamy's millenial worlds—and for the same

36. Perry Miller, "From Covenant to Revival," in *Nature's Nation* (Cambridge, Mass., 1967).

37. Nathaniel Niles, *Two Discourses on Liberty* (Newburyport, Mass., 1774), pp. 7–8, 17.

reasons. Individuals would be all of one mind, and thus work together for the same goals. "You and I shall perfectly unite in regard for your interest and for mine. . . . Every individual would choose to move in his proper sphere, and that all others should move in theirs."[38]

We are now in a better position to see why the ideal of a millennial utopia might complement Whig ideology yet fail to influence it significantly. As a vision of virtue triumphant, it could inspire colonists to preserve the probity requisite for a great future empire where everyone moved in his "proper sphere." But when the millennial perspective linked the coming of the thousand years with the regeneration of the human race, it was unable to deal effectively with the principal question of the day: whether British rule was so unregenerate, so corrupt, and so unwilling to remain within its "proper sphere," that revolution was necessary. Thus the developing Revolutionary ideology stressed the need for a government controlled by constitutional guarantees. As for lions lying down with lambs, the political theorists of the period would more likely have agreed with Jack Crabb's comment in *Little Big Man*: "That's O.K., son, so long as you add fresh lambs now and again."[39]

MILLENNIAL HISTORY, R.S.V.

Deteriorating relations between the colonies and the mother country did force millennialists to conclude that rulers re-

---

38. Ibid., pp. 26–27. Although personal regeneration and reformation shaped the contours of millennial logic, note that the converse was not always the case, as Niles's discussion here indicates. He united the emphasis on regeneration and reformation with Whig principles of constitutionalism, but the millennial impulse does not overtly intrude in his rhetoric. Where in Bellamy's election sermon the imagined land of holiness was explicitly the millennium, Niles's sermon spoke instead of heaven, where the "laws of Christ" would be engraved on every man's heart and hence "the same mind will be in them, that is also in Christ. Though there may be numberless ranks and stations in the heavenly world, yet no one will complain that he is not exalted according to his worth." (pp. 28, 48–54).

39. Thomas Berger, *Little Big Man* (New York, 1964), p. 439.

mained unregenerate usurpers, and that overt resistance was finally justified. To put the same proposition in millennial terms: the troubles with Britain were indeed part of the fore-ordained progress toward the millennium, but things were getting better and better only as they got worse and worse. Antichrist was raging as predicted and as he had during every past attempt to establish Christ's kingdom. Believers could comfort themselves with the thought that the present con-flicts were necessary to the accomplishment of good just as past evils had been.

The struggle of the American Revolution, in other words, fit nicely into that afflictive model of progress so much a part of the New England tradition, and colonial ministers used the millennial theodicy in the customary way. Izrahiah Wetmore, for one, spoke of the "sore and distressing events" which seemed to be approaching, and explained to the General Assembly of Connecticut that

> the only Way, that is left for us, to live with Comfort, in the present dark and perplexing State of Things, is to live by Faith upon the Word and Promises of the Gospel; which assure us, that . . . all the Affairs of Providence, are under the direction of a wise and skillful Manager. . . .

The period of deliverance was "doubtless near," but Wetmore noted that, first, the Elect needed to take "their Turn, of the bitter Cup of Affliction and Trial." Just as a sculptor could not work his stone with gentle taps nor the goldsmith refine his product with a lukewarm fire, so God would not achieve his goals painlessly.[40]

Since afflictions continued to mount, Wetmore's sermon was reprinted in 1775 and other voices joined his. Henry Cummings improved the times with a passage from the Psalms, noting that the biblical writer was laboring under troubles,

40. Izrahiah Wetmore, *Sermon Preached before . . . the General Assembly* (New London, Conn., 1773), pp. 5-6, 19.

"almost ready to renounce his hope in God," asking himself, "'Will the Lord cast off forever? And will he be favorable no more?'" Advised Cummings, "Whatever unfavorable conclusions, any persons, in the despondency and dejection of their spirits, may draw from the public troubles we are now involved in, the supreme Governor of all things may have intended them for the opening a way for the exaltation of the American colonies to the highest pitch of glory, opulence and renown."[41] Only a week before, Ebenezer Baldwin had preached to his congregation the same *Duty of Rejoicing Under Calamities and Afflictions*. The war with England was "doubtless the most calamitous Day the British Colonies ever beheld," and there were also "probably many fiery Trials" ahead before ultimate victory was gained; thus "we need all the Cordials Religion can afford, to keep our Spirits from drooping and Despondency." In the same vein, Jonas Clarke assured his parishioners that the prophecies promised triumph to God's people "notwithstanding the violence of their enemies against them, and the distress and sorrow their oppressors may have caused them."[42]

These pronouncements are out of the standard mold, and certainly, if eschatology influenced the coming of the Revolution, it did so as a rhetoric of history rather than as a blueprint for utopia, as a tale which both comforted the afflicted and at the same time goaded them into action against the enemy they perceived as antichrist. Yet even as history, the millennial logic could not function smoothly without undergoing alteration, for the simple reason that the Revolution made it a history that was out of date. In 1760, Samuel Lang-

41. Henry Cummings, *A Sermon, Preached at Billerica, on the 23rd of November, 1775* (Worcester, Mass., [1776]), pp. 6, 9.

42. Baldwin, *Duty of Rejoicing*, preface. Jonas Clarke, *The Fate of Bloodthirsty Oppressors* (Boston, 1776), p. 14. Note also the preface to Thomas Bray, *A Dissertation on the Sixth Vial* (Hartford, 1780), pp. iii–v.

don might well have spoken, as George Duffield later did, of a king "whose generous zeal for the rights of humanity inspired him, beyond the power of any meaner consideration"; of a sovereign designed "for distinguished honor, and raised . . . to the throne, to establish his name, and his glory, as lasting as the annals of time, as the PROTECTOR OF THE RIGHTS OF MANKIND." But Langdon would never have continued, as Duffield did in 1784, "let every American lip pronounce a VIVE LE ROI"! Louis XV of blessed memory, 1760, embodied the "enmity of the Beast and the false prophet," not the RIGHTS OF MANKIND.[43] Consequently, when England replaced France as the villain in the drama, millennial observers were forced into a painful revision of the history of redemption. They did not abandon the afflictive model itself, but they did need to change the cast of characters.

One relatively easy way of adapting to changing times was to fall back on the shop-worn device of "double" or "multiple" fulfillments. Prophecies, expositors noted, were certainly designed to refer to specific incidents; but they could also have a "springing and germinant accomplishment throughout the ages," and thus be fulfilled in a double sense.[44] By employing this broader standard of interpretation, ministers could link current events and biblical prophecies without committing themselves to a specific eschatological interpretation.

Jonas Clarke, for instance, took as his text a prophecy from Joel: "Egypt shall be a desolation, and Edom shall be a desolate wilderness, for the violence against the children of Judah, because they have shed INNOCENT BLOOD ." Since Clarke was memorializing the beginning of hostilities in Lexington the

---

43. Duffield, *Sermon Preached*, pp. 12, 21. Samuel Langdon, *Joy and Gratitude to God for the Long Life of a Good King and the Conquest of Quebec* (Portsmouth, N.H., 1760), p. 33.

44. Samuel Cooper, *A Discourse on the Man of Sin* (Boston, 1774), p. 26, 28.

year before, his listeners were well prepared to understand
parallels about the shedding of innocent blood. Clarke chose
to apply the prophecy only in a general manner, however. It
was "rational to suppose," he said,

> that though prophecies may have a special or immediate
> reference to particular persons, societies, nations or king-
> doms, and to events which they may be immediately
> interested: yet they may be fitly considered as having a
> further and more important interpretation, which may be
> of general use for the direction and edification of God's
> church and people. . . .

Thus he applied the general pattern of afflictive progress to
the battles of the Revolution. God's people never would have
been as successful had it not been for the oppressors who
chastened and roused them to action. The Reformation itself owed its existence to the papacy, whose oppressions had
risen high enough to excite the resentments of Luther and all
of Germany—and from that, "the power of the *beast* and the
false prophet received a shock [from] which it hath never
recovered." In the end, Clarke refused to say how literally his
listeners ought to believe the prophecy "'that *Great Britain*
shall be a desolation, and *England* be a desolate wilderness.'"
But he felt that proper repentance would surely deliver the
colonies from their troubles.[45]

In the same way, Timothy Dwight took another prophecy
from Joel, one where the Lord promised his people he would
"move far off from you the northern army, and will drive
him into a land barren and desolate," and applied it to the
recent defeat of Burgoyne. Like Clarke, he admitted that
Joel's prediction referred to biblical events concerning the
fall of the Assyrian Empire. But since it "almost perfectly
resembled" the circumstances surrounding Burgoyne's defeat,

45. Clarke, *The Fate of Bloodthirsty Oppressors,* pp. 8, 18-19, 30.

he used the story to underline the traditional call for moral regeneration, and ended by hoping that "God will not leave such mighty beginnings unaccomplished."[46]

Millennial history could also be adapted to the changing times of the Revolution simply by divorcing prophetic rhetoric from its interpretational context. Traditionally, expositors attempted to integrate each of the Revelation's vivid symbols and visions into a coherent, synchronous history. But the beasts, dragons, and whores of the prophecies posessed remarkable rhetorical power without the backing of meticulous scholarship, as some popular orators discovered.

One anonymous Son of Liberty put the technique to good use in a speech to his brethren at the Providence Liberty Tree. After decrying the Stamp Act as a plot against colonial freedom, he suggested that his comrades would be "better directed" in their pursuit of the men behind the troubles if they would follow a "guide" to the times "so infallible as that you shall not be mistaken." The Revelation, he noted, predicted that two "monsters in the shape of men" under "a pretense of governing and protecting mankind" would ravage the world. Were not the identities of these two beasts plain? The first one ascended from the sea and had seven heads and ten horns; surely it was common knowledge that "the wicked Earl of Bute, the first contriver of all our miseries" originally rose from a "despicable" island in the sea to the west of Scotland. The seven heads were likely the "capital posts or offices" he held for the crown, and the wound said to be given one of the heads, his disappointment at making so little money as head of the treasury. Yet the beast recovered from his wound, and as the Revelation predicted, all men wondered after him. "Yes, England wondered, Ireland wondered, and you know

46. Timothy Dwight, *A Sermon, Preached at Stamford ... December 18th, 1777* (Hartford, 1778), pp. 4–9, 14, 16.

we wondered," continued the orator, "and still wonder, that he had not been hanged long ago."

As for the second beast, the one with horns like a lamb and speech like a dragon, who else could that be but George Grenville, the man who assumed office meekly but later castigated his faithful North American subjects as rebels? Most striking of all was the Revelation's forecast that this beast would cause all, "both great and small, rich and poor, free and bond, to receive a mark in their right hand, and that no man might buy or sell save he had that mark." (Rev. 13th: 16-17)

> Here, my beloved brethren, he brings forth the Stamp-Act, that mark of slavery, the perfection and sum total of all his wickedness; he ordained that none amongst us shall buy or sell a piece of land, except his mark be put upon the deed, and when it is delivered, the hands of both buyer and seller must infallibly become branded with the odious impression: I beseech you then to beware as good christians and lovers of your country, lest by touching any paper with this impression, you receive the mark of the beast, and become infamous in your country throughout all generations. . . .[47]

Clearly the Sons of Liberty were roused by such stirring words, but it was the rhetoric more than the substance of the Revelation which the anonymous orator found useful. His interpretations were ingenious but hardly serious extrapolations from existing authorities like Moses Lowman or Thomas Newton. And while the speech capitalized on eschatological imagery, it was not concerned with putting current events into any continuum of history, culminating in either Armageddon or the millennium. The piece was effective rhetoric, pure and simple, and thus the speaker did not hesitate to tamper with Scripture, as when he added a "monstrous tail"

47. *A Discourse Addressed to the Sons of Liberty, February 14, 1766* (Providence, R.I., [1766]), pp. 3-6.

to the Beast of Bute, "which he used very flippantly, and which, for decency sake, could not be mentioned in holy writ."[48]

Other political harangues strayed even farther from a prophetic context. *Britannia's Intercession for the Deliverance of John Wilkes*, a popular tract, used biblical rhetoric as a satirical device. It told of a newly discovered "Book of Prophecies" written in London, which predicted that "there shall come a fox from the north, yea, and a lion shall rouze himself from the south, and they shall be at war, and shall not dwell at quiet." Since the authors were making up their text out of whole cloth, they hardly needed to be as clever as the Providence orator in fitting the facts to "scripture." The particular fox the text referred to was "the BOOT FOX," which had "an extraordinary long head, smooth tongue, and remarkable long eyes" (not to mention cloven feet). In contrast, the popular Wilkes was cast as the lion, an animal "unused to flattery and deceit, timidity and cowardice."[49] Along the same lines, the *First Book of the American Chronicles of the Times* treated readers throughout the colonies with Revolutionary rhetoric decked in biblical dress. The traditional patriarchs of Scripture were joined by men like Oliver Cromwell, who received lavish praise:

> thou shook the Holiness's [i.e. the Pope's] chair, made the triple crown of the dragon to totter . . . thou suffered not the haughty king of France to enjoy his boasted vain title . . . the invincible proud Spaniard thou humbled in the dust, and made their Donships, Don Palsey Benabio and Don Diego Surly Phiz, their ministers, as submissive as Spaniels. . . .[50]

48. Ibid., p. 4.

49. *Britannica's Intercession for the Deliverance of John Wilkes* (Boston, 1769), p. 13, 15.

50. *First Book of the American Chronicles of the Times*, 4:12. (Many editions are available, usually not paginated but divided, as are biblical scriptures.) Some

Undoubtedly, then, millennial rhetoric often diffused through Revolutionary ideology without explicitly intruding upon it an eschatological perspective: sometimes in a sustained application like the Providence oration, and other times merely in borrowed phrases, as when one minister urged his flock to separate from Britain's sinful conduct and "Come out of her my people" (Rev. 18:4).[51] When such allusions became a matter of nuance, separated entirely from their prophetic context, direct lines of influence are difficult to trace. Yet undoubtedly the millennial perspective reinforced the Revolutionary outlook in subtle ways. The prophecies heightened the illusion of a grand and conscious conspiracy directed and coordinated by Satan. Was it entirely a coincidence that Ebenezer Baldwin, a parson demonstrably fascinated by the grand battle, wrote what Bernard Bailyn has called "perhaps the most explicit and detailed explanation of the assault upon America by a conspiratorial ministry"?[52] Or that Samuel Sherwood believed it was the beast who incited agents to use "their enchanting art and bewitching policy, to lead aside, the simple and unwary, from the truth, to prepare them for the shackles of slavery"?[53] Many ideological elements contributed to the sense of conspiracy dominant in English and American political culture (not the least of them, the Popish Plot of the late 1670s), and surely the millennial rhetoric reinforced such perceptions.

Although prophecies could be used either as general meta-

of the rhetoric praising Cromwell is double tongue-in-cheek, we soon discover, for it turns out that this Lord Protector is not averse to flattery.

51. Peter Whitney, *The Transgressions of a Land* (Boston, 1774), pp. 39, 64. See also *The Watchman's Alarm to Lord N——h* (Salem, Mass., 1774), passim.

52. Bailyn, *Ideological Origins*, pp. 129–30, 141. See also the "Note on Conspiracy," pp. 144–59, and Bailyn, *Origin of American Politics* (New York, 1967), pp. 33–34.

53. Samuel Sherwood, *The Church's Flight into the Wilderness* (New York, 1776), p. 30.

phor or as simple rhetoric, men who studied eschatology seriously were forced to make a more thoroughgoing revision of the history of redemption. Gradually, the identity of antichrist and the beast shifted away from the traditional archenemy of France and to the corrupt morals and principles of the British government. And with the coming of independence, prophetic scholars provided new interpretations which replaced the British imperium with a Holy American Empire.

Throughout the eighteenth century, New Englanders had accepted the tradition, embodied in John Foxe's *Book of Martyrs*, that the English people were an elect nation and would play a key role in the downfall of the beast. Thus many expositors dated the pouring of the vials from the protests of John Wyclif. The revolt of Henry VIII marked another promising step along the way. Progress had not been uniformly upward, of course; the history of redemption never worked so smoothly. "In one, or perhaps in some part of one or other of the preceding reigns, the face of affairs wore a promising aspect; but soon the horizon was overspread with clouds," noted one minister in 1766. Yet the ever-present assumption was that the "clouds" of Mary Tudor and the Stuart tyrants served only to block temporarily the "daybreak" at the "induction of our glorious deliverers, King William and Queen Mary."[54]

At the end of the French and Indian War, antagonists East Apthorp and Jonathan Mayhew still at least agreed on England's place in the millennial world. Apthorp defended Anglican missions in New England with the hope that all missionaries, Anglican and Congregational alike, might "act in concert" to convert the continent. "How rapturous is the prospect to the true patriot," he exclaimed, "to behold this extensive Country, just won to the British empire, gradually

54. David Rowland, *Divine Providence Illustrated and Improved . . . Occasioned by the Repeal of the Stamp Act* (Providence, R.I., 1766), pp. 8-9.

acceding, among its numerous inhabitants, to the empire of JESUS CHRIST, and of consequence, flourishing in Arts, in Science and in Liberty both civil and religious!" Mayhew's 176-page rejoinder contained a few snide remarks about the Anglican's "rapturous" close, but it, too, ended with the hope that the Gospel would be preached throughout the land, and that the "grand event shall take place . . . even that HIS KING-DOM may come."[55]

As the dispute between Mayhew and Apthorp merged into the larger colonial quarrel, Whig eschatology separated itself from similar Loyalist aspirations by moving toward the conclusion that England resembled a corrupt appendage of the whore. To some degree, Americans had always been aware of the corruption in the mother country—the reprinting of pamphlets like *Britain's Remembrancer* guaranteed that.[56] But the inevitable judgments these sins would provoke were viewed as chastisements meant to reform and purify, as part of the afflictive progress toward the millennial day. By 1776 Jonas Clarke was forced to toy with the possibility that God's judgments against the mother country might actually be meant to leave her a "desolate wilderness." Samuel Cooke, who followed Clarke with another Lexington oration, demonstrated how history had been rewritten. All along, forces of the "great red dragon" in England had attempted to destroy New England's pure settlements. The regressive measures which before

55. East Apthorp, *Considerations on the Institution and Conduct of the Society for the Propagation of the Gospel in Foreign Parts* (Boston, 1763), p. 24. Jonathan Mayhew, *Observations on the Charter and Conduct of the Society for the Propagation of the Gospel in Foreign Parts* (Boston, 1763), pp. 173–74, 176. See also Apthorp's *The Felicity of the Times* (Boston, 1763), p. 19, where his millennial vision of the British Empire as a "refuge and asylum of Truth and Liberty," as well as a bulwark of "Civil Freedom and True Religion," parallels Mayhew's rhetoric at the close of the French and Indian War.

56. [James Burgh], *Britain's Remembrancer* (Philadelphia, 1747) and other editions.

had been the interruptions of a general trend upward now appeared as the governing tendencies of the land: the times of peace "gave our fathers" only "temporary relief." William and Mary became, not the capstones of progress, but only one fortunate and isolated reign, since "Monarchy, though under stipulated limitations, is pregnant with wo.—A crown, with its prerogatives and pomp, will soon darken the wisest head, and corrupt the soundest heart." Thus, even though William's new charter for Massachusetts "brought in the face of it, some appearance of liberty and safety," it also carried within it "the seeds of destruction."[57]

One reason why England's history seemed in need of revising was that the country still remained captive to the influence of the personal emissaries of the Whore. "The agents of Rome, ever restless and scheming, *compass sea and land to make proselytes*," noted Mayhew in one of his last sermons, "going about continually from country to country, *seeking whom they may devour*: and probably, there is no protestant country, in which there are not some of them, at least lurking, if they dare not discover themselves." In England, they were "making great strides," becoming bolder by the day. "Heaven only knows what the end of these things will be; the prospect is alarming!"[58]

The prospect became most alarming when England incorporated the Old Northwest into Quebec and guaranteed Roman Catholic inhabitants the right to their religion. For Samuel Langdon, the Quebec Act seemed to prove what everyone had suspected, "that all the late measures respecting the colonies have originated from popish schemes of men who would gladly restore the race of Stuart." Henry Cummings was even more outspoken. If the "Canada bill" were allowed to suc-

57. Samuel Cooke, *The Violent Destroyed: and Oppressed Delivered* (Boston, 1777), pp. 22–23.
58. Jonathan Mayhew, *Popish Idolatry* (Boston, 1765), pp. 50–51.

ceed, he warned, "the Scarlet Whore would soon get mounted on her Horned Beast in America, and, with the CUP OF ABOMINATIONS in her hand, ride triumphant over the heads of true Protestantism, making multitudes DRUNK WITH THE WINE OF HER FORNICATIONS." As America finally disowned her monarch, Samuel Sherwood published his belief that the frogs coming out of the mouth of the beast were undoubtedly "popish, jesuitical missioners," or their tools ("peeping and croaking in the dark holes and corners of the earth"), who could corrupt through their "free access to the Kings of the earth."[59]

Revolutionary ideology stressed the threat to constitutional principles as much as the corruptions of evil men, and prophetic rhetoric reflected the growing emphasis on the link between civil and religious liberty. "Popery can prevail only under an arbitrary government," said James Dana, in what was a truism of the day. "Should we lose our freedom, this will prepare the way to the introduction of popery."[60] The rising consciousness of this principle led those who studied the prophecies seriously to advance new interpretations of the Revelation's visions of the two beasts rising from the sea and the land.

Samuel Langdon had tried for a number of years to rally enough financial support to print his own analysis of the Revelation, and to that end he published a sermon in 1774 on the nature of the beasts. What he felt had not been stressed enough was the passage that described the first beast as one who received a mortal wound and then recovered to an even greater strength. The warning there seemed clear enough to

59. Samuel Langdon, *Government Corrupted by Vice, and Recovered by Righteousness* (Watertown, Conn., 1775), pp. 27–29. Cummings, *Sermon Preached . . . November, 1775*, p. 12 n. Sherwood, *Church's Flight*, pp. 13, 16.

60. James Dana, *A Sermon, Preached before the General Assembly* (Hartford, 1779), p. 15.

him: the beast represented the secular Roman Empire, and its wound, the successful invasion of the barbarians. What made the monster's recovery particularly strong was the mixing of ecclesiastical tyranny with civil despotism—a combination dangerous above all others. So far, the twin principles of slavery seemed to be prevailing; but Langdon hinted that his own exposition of the seventeenth chapter of the Revelation, if printed, would indicate that "the complete downfall of Popery may be much nearer than many have supposed," and that the present times provided some "remarkable signs of its approach."[61] Much to his disappointment, Langdon did not get his analysis to the press for more than a decade.

Other men reiterated his views, however; among them, the eccentric and energetic Samuel West, pastor at Salem. West exhibited a lively interest in the prophecies. His own calculations, the details of which he circulated in manuscript among clerical friends, deduced 1775 as the year inaugurating the chain of events leading to the millennium. The overthrow of the Turks and Russians was coming soon, and he estimated 1813 as the date when the Pope would finally be reduced to his proper status as Bishop of Rome.[62] In 1776, however, West was more directly concerned with demonstrating that submission to political tyrants was as dangerous as giving in to religious despotism. He argued that although the second beast represented the papal Roman Empire and should be shunned as such, so also should the first beast, which stood for the "tyranny of arbitrary princes." Those who worshiped her did so by paying "an undue and sinful veneration to tyrants" and were thus "properly servants of the devil."[63]

61. Samuel Langdon, *A Rational Explication of St. John's Vision of the Two Beasts* (Portsmouth, N.H., 1774), Advertisement, pp. 11-12, 14.

62. Clifford Shipton, *Sibley's Harvard Graduates*, 13:503. In holding these views, West was more hopeful about the coming millennium than the majority of the clergy, who placed its beginning around 2000.

63. Thornton, *Pulpit of the American Revolution*, pp. 316-18.

Another anonymous author brought the connection even closer to England by focusing on Henry VIII. Traditionally, Henry received honors for striking the first major blow against Rome; but now he was cast as the second beast from the earth, who had separated from the Pope for reasons "of a very terrene, sensual," earthly nature. The two horns of the beast could be "decyphered" to represent the king's dangerous "headship in the church as well as the state." What, concluded the pamphleteer, could be a

> more clear, plain and express fulfillment of this prophecy, than that supremacy in the church, given to our kings . . . by the British ecclesiastical constitution? . . . Nothing but a fond partiality, of applying every thing that is bad, to the Pope, can, I conceive, prevent our embracing this application of the prophecy.[64]

By the time the war was in full swing, many pious patriots had willingly expanded their apocalyptic mudslinging to targets other than the Pope. It only remained for Thomas Bray, veteran of the French and Indian War and chaplain in the Revolutionary Army, to publish a systematic analysis of the prophecies which incorporated the emphasis on civil and ecclesiastical tyranny into the revised history of redemption. Bray's *Dissertation on the Sixth Vial* examined a prophecy whose fulfillment had usually been linked to the fall of the Turkish Empire. When Samuel Sewall at the beginning of the century proposed the unorthodox theory that the sixth vial might refer to events in America, he met with a chorus of objections. Years later, Jonathan Edwards had suggested that the vial (said to be poured out on the Euphrates River) referred to the drying up of the streams of papal revenue.[65]

64. Appendix "by another hand" in Sherwood, *Church's Flight,* pp. 51–53. This might have been Ebenezer Baldwin, who had contributed an appendix to a sermon by Sherwood in 1774, and shared an interest in matters eschatological.

65. Bray, *Dissertation*. He denies Edwards's interpretation, p. 18n.

Now Bray found an audience receptive to an even broader meaning. The Euphrates, he thought, symbolized the over-grown powers of antichrist and the false prophet "in any part of their vast dominions"; and the key characteristic of this power was the combination of civil and ecclesiastical despo-tism. Heathen tyrants were just as guilty as Rome on this count, since "having had originally in their hands, the [cultic] offices of religion, [they] turned the whole into state policy."[66]

If the nature of antichrist's power was to be taken in a general sense, so too ought the power that would vanquish it. Thus, although Bray was willing to grant that the vial referred to the downfall of the Turks, he also argued that the two other antichristian powers, Islam and the papacy, would meet disaster at the same time, just as they had risen together. "So," he concluded, "the breaking of the power of civil and ecclesiastical tyranny in both parts of the great Roman em-pire . . . all come to one grand period which harmonizes with my hypothesis of the import of the sixth vial." The only ques-tion remaining was precisely where this grand blow would begin. Bray noted that the tyranny had spread from east to west, and suggested, with an eye to the Revolution, that Christ would probably "turn upon his pursuers" and chase tyranny back from west to east. Americans were thus justified in leading the attack on antichrist, and the subject of the sixth vial would "animate and support the faithful" in their cause.[67]

66. Ibid., p. 23.
67. Ibid., pp. 59, 75, 102–03. It may be worth noting in passing that the pat-riots' use of the beast imagery is yet another example of the way millennial thought reflected rather than influenced political ideology. As rhetoric, prophetic interpretations underlined the general concern with the connection between civil and religious liberties, but the millennial vision itself allowed a good deal of lee-way on the specific ways in which religion and the state deserved to be separate. East Apthorp could defend the Anglican system as part of a millennial era of "lib-erty both civil and religious"; Timothy Dwight could agree with Bray that the task of the sixth vial was the separation of civil and ecclesiastical powers; and

Prophetic expositors engaged in relocating antichrist in England were perhaps most uneasy about the new role of France, whose inclusion within the empire of righteousness required a good bit of gerrymandering, at least by the lights of previous prophetic calculations. "France has been satiated with the blood of Protestants," admitted Samuel Sherwood, "and 'tis to be hoped, [she] will never thirst after it any more. She has already shewn some tendency towards a reformation and therefore may be judged very likely to effect such a revolution." In any case, he argued, America's association with France could not but help spread the spirit of liberty. David Rowland was similarly defensive. "Doubtless every one that is an enemy of the alliance will make [Catholicism] the ground of their objections, even though they were Catholics themselves, or equally superstitious, and not a whit better." But Rowland argued that England had made alliances with Catholic countries before, and concluded that "Differences in religion have no operation on the political system"—a principle which directly contradicted the eschatological rhetoric linking ecclesiastical and religious tyranny in England![68]

Much easier to accept was the notion of America as the locus of the coming kingdom. As the hostilities with Britain opened, ministers began to express theories which they had not dared to utter before the final rupture. In November of 1775, Ebenezer Baldwin hesitatingly suggested that the colonies were likely to be

the Foundation of a great and mighty Empire; the largest

Isaac Backus could use the prophecies to defend religious liberty. Yet each of them drew different lines between church and state. Apthorp, *Considerations*, p. 24; Dwight, *Sermon Preached at Northampton*, p. 28; Backus, *The Testimony of the Two Witnesses* (Boston, 1786).

68. Sherwood, *Church's Flight*, p. 36. David Rowland, *Historical Remarks, with Moral Reflections* (Providence, 1779), pp. 31–32.

the World ever saw, to be founded on such principles of Liberty and Freedom, both civil and religious, as never before took place in the World; which shall be the principal seat of that glorious Kingdom, which Christ shall erect upon the Earth in the latter Days.

Baldwin noted that he had "thoughts of suppressing this Conjecture" for fear it would "appear whimsical and Enthusiastical"; but once out, his expansive ideas flowed over into a long footnote. As everyone knew, the colonial population was doubling every twenty-five years; that meant a nation of 48 million in 1876. Allowing for growth "but half so fast" in the next century, the empire would in 1976 boast 192 million. "About this time," concluded Baldwin, "the American Empire will probably be in its Glory." Since Moses Lowman had predicted that the millennium would arrive shortly thereafter, what other continent was as likely a candidate? Civil liberty would of necessity be present in such a paradise, and there was "little Reason" to think that liberty would be enjoyed "in any great Extent of Territory save in America." Thus, although the outcome of the war with Britain was still uncertain, Baldwin believed the conflict was "remotely preparing the Way" for the millennium.[69]

The same considerations bore weight with Samuel West, who admitted he could not "help hoping, and even believing, that Providence has designed this continent for to be the asylum of liberty and true religion." God would never suffer liberty to die out entirely, and it was "expiring and gasping for life in the other continent." West supplemented his conjectures of 1776 with more detailed ones the following year at the anniversary celebration of Plymouth's founding. It seemed to him that a text in Isaiah was finally being fulfilled by current events: a prophecy which predicted that the peo-

69. Baldwin, *Duty of Rejoicing*, pp. 38-40 n.

ple of God, after being hated and persecuted by their own brethren, would be driven out of their land and only long afterward delivered. With the founding of Plymouth foremost in everyone's mind, it took little effort to imagine which "brethren" had been driven from their own land, and which descendants were now fighting for deliverance. West noted that "many judicious persons" thought that "some grand events" were about to take place, and he predicted that upon

> establishing our independence, pure religion will revive and flourish among us in a greater degree than ever it has done before: that this Country will become the seat of civil and religious liberty; the place from which Christian light and knowledge shall be dispersed to the rest of the world; so that our Zion shall become the delight and praise of the whole earth, and foreign nations shall suck of the breasts of her consolations, and be satisfied with the abundant light and knowledge of Gospel truth which they shall derive from her.[70]

The Plymouth anniversary was an ideal occasion to revise millennial history, because its image of persecution and flight harked back to the Revelation's prophecy of the woman who fled into the wilderness to escape the Satanic dragon. Prophetic interpretations usually viewed the woman as a general symbol of the true church, and saw her time in the wilderness for 1,260 days as the period of trial preceding the millennium. While relations with Britain remained peaceful, colonists readily adopted that nonspecific explanation, but as Henry Cummings noted when the crisis came to a head, one could "hardly think of being thus pursued from Britain into the deserts of America without recollecting that passage in the Revelations, 'And to the woman were given two wings of a

70. Thorton, *Pulpit of the American Revolution*, p. 311; Samuel West, *An Anniversary Sermon Preached at Plymouth, December 22nd, 1777* (Boston, 1778), 31 ff., pp. 49–50.

great eagle that she might fly into the wilderness into her place, where she is nourished.'"[71] And just as Thomas Bray provided a systematic treatise that reshaped the imagery of the two beasts to the Revolution, so Samuel Sherwood, pastor at Fairfield, Connecticut, methodically overhauled the image of the woman.

Sherwood had felt the need to enlarge the definition of popery, as many other Americans had, and so assumed it had spread "in a greater or less degree, among almost all the nations of the earth"—a point, he remarked, which had not "been suitably noticed and attended to by expositors." The next logical step was to identify America as the wilderness to which the woman had fled to escape this universal diffusion; but previous expositors had associated the wilderness with "bondage, persecution and distress." Sherwood argued that this was a mistake: the wilderness in truth symbolized "a land of liberty, peace and tranquillity." Just as the Jews had been promised Canaan, the land of milk and honey, after fleeing into the desert, so the Christian church would receive its own promised land.[72] We need not be detained by the more intricate arguments meant to reconcile the new interpretation with earlier ones: suffice it to say that by the time Sherwood finished, he had made a case for a millennial America which other patriots found convincing. Samuel West adopted the image of the woman in his Plymouth sermon; Samuel Cooke used it at his Lexington oration; and when Ezra Stiles, president of Yale, preached at the conclusion of the war on *The United States Elevated to Glory and Honor*, he too compared true believers in America with the woman who "should 'flee into the wilderness, where she hath a place prepared of God.'"[73] Like many other Americans, he saw his country leading the way toward the millennial world.

71. Cummings, *Sermon Preached . . . November, 1775*, pp. 11-12.

72. Sherwood, *Church's Flight*, pp. 10, 14, 22-23.

73. West, *Anniversary Sermon*, p. 17; Samuel Cooke, *Violent Destroyed*, p. 22;

As we can now see, the millennial orations of 1783 were not the same as the paeans given at the conclusion of hostilities in 1763. The history of redemption had moved in unexpected directions, and it took the labors of Sherwood, Bray, and others to readjust the interpretational schemes which underlay the eschatological rhetoric. Yet the basic thrust of revised millennial history remained the same. It was a message designed to provide comfort and strengthen commitments in a time of adversity and conflict. "Can we, my brethren," asked Samuel West,

> once entertain a thought of being discouraged, even though our tribulation should become greater and severer than it ever yet has been? Surely to be dismayed when we have such glorious encouragements [from the prophecies], must discover a great degree of ingratitude. . . . Ought we not rather in a firm belief in the word of God . . . reflect upon that happy and glorious state which is to take place when our deliverance is compleated?[74]

The Revelation did not supply the ideology which underlay the Revolution, but it surely viewed the conflict as part of the necessary affliction on the road to the millennium.

That, in fact, was a worry that underlay the triumphant tones of the victory sermons. If affliction and conflict were an integral part of redemptive progress, what would happen when they disappeared from the scene? James Dana wondered even before the war was over. "We may image to ourselves the future glory of these rising states," he mused. "A rapid population—a vast wilderness turned into a fruitful field—a respectable navy—a well disciplined militia—the progress of science." But that was just the problem: peace and plenty gave

---

Ezra Stiles, *The United States Elevated to Glory and Honor* (New Haven, 1783), reprinted in Thorton, *Pulpit of the American Revolution*, p. 472.

74. West, *Anniversary Sermon*, p. 54.

all too much opportunity for degeneracy. "Methinks I see profusion and luxury coming in like a flood—corruption and bribery invading all ranks—public measures carried by influence—houses of worship forsaken."[75] And so on. In the millennial logic, nothing failed quite so much as success.

So it was that David Tappan's victory sermon, which told how "every wheel of Providence" seemed in motion to "hasten on the downfall of tyranny," was followed only two weeks later by another prophetic tract in which he conjured up the old threats: "When we look abroad and see all the world around . . . still overspread with that darkness of Popish, Mahometan and Heathenish ignorance and superstition . . . are we not constrained to pronounce the present time a dark night . . . ?"[76] Tappan's logic and rhetoric echoed (more than coincidentally) the strains of James Dana's earlier plea,[77] reiterating the fears of what men might do (the afflictions and "restraints" of the war having been removed) if they actually *did* achieve a millennial land of peace and plenty.

> What are we to expect, now these restraints are taken off, and our unsubdued lusts permitted to range and riot at large among the tempting sweets of a fertile, peaceful country, and to call into their entertainment the delicacies and luxuries of all foreign climes? . . . Is it fancy, or do I really see luxury and vain magnificence coming in upon us like a flood . . . ?[78]

Some of it indeed was fancy. In the decades to come, the

---

75. Dana, *Sermon Preached before the General Assembly*, p. 31.

76. Tappan, *Discourse Delivered at the Third Parish*, p. 12; and *The Question Answered, Watchman, What of the Night?* (Salem, Mass., 1783), p. 9.

77. More than coincidentally because Tappan plagiarized from Dana's 1779 sermon! Compare Dana's rhetoric (*Sermon Preached*, p. 31) with Tappan's phraseology (*The Question Answered*, pp. 14–15), which copies it verbatim, adding only an adverb or two to dress up the text.

78. Tappan, *Watchman*, pp. 14–15.

"foreign" threats, like the conspiratorial Bavarian Illuminati, would generally prove to be figments of an overheated imagination. Yet if the dangers themselves were illusory, the perceptions of them were frighteningly real. The late 1780s and the 1790s were to prove that self-manufactured apocalyptic afflictions could subvert the millennial dream far more easily than the concrete conflicts of the Revolution.

7

The End—and the Means

Among the many tangled urges which impelled men to return again and again to the prophecies, surely one was the simple pleasure derived from unraveling a great and labyrinthine puzzle. The tantalizing obscurity of numerical predictions, the oblique hints for those who had "wisdom," the allusive interrelationships between the Revelation and the other apocalyptic writings—all these provided challenge sufficient to engage minds as great as those of Mede, Newton, Whiston, and Edwards. What further spurred men to attempt such minute and complete expositions was the sure knowledge that there *was* a complete solution: God had inspired each of these predictions, no matter how obscure or seemingly unrelated, and each had its place in the grand scheme. Hence the admiration of other scholars when Joseph Mede pulled together so many disparate elements in his synchronisms; hence the willingness of Moses Lowman to sift ancient chronicles in order to mesh fulfilled predictions with the minutest events in history; hence the obstinacy of William Whiston in working his calculations to prove that a comet would effect, not only the conflagration, but the deluge and virtually every other major celestial event in the history of the earth.

Men today are less sure about the existence of an all-directing mind behind nature, let alone one behind the prophecies; yet the fascination for chronology, puzzles, and periodization remains with us. Surely Gerald Hawkins enjoys comput-

255

ing the lunar and solar configurations at Stonehenge as much as the people must have who erected them in the first place. Immanuel Velikovsky cites history and mythology as proof of a comet's role in the Flood with a tenacity equal to Whiston's. Historians, too, prefer to divide their accounts into distinct periods, and are willing to tout apparently insignificant events or books as "subtle but profound" watersheds in political or intellectual history.

The present study has succumbed, at least in part, to the pitfalls of periodization by taking the eighteenth century as its area of focus. The attraction of enclosing a study in double zeroes is surely no less specious than beginning the 1,260 years of the witnesses in 756 so they will end at an appropriate time. Hopefully, however, the vestigial habits of chronology have not entirely blunted the worth of this inquiry. While 1700 and 1800 have served as rough guideposts, they have not prevented excursions on the far sides of either border; and while we have proceeded in approximately chronological order, the organization of this book has been primarily thematic.

The investigation initially advanced an assumption and a question. It assumed that many eighteenth-century divines shared an interest in biblical prophecies about the latter days; and it questioned whether this interest affected in any consistent way New Englanders' perceptions of their social situation. The query was meant to be taken seriously, and not merely as a straw man to be knocked handily about as the book progressed. That millennial interpretations might be (like Rorschach inkblots) mere reflections of social concerns rather than determinants of them seemed a definite possibility, especially in light of the common admission that prophecies were naturally obscure and hence needed to be interpreted by events.[1]

1. Readers have a right to be skeptical of any highminded professions regarding

The prophecies, however, did not turn out to be as amorphous as Rorschach blots. They possessed a consistent social function acknowledged by all expositors, and that was to serve as promises that God would ultimately deliver his church, as "cordials" for the times when the faithful were suffering in their war with Satan. "It will be found, on inquiry," noted one man who surveyed expositors of the previous centuries, "that most of the authors from whom the following extracts are selected, wrote either during times of persecution, or in the immediate prospect of them."[2] And in a broad sense, this was true. Sometimes the rhetoric of comfort functioned in concrete and intensely personal ways, as in Cotton Mather's ecstatic reassurances through particular faiths that, despite the opinions of his enemies, he would play an instrumental part in bringing in the kingdom; or as in Gilbert Tennent's words of encouragement (it was "darkest before the dawn") to Peter Thacher, whose barren ministry stood in sharp contrast with the successful revivals all around him. The same rhetoric functioned well to provide corporate reassurance of a similar kind, as when Thomas Foxcroft used Robert Fleming's book to reassure New Lights that oppositions to the true Gospel were always to be expected; or when ministers like Aaron Burr and Ebenezer Baldwin comforted New Englanders in the darker stages of both the French and Indian War and the Revolution. Prophetic rhetoric functioned in a more intellectualized setting when Bellamy and Hopkins used the history of redemption as their centerpiece in the construc-

---

straw men. But one indication that this question was indeed taken seriously is my original inclination to accept the Rorschach explanation as a convincing one. See James W. Davidson, "Searching for the Millennium: Problems for the 1790's and the 1970's," *New England Quarterly* 45, no. 2 (1972):241-61, especially 255, 257-58, where the treatment of the problem conflicts with the answers given in the present study.

2. *Prophetic Conjectures on the French Revolution* (Philadelphia, 1794), pp. 4-5.

tion of a formal theodicy demonstrating God's widom in the permission of sin.

But we can make the terms of the argument even stronger. Not only did the millennial perspective play an important part in explaining existing social realities, it also worked to bend those social realities into line with the situations it predicted. The prophecies warned that agents of the devil and carnal men would oppose the Gospel in all ages, and when New Lights used such unconsciously grating rhetoric to describe those who had reservations about the Awakening, they virtually guaranteed the existence of an aggrieved and vocal opposition. Both the smaller model of conversion and the larger history of redemption worked to create the polarized conditions they anticipated. In another context, the same vision of history united providences of both the moral and physical world under the rubric of God's judgment, and thus insured that disasters such as earthquakes would contribute to the feeling that history was approaching its consummation in accordance with the laws of the afflictive model of progress; surely that was the case when the French and Indian War followed shortly on the heels of the tremors of 1755. And afterward ministers recounted how the North American continent was finally delivered from the hands of the beast only after England had been forced to a position of utmost extremity. In their telling, divines stretched realities to fit the stylized framework of redemptive history.

One realm, that of political affairs, was shaped less by millennial theology than we might have expected. Certainly the traditional rhetoric continued to comfort saints, sanctify their struggles, and spur them to fight through the dark times of the Revolution. In essence, however, a millennial model of history was employed to support *a* cause; it did not, from principles inherent in its own theology, supply the tenets which were peculiarly characteristic of *the* Revolutionary cause. In part, this apolitical bent of the history of redemption can be explained by its close affiliation with the conversion morphology. Dwight, Bellamy, and others saw the promotion of virtue in rulers as more central to the cause than safeguarding the constitution or reordering political structures.

But there is another, broader explanation of why the expectation of an American Revolutionary millennialism has not been completely fulfilled. It lies in the assumptions we are likely to make, or want to make, about eschatology as a motivating force. The bulk of recent scholarship has focused on the millennium itself as an inducement for social action—a utopian vision that would goad believers into transforming their society. In many instances, eschatology has indeed served this purpose—witness Gerrard Winstanley's statement during the English Revolution that the "government that gives liberty to the gentry to have all the earth, and shuts out the poor commons ... is the government of imaginary, self-seeking Antichrist," and that during the millennium, "this enmity of all lands will cease, and none shall dare to seek dominion over others."[3]

We must avoid, however, the temptation to analyze all eschatological rhetoric as millennial rhetoric. The message contained in John's Revelation, after all, was in one sense precisely the opposite of what one might expect to find in a "millennial" tract. Those to whom it was originally addressed were indeed expecting an imminent end to the world they knew and the beginning of a new one ruled by Christ. But the Revelation warned that peace was not coming as soon as they hoped. The bulk of the visions had little to say about the mil-

3. Quoted in Christopher Hill, *Antichrist in Seventeenth-Century England* (London, 1971), p. 117. A comparison of both the quality and quantity of millennial writings produced by the English and American revolutions is instructive.

lennium: only six verses in all of the twenty-two chapters dealt directly with the subject. Most of the book was devoted to a history, centering on the trials and sufferings of the faithful in years to come. Believers had been hoping for a Christ who would deal immediately with the Caesars of the world; instead, John gave them a once and future king. They had been hoping for a millennium that would end their present troubles; John gave them the burden of a once and future history.

The thematic organization of this study, then, has not been built on the utopian and revolutionary dynamics of seventeenth-century English eschatology, nor upon the progressive, even imperial, visions of nineteenth-century millennial missions. It has centered on a psychological stance: a perception of the world shaped by an afflictive model of progress gleaned from the Revelation itself and reinforced by the Puritan morphology of conversion. That stance was certainly nurtured by the social situation which spawned American Puritanism—the faithful had been harried out of England even as the afflictive model predicted. Yet the model persisted long after the persecuted minority had become a ruling establishment. Throughout the eighteenth century, the emotional temperament and the historical viewpoint remained remarkably consistent, and hence the chronological divisions of this book have been used not so much to chart basic shifts as to provide convenient guideposts from which to spin out the implications of a unified perspective.

Yet the question remains: why choose 1800 as the approximate guidepost at which to end the thematic treatment? Apart from the undeniable lure of double zeroes, there are two reasons. In the first place, the nineteenth century witnessed the development of a millennial logic more familiar to most American scholars, one predicated on a division between pre- and postmillennialism. The present author might rightly be accused of being less than charitable if, after having dispensed with these concepts in his own study, he left his readers at the far borders of the eighteenth century without any hint of how they might make their way to the more familiar contours of the nineteenth. The circumstances which brought an alteration in outlook were indeed gradual ones, accomplished over the span of more than half a century; but many of the realignments and shifts of interest can be seen taking place in the 1790s and early 1800s. The discussion of earlier developments has deserved to wait until the conclusion of this study, in order that the perspective of the nineteenth century not obtrude on that of the eighteenth.

The second reason for concluding with the final decade of the eighteenth century is that, in one sense, it does provide an ending to the drama. Not a chronological one, to be sure: Edwards was right in viewing the history of redemption as a series of "connected, successive events" whose conclusion properly came only with the end of history. But in a thematic sense, the 1790s bear witness to some of the ultimate (and darker) ends to which the millennial logic might be taken. While the Revelation comforted Christians by giving them a savior and general to direct the armies of the faithful, it also gave their opponents a general: Satan, the grand dragon and father of lies. In the 1790s, some New Englanders demonstrated what might be the consequence of viewing history in terms of an overarching war between the Lamb and the beast.[4]

PROSPECT

The development of a postmillennial perspective depended not so much on a new system of prophetic interpretation (such as Mede's discovery of the synchronisms or Whitby's

4. Some readers may conclude that by organizing this chapter so as to treat the development of the more sanguine ideas of progress in the section which precedes rather than follows the one dealing with the darker sides of the 1790s, the present author betrays in his own way a predilection for the apocalyptic. They have a point.

theories about the Jewish millennium), as on the synthesis of several long-familiar tenets into a coherent view of history. The idea that Christ would come only after the millennium, for instance, was common enough at the end of the seventeenth century, but it was not used as a linchpin on which to hang a rationalized psychology of motivation. Postmillennialism thus came into its own only when divines consciously argued that Christ's figurative millennial reign demanded human action; that natural catastrophes were inappropriate means of providential accomplishment in such a scenario; and that, consequently, history was to be seen as a series of gradual, progressive steps toward this-worldly perfection.

In some ways, it would be natural to expect that theological liberals would lead the way toward the new postmillennial position. The afflictive model of progress, which viewed chastisement of the faithful as a necessary part of the consummation of history, was more closely allied with New Light theology. Rational religion, on the other hand, played down the role of humiliation in the conversion process, and also leaned the same way in terms of the larger history of redemption. Hence Samuel Moody, Samuel Webster, and other liberals could not understand why Joseph Bellamy thought them blasphemous for believing the world would have been better had Adam not fallen. The necessity of evil as a counterpoint which heightened—indeed made possible—Christ's redemptive act was not a central part of their theological system, nor even of their psychological temperament. Consequently, various liberal pronouncements of the 1750s and 1760s do reveal a move in the direction of a postmillennial logic.

The ambivalence of liberals toward the afflictive model is neatly illustrated in Thomas Barnard's French and Indian War sermon, a theodicy which explicitly separated itself from the doctrines of wisdom in the permission of sin.[5] Barnard

5. Barnard, *Sermon Preached to the ... Artillery Company.* See especially his comments, p. 9.

divided his presentation into two sections, the first of which dealt with the present evil state of the world, "by itself considered." From this limited perspective, Barnard admitted that calamities could be justified because "Afflictions shall soften the Heart and mend the Manners." In that sense, "the present Condition of Men is so proportional, as to be productive of Good and Happiness on the Whole." This was a rather lukewarm endorsement of the afflictive model, but recognition nonetheless.

The second part of the discourse considered the present days "as Part of a Plan, or connected Series of the divine Proceedure, tending gradually to a Perfection worthy of its Author." Here Barnard expanded a much more optimistic vision of progress, where virtue was spread not so much by the conversion process as by the example of a righteous nation. It might be asked, Barnard admitted, why God arranged for gradual progress toward perfection instead of letting man possess it immediately. The reason was that God blessed activity per se as a virtue; and

> Activity is preserved by having Objects in View to pursue, by Hope, by the approach of joyful Scenes, by surmounting Difficulties, by escaping Dangers, by possessing Happiness as the Prize of Labour, by comparing their Situations at different Times, and the consciousness that they have something further to attain.

Hence the millennium would be accomplished by sufficiently motivated men in a set of gradual steps reaching toward perfection.[6]

Near the end of the war, Jonathan Mayhew exhibited a similar optimism. His view of history, like Barnard's, painted progress on the American shores as one of gradual improvement.

6. Ibid., pp. 17, 7, 19.

> Even these days, my brethren, wherein we live . . . are far
> more joyful than any which our fathers saw; tho' far less
> happy than those times which busy fancy, the love of my
> dear country, and charity to unborn posterity, would
> paint out to me, and almost compel me to believe are
> actually to follow.[7]

To the south, William Smith combined such optimism with
an awareness that supernatural judgments might not be
appropriate means for bringing in the kingdom. "Except in
extraordinary cases," he noted, "the supreme Being seems to
conduct all his operations by general laws; and both in the
Natural and Moral world, the advances to Perfection are
gradual and progressive." God might have spoken "once in
thunders and lightnings from Mount Sinai," but in the present
age he had left "the conversion of nations to the ordinary
methods of his providence."[8]

Despite these preliminary advances, liberals by and large
did not figure in the development of a full-fledged postmillennialism. Although the victory of the Revolution elicited
their predictions of a great American empire, more orthodox
divines were the ones responsible for the new rationale. Paradoxically, liberals deserted the prophetic cause for the same
reasons they moved away from the afflictive model in the
first place: their increasing reliance on Reason.

At the beginning of the eighteenth century, study of the
prophecies ranked along with the study of the natural world
as endeavors accorded the highest respect. Isaac Newton
turned easily from the predictions of elliptical orbits to predictions in the book of Daniel; and Whiston followed in the
master's steps with his own comets and calculations. Joseph
Mede applied linguistic and textual analysis in his attempt at

7. Mayhew, *Two Discourses . . . October 25th, 1759*, pp. 60–61.

8. William Smith, *A Discourse Concerning the Conversion of the Heathen* (Philadelphia, 1760), pp. 11, 12.

rigor. The tone of these inquiries, with their postulates, lemmata, and synchronisms, was one of scientific exactitude. By the end of the eighteenth century, the frontiers of science and prophecy were not being directed by the same people. In the area of biblical criticism, prophetic commentaries continued to appear, but the textual methods Mede employed would increasingly be used by the Higher Criticism to undermine older assumptions. And the only major figure left in the lineage of Newton and Whiston was Joseph Priestly, who combined a talent for chemical experiments with a strong interest in the Revelation. Priestly had to defend his belief in revealed Scripture to his more enlightened friends;[9] and it is a measure of how far radicals were willing to question Scripture that during the same year in which Priestly published his *Present State of Europe Compared with Antient Prophecies*, Tom Paine's *Age of Reason* appeared in the United States.

Paine painted with a broad brush, and tarred just about every book in the Bible. He certainly did not miss John's Revelation ("which, bye the bye, is a book of riddles that requires a Revelation to explain it").[10] *The Age of Reason* hit expositors on two particularly soft spots, the first being their proclivity for making into "predictions" those scriptural passages which plainly referred to events contemporary to the original biblical writers. "Scarcely any thing can be more absurd," Paine noted,

> than to suppose, that men situated as Ezekiel and Daniel were, whose country was over-run and in the possession of the enemy, all their friends and relations in captivity abroad, or in slavery at home, or massacred, or in continual danger of it; scarcely any thing, I say, can be more

9. E.g. Joseph Priestly, *Letters to a Philosophical Unbeliever* (Philadelphia, 1795).

10. Thomas Paine, *The Age of Reason* (Worcester, Mass., 1794), p. 22.

absurd than to suppose, that such men should find nothing to do, but that of employing their time and their thoughts about what was to happen to other nations a thousand or two thousand years after they were dead. . . .[11]

Paine also waxed sarcastic about the traditional dictum on prophetic obscurity, observing that if an alleged biblical seer "happened, in shooting with a long bow of a thousand years, to strike within a thousand miles of a mark, the ingenuity of posterity could make it point blank." Thus everything unintelligible in the Bible became "prophetical," and "every thing insignificant was typical. A blunder would have served for a prophecy; and a dishclout for a type."[12]

Americans may have been shocked by this sort of rhetoric, but skepticism over the worth of the prophecies had been increasing in England throughout the century. When Bishop Thomas Newton published his influential *Dissertations on the Prophecies* in 1758, he noted Voltaire's condescending remark "that Sir Isaac Newton wrote his comment upon the Revelation, to console mankind for the great superiority that he had over them in other respects." Worse yet, ministers in the church were suggesting that John's Apocalypse "either finds a man mad, or makes him so."[13] Some ministers, of course, had always been hesitant about applying the prophecies to current events, but the rising number of radical doubters led expositors to frame their discourses as often along the lines of apologetics as of theodicies.

11. Paine, *The Age of Reason (Part the Second)* [Paris, 1795], pp. 78–79. Paine originally wrote *The Age of Reason* while in prison, without a Bible at hand. When he got out and actually read the Bible over again, he was even more convinced of its contradictions and absurdities, and so wrote a second part to his study, published separately.

12. Paine, *The Age of Reason* (1794), pp. 88–89.

13. Thomas Newton, *Dissertations on the Prophecies Which Have Remarkably Been Fulfilled*, 2 vols. (New York, 1794), 2:103.

Although apology and theodicy both address themselves to doubters, their audiences—the doubters—are of two different sorts. Theodicies speak directly to the questions of believers, who wonder why an omnipotent God would allow evil to triumph. Such a question, as C. S. Lewis has pointed out, assumes a belief in God in the first place: evil can be easily enough explained in a world uncontrolled by a deity. Apologies, on the other hand, are directed primarily toward those who do not believe in the first place. Thus, while Thomas Newton's *Dissertations* were written partly as theodicies to comfort believers, they also marshaled evidence to convince skeptics like Voltaire that with so many prophecies having already been fulfilled, disbelief was not rationally possible.

The new, somewhat defensive tone in prophetic expositions can be seen clearly in Richard Hurd's course of lectures published in London in 1776. Hurd's primary interest lay in rebutting the skeptic's traditional complaint that the "prophecies are expressed so ambiguously or obscurely, are so involved in metaphor and darkened by hieroglyphics, that no clear and certain sense can be affixed to them." Thus the lectures treated predictions, not by deciphering their actual meanings but by debating whether they were decipherable at all. In the past, expositors had disposed of this kind of argument briefly in the introduction, but Hurd's two volumes returned to it repeatedly. Ancient languages, he argued, were based not on an alphabet, but on hieroglyphic symbols, which meant they were inherently pictorial. Writers of those days were thus forced to use metaphor to communicate, and it was wrong for infidels to suppose that the Bible contained such language simply because it was conveniently vague.[14]

Hurd's response to the rising tide of skepticism was an ac-

14. Richard Hurd, *An Introduction to the Study of the Prophecies Concerning the Christian Church*, 2 vols., 4th ed. (London, 1776), 1:16; 2:83–86.

tive defense of the prophecies; another, easier way out of the problem was silence. This was the route many liberals took in light of rationalist attacks on the prophecies. In 1773, Samuel Cooper dutifully preached the annual Dudleian lecture (established at the beginning of the century to prove "that the church of *Rome* is that mystical Babylon, that MAN of SIN"), but his examination of the prophecies kept well away from current events. The general predictions of Rome's rise, he felt, were "solid and convincing" arguments of the papacy's malevolence; "yet," he added, "it is only one [proof] , among many; and not so essential to the Protestant cause" that if it should fail, the cause would go with it. The principal arguments to be adduced against popery arose from its "own intrinsic absurdity," from other clearer parts of Scripture, and from the whole "genius and spirit" of the Gospel.[15]

As the century progressed, more and more men found the old detailed applications to current events less a part of the "genius and spirit" of their gospel. Ebenezer Hazard joked with his friend Jeremy Belknap about the foibles the Mathers revealed in their diaries. Hazard granted Increase a certain genius, but added, "I don't wonder he complains his prayers were not heard when, 'Lord, pour out a vial on the House of Austria' formed a part of them."[16] A similar distrust of the prophecies is betrayed in William Bentley's cautions to his friend James Winthrop. Winthrop (the son of the Harvard professor) "had employed his singular abilities upon the Revelation of John" in a way Bentley evidently thought was unsatisfactory. "According to the account I received," he wrote in his diary, Winthrop

has not touched the supposed history of the period included in the life of the writer [i.e. of the Revelation—

15. Cooper, *A Discourse on the Man of Sin* (Boston, 1774), pp. 12, 17.
16. Belknap Papers (Coll. MHS, 5th ser.), 2:155. See also pp. 198-99.

note Bentley does not identify him as John], but about the fourth chapter in a paraphrase, illustrated by General History, Coins, &c., has shewn the History of the Church till the present period. A Presumptive argument of the nature of the work is taken from the particular politics of the Author, which find a place in the Paraphrase, which explains the agreement with present times. I wrote a Letter to Mr. Winthrop, expressing my fears that he had attempted impossibilities.[17]

Thus, by the beginning of the nineteenth century, most theological liberals had set the prophecies firmly on the periphery of their theology, adopting the position expressed by Connecticut pastor Stanley Griswold in a sermon to his congregation in 1800. Biblical predictions might well refer to events that would be truly "important when they come to pass"; but speculation over specifics only belittled that importance. If men were to give credence to all the interpretations of the Revelation ever advanced, they would be forced to conclude that "a more wild, incoherent book never was written." Among the "jargon and nonsense . . . dealt out to admiring congregations" by ministers "speaking from the sacred oracular" were many "whimsical notions" of the millennium; when the absurdity of these and other predictions became evident, it could only drive men to "sad gloom and despondence." Thus Griswold argued that "*We* are not the people" to understand the prophecies concerning the fall of Babylon, the return of the Jews, or the millennium. They

17. *The Diary of William Bentley*, 4 vols. (Salem, Mass., 1905), 1:155. Bentley's dissuasion was unsuccessful. Winthrop published his study under the title of *An Attempt to Translate the Prophetic Part of the Apocalypse of St. John into Familiar Language* (Boston, 1794). Bentley is right that Winthrop's politics show through; see, e.g., his paraphrase of Revelation 4:18 or 21:21. See also, James Winthrop, *A Systematic Arrangement of Several Scripture Prophecies* (Boston, 1795).

might be of "general encouragement," but God would ultimately "choose his own way, his own time and his own
means" to fulfill history.[18] With that sort of outlook, there
was no need to spend time formulating either a pre- or postmillennial scenario—and most liberals did not.

It remained for the more orthodox, who still trusted in the
prophecies, to develop a coherent doctrine of postmillennialism. Yet the strong tradition of an afflictive model of progress
hampered any quick movement toward a new position.
Jonathan Edwards, as we have seen, was one of the first
Americans to argue explicitly that a noncatastrophic interpretation of Christ's coming would provide believers with the
confidence necessary to establish the kingdom, but even so
influential a man as he remained unable to win acceptance of
his theories from his principal colleagues, including Bellamy,
Hopkins, Aaron Burr, and Jonathan Parsons.[19]

Their reluctance may have lain partly in the social climate
of the times: Edwards began his speculations near the height
of the Awakening's optimism but published them only in
1747, when the afflictive model seemed to explain well the
reverses suffered under the attacks of both heretical rational-
ists and French papists. By the 1820s the perspective had
changed considerably. Postmillennialism had become a well-
established, coherent position, and Sereno Dwight could look
back and see Edwards's departure as a significant milestone in
eschatology.[20] In a sense, he was right—so long as we keep
the dominant perspective of the eighteenth century in mind
and remember that, as late as 1793, Samuel Hopkins was still
respectfully dissenting from the master's opinions.

One question that naturally arises is why a coherent postmillennialism developed fully only in the 1790s and early

18. Stanley Griswold, Griswold Manuscript Collection, Houghton Library, Harvard University, Sermon no. 542.

19. See above, chap. 4, n. 73.

20. Edwards, *Works* (Dwight ed.), 1:211 ff.

1800s, when the basic ingredients for the position had existed throughout the century. For the reluctance of the liberals, an explanation has been offered; for the Calvinists, the suggestion that the afflictive model of progress remained strong. Yet that model remained equally attractive during the 1790s; why, then, does the rationale for postmillennialism begin to appear? I can offer several reasons for the shift in thinking, although ultimately these must remain conjectures until better evidence comes to light.

In the first place, expositors writing in the 1790s focused increasingly on the qualities of the millennial reign instead of on the history of redemption as a whole. We have already noted the slight attention Edwards gave the thousand-year reign; the same general neglect held true in other commentaries. (Lowman's *Paraphrase*, for instance, devoted only about three pages in eighty to it.) In 1793, Samuel Hopkins explicitly recognized this lack and thus narrowed his discussion to "the events which, according to scripture, are to take place between the present time, and the introduction of the happy state of the church, which have not been before so particularly considered." In so doing, he encouraged his readers to think out more specifically the contours of the coming ideal world. A similar emphasis marked the expositions of Elhanan Winchester, an English Baptist whose two-volume commentary, published in New England in 1794-95, devoted fully half its survey to the nature of the millennium. Sometimes both Hopkins's and Winchester's imaginations lit on rather whimsical conceits: Hopkins cherished the day when men would rediscover how to move big stones to great heights (just as the Egyptians had done with the pyramids); Winchester suggested that the Great Lakes fisheries had been spared until the thousand-year reign so that men might not have to depend so heavily on animal meat for sustenance.[21]

21. For Hopkins's descriptions, see *A Treatise on the Millennium*, (Boston, 1793), pp. 42–83. Hopkins also explicitly classifies previous expositors according

But farfetched or not, these speculations drew attention to the millennium itself, and that was a necessary precondition for a psychology of motivation which used utopian visions as an impetus to social action.

A second factor that helps to explain the development of a more rationalized postmillennialism was, paradoxically enough, a rise in the number of literal premillennial interpretations of the Second Coming, which forced postmillennialists to examine more closely the reasons for their own position. Elhanan Winchester's long commentary argued that the prophecies refuted "the opinion of those who suppose that *that flourishing state of the Church*, so largely spoken of in the Scriptures, will take place before the coming of Christ; whereas one of his principal designs in coming to earth, is to introduce that state."[22] Bishop Thomas Newton's respected commentaries, which predicted Rome's literal decimation and a day of judgment coterminous with the millennium, achieved wider circulation in the colonies for the first time in the 1790s.[23] So also Joseph Priestly's opinion that the mil-

---

to their views of when Christ will literally descend to earth (pp. 5–8). For Winchester, see *A Course of Lectures, on the Prophecies*, 2 vols. (Norwich, Conn., 1794–95), 2:53. Winchester made good use of America in his future scenario. In noting that John predicted the appearance of many vultures at Armageddon, he remarked that he had lived for some years in South Carolina ("a warm, flat country, much like Egypt"), and that when rivers there flooded and drowned many cattle and swine, "you will see vast numbers of a kind of vultures, called there turkey-buzzards. . . . It is almost incredible what numbers of those birds assemble at such times; and it is surprizing what a quantity of flesh each of them daily devours, 'till they have cleared the land. From whence they come, and whither they go, I could never discover; but as soon as any carcase begins to be offensive, they find it out" (1:258). So also at Armageddon!

22. Winchester, *A Course of Lectures*, 1:196. Winchester's volume indicates a change in view; originally he had been convinced that all men would be saved by a "universal restoration" at the end of time; but the prophecies forced him to concede an eternal hell (1:291–92). For his earlier views, see *Two Lectures on the Prophecies* (Norwich, Conn., 1792), pp. 3–4.

23. Newton, *Dissertations on the Prophecies*, 2:268–70, 239. The work was published originally in London in 1758, and appeared first in the colonies in 1794.

lennium would be more than a "purely spiritual kingdom," and that "as the ascent of Jesus was conspicuous, and probably leisurely, so will be his descent." A host of lesser figures appeared in print with similar views.[24]

The increase of these divergent opinions, which in New England had been in the minority throughout the century,[25] may well have forced postmillennialists to rationalize what were until then much less coherent theologies. Near the end of the seventeenth century, when Henry More wrote his commentary on the Revelation, the differences between the various interpretations had not crystallized around the nature of Christ's second coming; as a result, More could defend Joseph Mede's dramatic scenario from the attacks of men he deemed literalists—even though More himself spiritualized the millennium much more than Mede had.[26] But now premillennialists found the gulf much wider. Winchester, for one, attacked the prevailing tendency toward metaphorical, nonliteral interpretations of future events. After all, he argued, if the expositors applied the same metaphorical method to other parts of the Bible, wonders like the virgin birth would be explained away by claiming that "the virgin is a pure undefiled mind; this

24. Priestly, "The Present State of Europe compared with Antient Prophecies," in *Two Sermons* (Philadelphia, 1794), pp. 30, 52. See also, for premillennial works, Benjamin Gale, *A Brief Essay, or an Attempt to Prove . . . What Period of Prophecy the Church of God is Now Under* (New Haven, [1788]); Charles Crawford, *Observations Upon the Fall of Antichrist and the Concomitant Events* (Philadelphia, 1788); Francis Benjamin, *The Conflagration* (Philadelphia, 1787); John Watkins, *An Essay on the End of the World* (Worcester, Mass., 1795), which revives Whiston's theory of comets; Simon Hough, *An Alarm to the World* (Stockbridge, Mass., 1792) and *The Sign of the Present Time* (Stockbridge, Mass., 1799). See also the numerous works of David Austin, beginning with his conversion to premillennialism in *The Voice of God to the People of the United States* (Elizabethtown, Pa., 1796). For further information on Hough and Austin, see Davidson, "Searching for the Millennium," pp. 245–48, 253–54.

25. In addition to Cotton Mather's comments to this effect (above, chap. 2), see Ezekiel Cheever, *Scripture Prophecies Explained*, pp. 7–8; and the assessment by Joshua Spalding discussed later in this chapter.

26. More, *Apocalypsis Apocalypseos*, pp. 249 ff., 337–38.

conceives and brings forth the living child of truth . . . &c."[27]

Even more to the point, premillennialists attacked what they felt were the pernicious psychological consequences of believing in a metaphorical Second Coming. Joshua Spalding thought people's ideas of the last days before the millennium

> must be very different according to their different ideas of the Millennium itself. They who expect the Millennium will be merely a reformation and melioration of the world will have no greater ideas of the battle [of Armageddon] . . . than of some remarkable revolutionary struggles, between patriots and tyrants, about forms of government; and about civil judgments upon anti-Christians . . . which shall destroy their civil powers, and favour the spread of the Christian religion.

Spalding, on the other hand, expected "the dissolution of the whole frame of this world, political, moral, and natural." He knew that his was an uphill fight, and that the belief in a metaphorical Second Coming had "constantly prevailed: all hands, learned and unlearned, have been employed to propagate it, and for about half a century, it has been the most common belief." The psychological consequences to him seemed obvious: "People have laid aside all expectation, that the day of the Lord is nigh," and thus would be too complacent to seriously reform their lives.[28] Priestly also viewed "the certainty of this great catastrophe" (which he felt was "really *near*") as "a sufficient motive with all Christians . . . to regulate their whole conduct with a view to it."[29]

27. Winchester, *A Course of Lectures*, 1:29.

28. Joshua Spalding, *Sentiments Concerning the Coming of Christ* (Salem, Mass., 1796), pp. 85–86, 46.

29. Priestly, *Two Sermons*, pp. 52–53. See also, Edward King's attack against the idea of "a gradual progressive improvement of human nature, and a regular slow melioration of the state of things on earth produced by that means," quoted in Elias Boudinot, *The Second Advent* (Trenton, N.J., 1815), p. 507.

If the new spate of premillennial tracts forced postmillennialists to rationalize their motives, so did the fast-growing missionary movement. Missions in New England had a long history reaching back to John Eliot; yet it was only in the 1790s that missionary societies began to spread in earnest.[30] The goal of these societies—the conversion of the entire world—was something millennialists had always anticipated (Prince's *Christian History* had printed optimistic reports of natives converted in far-flung lands); but now as the societies began to conceive their own roles in grander terms, premillennialism appeared to many as a theology incompatible with the new evangelical impulse.

Timothy Dwight combined the motivation of missionary and millennial endeavors as well as anyone when he painted the history of redemption for the American Board of Commissioners for Foreign Missions in 1813. During the millennium, he noted, the world would be united in love; and that unity would be accomplished "not by miracles, but by means."

> Should we fasten upon the year 2000, as the period . . . concerning this wonderful event, how evidently is it necessary, that all the measures, by which it is to be accomplished, should be now formed, and immediately begin to operate. . . . Think of the changes, which have been mentioned in this discourse: how numerous; how vast; how wonderful; how evidently indispensable.[31]

Eliphalet Nott, president of Union College, made the same connections. He was not impressed by predictions of conflagration and catastrophe which some expositors offered. Cer-

---

30. J. A. deJong, *As the Waters Cover the Sea* (Kampen, 1970) discusses the connections between millennialism and the Anglo-American missionary impulse, 1640–1810.

31. Dwight, *Sermon Delivered in Boston, September 16, 1813* . . . (Boston, 1813), pp. 7, 20, 25–26.

tainly "the sun is burning out its splendours—subterranean fires are consuming the bowels of the earth," and there is "a constant and solemn advance towards that dreadful catastrophe, of which revelation pre-admonishes the saint." But the world was to sustain a millennium before the fires broke out—perhaps even one lasting 360,000 years. More significantly, Nott emphasized that the "extent and perpetuity" of the kingdom was "to be introduced BY HUMAN EXERTIONS."[32] To men like Nott and Dwight, a postmillennial scenario seemed the one most consonant with the missionary impulse.[33]

All these factors—the attention given the millennial period itself, the resurgence of literal interpretations of Christ's coming, the growing missionary movement—undoubtedly promoted the growth of consciously held pre- and postmillennial eschatologies. In that sense, the millennial logic of the eighteenth century gave way to a new, different logic of the nineteenth. Yet some of the lessons learned from the present study may provide a useful caveat or two for historians working in later periods.

Pre- and postmillennialists both developed rationalized psychologies of motivation which explained, not only how their own chronologies encouraged the right sort of behavior, but also how their opponents' chronologies encouraged the wrong sort of behavior. If historians are rightly wary of accepting anyone's explicitly rationalized theory of motivation

32. Eliphalet Nott, *A Sermon Preached before the General Assembly of the Presbyterian Church* (Philadelphia, 1806), pp. 17–19.

33. For further ties between postmillennialism and the missionary impulse, see the sermons of John Henry Livingston, John McKnight, John M. Mason, and William Linn, all involved with the New York Missionary Society. Livingston, *Two Sermons Delivered Before the New York Missionary Society* (New York, 1799); McKnight, *Life to the Dead* (New York, 1799), and *A View of the Present State of the World* (New York, 1802); Mason, *Hope for the Heathen* (New York, 1797); and Linn, *Discourses on the Signs of the Times* (New York, 1794).

as *sufficient* explanation of his own behavior, they should be doubly wary of theories advanced to explain an opponent's actions.[34] Joshua Spalding, who believed that Christ's literal coming would precede the millennium, refused to accept a metaphorical interpretation because he feared it would lull men into complacence, just as Cotton Mather argued that men would be "all Asleep" if they felt they could postpone the conflagration to the far side of the thousand years. Yet obviously these two premillennial predictions of how post-millenialists ought to think are wide of the mark.

Most historians have perceived this, but they have not always been equally astute in rejecting postmillennial ideas of how premillennialists ought to behave. Cotton Mather was as active as any man in the colonies, with his projects for converting the Indians and the Spanish, or with his letters to August Francke attempting to unite the pietistic movements of two continents. According to postmillennialists' theories, Simon Hough of Stockbridge, Massachusetts, ought to have remained withdrawn and despondent, because he felt the world could be purged of its sin only through Christ's literal coming. But no one within earshot of Simon Hough took him for despondent or withdrawn—not once they heard him preach his ideas of social equality and a nonsalaried ministry![35]

Nineteenth-century premillennialists also fail to fit the stereotypes postmillennialists provided for them. Joseph

34. I emphasize "sufficient" here because I do not wish to enter a debate on the question of how much expressed, rationalized motives serve only to cover deeper, subconscious motives of a different sort. Postmillennialists may have done the things they did for reasons beyond those they enunciated; but it surely contributes to our understanding of them to know the motives they consciously professed. My present point is concerned with the validity of postmillennial classification of premillennial motives, and vice versa.

35. Hough, *An Alarm to the World*, p. 6; *The Sign of the Present Time* (Stockbridge, Mass., 1799), passim.

Clarke, a Saturday-keeping Adventist, wrote in a militantly activist tone when the Civil War broke out:

> I have been very anxious to know duty respecting the war, not so much for fear of the draft, as because I want to see treason receive its just deserts. . . . Consequently, I have written to Bro. White, to know if it would be allowable for us to go into the ranks. . . . Often as I have thought of the baseness of slave treason, and how it hinders the message from moving forward, how it instigates Kansas raids, how it prompts to fugitive slave laws, and Dread [*sic*] Scott dicisions [*sic*], how it separates families, how it does violence to innocence, how it tars and feathers, and hangs, innocent travelers, pedlars, schoolmasters, &c. . . . I have wished sometimes that I had it where Joab and Absalom, and almost fancied that the time might come when a regiment of Sabbath-keepers would strike this rebellion a staggering blow, in the strength of Him who always helped his valiant people when they kept his statutes.

Obviously, premillennial beliefs did not keep Clarke from wanting to go to war against the slave tyranny. Most Adventists' principles did keep them from enlisting (ought we to consider pacifism the most revolutionary method of ushering in a thousand years of peace?) but the majority were nonetheless strongly opposed to slavery.[36] The recent

36. *Review and Herald* 20 (September 23, 1862):132. See also, Ellen White's reproof of an Adventist who did favor the Southern cause, in Ellen G. White, *Testimony for the Church, No. 9* (Battle Creek, Mich., 1863). The complexity of the problem is increased because many Adventists assumed that the world might well end before the North could free the slaves; and some Adventists used this argument to discourage others from exercising their franchise rights. But the church never forbade voting. I am indebted to Ron Graybill, graduate student in history at Johns Hopkins University and research assistant at the General Conference of Seventh-Day Adventists, for directing my attention to these citations in Adventist literature, and for his helpful and stimulating discussion of these points.

excellent work of Ernest Sandeen has also done much to show that nineteenth-century premillennialists participated vigorously in worldwide missionary movements and that, far from withdrawing from American culture, they reflected and championed its values in an attempt to win respect.[37]

A second caveat to be made concerns the relationship of nineteenth-century postmillennialism and the afflictive model of progress. As postmillennial expositors began to perceive their chronology as part of a philosophy which viewed history as "constantly progressive towards what may be termed natural perfection" (to use Dwight's words), the older notion of progress through affliction became less central to the rationalized psychology of motivation. But it still retained much force in terms of actual rhetoric, and understandably so. The Revelation—indeed much of the Old and New Testaments—reflected the theme of salvation through judgment, and no student of the prophecies could escape that influence, no matter how much he might believe that "a grand feature of our times is that *all* is *Progress.*"[38]

Thus even as expositors conceived of the millennial carrot as a prime stimulus for action, the stick of chastisement forestalled any complacence that might be built into a theory of gradual, inevitable progress. Edward Beecher believed the gospel light was inexorably spreading, but he also saw antichristian bishops and priests in every dark corner, burning Bibles and undermining the foundations of free schools wherever they could.[39] Timothy Dwight, too, warned against complacence. Although he felt the day when millennial blessings were "to be ushered in, has arrived," he also warned that, should the concomitant human "efforts cease; should this

37. Ernest Sandeen, *The Roots of Fundamentalism* (Chicago, 1970).

38. *The Independent*, January 16, 1851, quoted in Timothy L. Smith, *Revivalism and Social Reform* (New York, 1957), p. 226.

39. Edward Beecher, *The Papal Conspiracy Exposed* (Boston, 1855). In addition to the text, see the engravings to this effect, complete with pick- and spade-wielding papists in back of the schoolyard!

spirit expire; how many generations of men may pass before the same mighty advantages will return. . . . There is a crisis in all human affairs. If seized, it almost insures success: if lost, everything is lost with it."[40] This heightened sensitivity for eschatological drama—that present events had brought history to a crisis, that the enemy was preparing yet one final grand (but insidious) stroke—persisted in many postmillennial tracts, no matter how apparently incongruent it seems to be with the logic of an optimistic gradualism. A familiarity with the same combination in eighteenth-century rhetoric makes this incongruence easier to comprehend.

THE END

All histories should have an end, but the obvious conclusion to this one is the end of history. Providence has not seen fit to provide that; and the conclusion is obvious, after all, only because history tends to let chronology shape the contours of an interpretation. Since this study has been concerned more with the components of a broadly consistent millennial logic than with a sequential history of eschatological interpretations, it makes good sense to finish with the logical, rather than chronological, ends of the eighteenth-century millennial vision. The first section of this book analyzed the roles played by three potential components of eschatology; and the decade of the 1790s illustrates well some of the logical ends that might be derived from each of these components: chronology (the sequential ordering of latter-day events), conversion (the psychological pattern which gave shape to the larger history of redemption), and judgment (the means by which ordinary and extraordinary providences were combined to accomplish God's plan). The 1790s are by no means the only period in which the ends of these topics become apparent; nor are the ends described the only logical ones to which eschatology

40. Dwight, *Sermon Delivered in Boston*, p. 28.

may be taken. But they are ends relevant to the themes pursued thus far, and so we conclude with them.

When Joseph Mede used the chronology of his synchronisms to order the obscurities of the Revelation, he hoped that he had laid the groundwork for finally unraveling the precise order and meaning of latter-day events. The variety of subsequent interpretations (many appearing with their own precise theorems) guaranteed that chronology would not provide the unified outlook everyone had hoped for. Yet chronologies, if not a single chronology, comprised a large part of prophetic expositions. Men were fascinated by the challenge of divining who the frogs, beasts, or witnesses might be, even if they could not agree on the answers. In this sense, although chronology failed to provide the impetus to any one type of concerted action, it did foster a conviction that current events were extremely important parts of salvation history, if only their prophetic meaning might be understood. The very existence of the prophecies, cloaked in allusive metaphorical language, confirmed and encouraged in readers a feeling of imminence.

The word *imminence* is commonly associated in eschatological discussions with the belief that Christ's literal second coming was momentarily impending, a conviction that the end was temporally close. That is accurate enough, but it is well to remember that the root of the word comes from a verb meaning to project, lean over, or overhang; and in this broader sense imminence points to a psychological perspective which need not be wedded to a belief in the premillennial appearance of Christ. Certainly, for men like Cotton Mather or David Austin, Christ's descent was a central element in their feeling of imminence. But other chronologies, merely by clothing current events in the dramatic language of the Revelation, encouraged the belief that (as Jonathan Parsons put it) "some great event is nigh at hand"; or that (as Dwight put it) a juncture in history had been reached that the faithful dared not ignore, lest the opportunity never appear again. Thus the dictum on prophetic obscurity, which was meant to control speculation by insisting that prophecies could only be interpreted after the event, actually encouraged a feeling of expectation. Men searched every event for clues: is *this* the critical juncture indicated by the slaying of the witnesses?—the final battle of Armageddon?—the sixth vial? It is not surprising, then, to find that the French Revolution is a prime example of an event whose significance was heightened by expositors' intricate chronological calculations.

One of the favorite numbers for manipulation was the standard 1,260 years of trials for the faithful, which Lowman had persuasively argued began in 756. But Charles Crawford, an Englishman, pointed out that in the 1790s, many prophetic interpreters had begun to suppose that, contrary to Lowman, the period approached its expiration date. If that was so, then "the French revolution is the precursor to the total and final extirpation of papal power."[41] William Linn, the president of Queen's College (later Rutgers), arrived at just such a conclusion because the "most extraordinary events" that were taking place forced him to reassess their "connection and consequence." His calculations led him to agree with Harvard's president, Samuel Langdon, that "the fall of Antichrist, and the glorious days in the church which are to succeed, may be expected, at least in part, much sooner" than the "most commonly received" opinions would have it.[42] Elhanan Winchester also realized the value of the French Revolution for chronology. The "late events in France" marked

41. Charles Crawford, *Observations upon the Revolution in France* (Boston, 1793), p. 13.

42. Linn, *The Signs of the Times* (New York, 1794), pp. 7, 152–153 ff. Langdon, *Observations on the Discourses on the Revelation of Jesus to St. John* (Worcester, Mass., 1791), pp. 266 ff.

"the close of the preceding [prophetic] period with great exactness; and in this light the consequence is very great: they shew us whereabouts we are."[43]

The French Revolution spurred chronological calculations for another reason: it seemed to have been predicted not only by the Apocalypse but by many older expositors. On the more sensational level, the prophecies of Christopher Love which had appeared during the late 1750s reappeared in many editions throughout the 1790s, with the world's expiration dates suitably amended.[44] More reputable was the publication of a prophetic tract by Robert Fleming, son of the Scotsman whose eschatology had comforted so many New Lights during the Awakening. *A Discourse on the Rise and Fall of the Papacy* was what the younger Fleming had titled his work when it was issued in 1701, but in 1794 the new edition added an explanatory *wherein the Revolution in France and the abject State of the French King is distinctly pointed out*. The editor of the new edition excitedly noted that the calculations of 1701 had given proof, "tantamount to mathematical precision . . . *that the King of France, about the year 1794, shall be reduced to a state inferior to all the Kings of the earth*."[45] Had that not been fulfilled? Surely no one would deny that having one's head sundered from one's body was about as inferior a state as could be conceived! Other venerable and hoary sources were cited. Pierre Jurieu's prediction of 1687 seemed remarkably close to the facts:

> The tenth part of the city which here fell, will at some future time appear to be the kingdom of France, where a

43. Elhanan Winchester, *The Three Woe Trumpets* (Boston, 1794), p. 38.

44. Christopher Love's prophecies were republished in 1791, 1793, 1794, 1795, 1797, and 1798. For more information, see above, chap. 5.

45. Robert Fleming, *Discourse on the Rise and Fall of the Papacy* (Boston, 1794), introduction; also p. 46. The 1701 edition was published in Edinburgh and apparently never received much notice in the colonies earlier in the century.

revolution will take place about the year 1785, and a separation from the Papacy follow; when the names of monks and nuns, of Carmelites, Augustines, Dominicans, &c. shall perish forever; and all these vain titles, and armorial bearings, which serve for ornamental pride, shall vanish; and brotherly love shall make all men equal.[46]

Others noted that Isaac Newton had supposed, long before events would prove him right, that when the Roman Catholic antichrist waned, infidelity would rise to take its place.[47] In Philadelphia, an avid student of the prophecies gathered together excerpts from the expositions of Thomas Goodwin, Henry More, John Knox, as well as Jurieu, Fleming, and others—all purporting to be accurate predictions of the French Revolution. The first edition was sold "in a few days," and two more quickly followed, one of them in German.[48]

For our purposes, then, the ultimate importance of chronology lay not in the answers it provided but in the process by which the answers were deduced. Expositors, given a pseudo-scientific method by which to fit current events into salvation history, played with numbers in hopes of confirming what they suspected: that a crisis in history was at hand. The more the numbers dropped into their proper slots, the more the feeling grew; events and arithmetic meshed to compound the conviction of imminence.

Nowhere is this more apparent than in James Bicheno's *Signs of the Times*, a popular English tract that went through six American editions. Bicheno, like many others, decided to test his hunch that the French Revolution was one of the most extraordinary events in history. Having fixed on Louis

46. Samuel Stillman, *Thoughts on the French Revolution* (Boston, 1795), pp. 17-18; see also, Linn, *Discourses on the Signs*, pp. 25-26n.

47. Priestley, *Two Sermons*, p. 48; Crawford, *Observations*, p. 13; James Bicheno, *The Signs of the Times* (Providence, R.I., 1794), p. 8.

48. *Prophetic Conjectures on the French Revolution* (Philadelphia, 1794).

XIV as the second beast who rose from the earth (and the "master key to unlock the greater part of the prophecies before us"), Bicheno somehow had to work his calculations so that the witnesses rose properly as he expected, at the French Revolution. But no matter how the three and a half year-days were manipulated, or the 1,260 days shifted, the solution refused to come—until Bicheno struck on the thought that the three and a half year-days each signified "a *month*, or if you please, *lunar days*, reckoning, as the Jews did, thirty days to a month." That was all he needed—and we can watch him set his calculating machine into full gear:

> *Thirty* multiplied by *three*, adding *fifteen* for the half day, makes 105. When this reckoning first occurred to my mind, I had no idea of the events which this number connected; for I did not recollect the year when the Edict of Nantes was revoked. But looking over Quick's Synodicon, I found it to be October 18, 1685, to which if 105 be added, it brings us to 1790; take off a few months (if that should be thought necessary) for the event taking place before the half day is quite expired, and it brings us to 1789, when the witnesses were to be quickened. Whether this may strike others as it struck me, when I first observed the coincidence, I cannot tell; but from this agreement of the number 105. . . . a thousand ideas rushed upon my mind. Is it probable, is it possible, that this can be the quickening of the witnesses? What! the olive trees? the candlesticks? I have always supposed these to be all saints! Is this resurrection, in the vision, the rising to this civil and religious liberty, previous to better days?[49]

Thus did chronology conform events to the larger pattern of

49. Bicheno, *The Signs of the Times*, pp. 30-31, 46-47.

redemption, even if it required a double-jointed contortionist to do the job!

Conversion, we have seen, provided the implicit (and sometimes explicit) shape of that larger pattern; the psychological last on which chronological calculations were shaped. Just as the state of conviction forced a man to wrestle with sin and the devil, so the pattern of history pushed affairs to a climax. "What is our present situation?" asked John McKnight. "A crisis, where proper encouragement will send us up, wrong acts will doom us."[50] It was this perspective—that Satan was readying himself for one fierce, final rage—which led many students of the prophecies to view the events of the 1790s from a particularly distorted perspective. If one granted, as David Tappan did, that "the empires, and nations, and great things of the globe" were "to the grand scheme, which the Deity is carrying on, just what the scaffoldings are to a magnificent building: they are but so many temporary stages employed in erecting the glorious kingdom of God and of Christ on the ruins of Satan's empire of falsehood"—if one granted that, what followed?[51] Christ was the superintending architect of the history of redemption; was not Satan architect of another plan? Each saint consciously united himself with the whole church in its war against the devil; did not all opposers, be they infidel, deist, latitudinarian, or Jesuit, unite in their war against Christ? The conversion-oriented pattern of redemption tended to assume that history's climax would be attended not merely by resistance but concerted resistance.

Thus, in 1798 Joseph Lathrop took for his text Revelation 12:12, to warn the public of the dangers of the times: "Wo to the inhabitants of the earth, and of the sea: for the devil has come down to you, having great wrath, because he knoweth he hath but a short time." Lathrop took his text

50. McKnight, *A View of the Present State of the World*, p. 35.
51. David Tappan, *A Sermon, Delivered to the First Congregation in Cambridge . . . April 11, 1793* (Boston, 1793), p. 11.

quite literally, arguing that tradition among all nations, as well as Scripture itself, assumed that "there are evil spirits acting invisibly on the passions and imaginations of mankind, and thus producing vice and misery among them." Although evil was caused in part by "the native corruption in men's hearts, . . . the tempter, by exciting and inflaming this corruption, increases the mischief." And surely, Lathrop argued, the devil knew his time was short. That was why he was raging so strongly now, just as he had before the church's triumph under Constantine. Revelation 12:12 was clearly being fulfilled by the outbreaks of infidelity, war, and revolution.[52]

In 1799 David Osgood, a preacher notorious for his pro-Federalist sermons, took the same text for his sermon, *The Devil Let Loose*. Osgood agreed with Lathrop that Roman Catholicism had ceased to be the devil's major weapon: the whore of Babylon, in fact, seemed to be acting more like a "reformed prostitute"! But why, asked Osgood, did so many people "affect to rejoice" in the French Revolution's blow to the papacy as the "fall of Antichrist"? There were many antichrists, not just one: the Dragon, the Beasts, the False Prophet, Babylon the Great; and now with "these arts being either exhausted or worn out, or mankind arrived at a state in which they are no longer liable to be hoodwinked by former impositions, the devil seems to have thrown off the mask. He now ceases to hide his cloven foot." Thus France was the scene of crimes and miseries perpetuated "to a degree beyond what any nation" had seen before; and the fires of the "volcano" there were spreading. As the armies of Gog and Magog gathered, Osgood gloomily predicted that the millennial scene would be consummated only after an "immense waste and depopulation of the human race."[53]

52. Joseph Lathrop, *Sermon on the Dangers of the Time* (Springfield, Mass., 1798), pp. 5, 7, 11.

53. David Osgood, *The Devil Let Loose* (Boston, 1799), pp. 8, 10, 11, 13-14.

Of the many New Englanders who looked with horror on Satan's machinations, none excelled Timothy Dwight's ability to transform the conspiracies of the devil into intensely palpable realities. If Jonathan Edwards charted the magisterial course of the History of Redemption, then his grandson created the logical complement in his poem, "The Triumph of Infidelity," which constituted a satanic History of Unredemption. The narrator was none other than the devil himself, who dedicated the poem to Voltaire because he taught "that the chief end of man was, to slander his God, and abuse him forever." The notes to the poem supplied the appropriate prophetic chronology in the annotated marginalia. ("State of Infidelity at the birth of ———," explained Satan, who would not mention Christ's name even in a footnote; "Progress of infidelity after the death of Constantine the Great"; "New progress of infidelity under the papal hierarchy"; and so on.)[54] The annotations indicated that as early as 1788 Dwight had put infidelity in the place of Catholicism as the central antichristian principle. The poem ended with the pernicious doctrines taking root even in America, and the archfiend gloating over his triumphs.

Some of Dwight's vision was merely poetic metaphor; all the same, it was a vision he absorbed and used in his ostensibly rational arguments on behalf of the faith. When he warned Yale students of the dangers of infidel Philosophy (with a capital *P*), he argued that the sophists were self-contradictory. "If Natural Religion be truth, then Scepticism cannot be truth; the Animal System cannot be truth; mere Infidelity cannot be truth; Atheism cannot be truth. The very face of this Philosophy is, therefore, suspicious." Dwight took for granted that all arguments by infidels reduced to one philoso-

54. Dwight, *The Triumph of Infidelity* ("Published in the World," 1788), pp. 6–8.

phy, and that the proponents of each system were secretly and consciously united in the same antichristian cause.[55]

With such a frame of mind prevailing, men like Dwight, Osgood, and Lathrop were ready to believe the wildest assertions from abroad that the French Revolution was nothing less than a concerted effort at world revolution by a cadre of artful, designing agents of the devil. That, in essence, was the news brought to America in 1798 by John Robison's *Proofs of a Conspiracy Against All the Religions and Governments of Europe.*[56] Robison, a Scottish professor of natural philosophy, sought to prove that for fifty years, subversive groups had been circulating heretical and immoral ideas "under the specious pretext of enlightening the world by the torch of philosophy. . . . till, at last, AN ASSOCIATION HAS BEEN FORMED for the express purpose of ROOTING OUT ALL THE RELIGIOUS ESTABLISHMENTS, AND OVERTURNING ALL THE EXISTING GOVERNMENTS OF EUROPE."

The society in question was the Bavarian order of "Illuminati," founded by Adam Weishaupt in 1776. Its actual influence was minor, for it had soon been suppressed by the Bavarian monarch; nevertheless, Robison thought he had proved that "the most active leaders in the French Revolution" were members of it and that "the Association still exists, [and] still works in secret" all over the world.[57] Jedidiah Morse of Charlestown led the way in publicizing

55. Timothy Dwight, *The Nature and Danger of Infidel Philosophy* (New Haven, 1798), pp. 68-69.

56. John Robison, *Proofs of a Conspiracy* (New York, 1798). The controversy over the Bavarian Illuminati has been told fully elsewhere, and there is little need for a detailed account here. See Vernon L. Stauffer, *New England and the Bavarian Illuminati* (New York, 1918). Richard Hofstadter discusses the episode from a viewpoint similar to the present one, although he does not analyze the role that eschatology played in disposing men like Morse and Dwight toward a conspiratorial explanation of events. Hofstadter, *The Paranoid Style in American Politics* (New York, 1970), chap. 1.

57. Robison, *Proofs*, pp. 14-15.

Robison's theories, and he undoubtedly found it plausible
to believe in such societies because that fit into the established
plan of redemption. "By these awful events—the tremendous
shaking among the nations of the earth," Morse explained,
"God is doubtless accomplishing his promises and fulfilling
his prophecies."[58] Dwight received Robison's book too late
to incorporate it in his remarks on the *Nature and Danger of
Infidel Philosophy*, but his famous Fourth of July speech on
the *Duty of Americans at the Present Crisis* was, quite simply,
an eschatological rendering of Robison. Dwight concluded
that recent events fit perfectly the Revelation's prediction of
the frogs coming out of the mouth of the beast to gather
Satan's forces for the final struggle at Armageddon.[59]

Just as the conversion model of redemption viewed the
whole course of history in terms of the battle between the
Lamb and the beast, so on an individual level it imputed consciously evil motives to the enemy. We have seen, in chapter
4, that the conversion psychology encouraged saints to view
opposers like Charles Chauncy as sleepy worldlings dead in
sin rather than conscientious men whose differing views were
nonetheless sincerely held. In 1788 Chauncy the universalist
was back in Dwight's drama as one of Satan's key agents in
America. What better way to subvert the Gospel, mused the
devil, than with "a preacher's wield;/False friends may stab,
when foes must fly the field." Dwight at his most charitable
could only assume that "palsied age" had dimmed Chauncy's
faculties, but he also supposed there was a "love of system"
and "lust of fame" at work.[60] The motives of the English
Deists, of course, were beyond doubt:

Herbert, Hobbes, Shaftesbury, Woolston, Tindal, Chubb,

58. Jedidiah Morse, *A Sermon delivered at the New North Church* (Boston,
1798), p. 25.
59. Timothy Dwight, *The Duty of Americans at the Present Crisis* (New Haven,
1798), pp. 6–7.
60. Dwight, *Triumph of Infidelity*, pp. 23–24.

and Bolingbroke, are all guilty of the vile hypocrisy of professing to love and reverence Christianity, while they are employed in no other design than to destroy it. . . . All hypocrisy is detestable, but I know of none so detestable as that, which is coolly written, with full premeditation, by a man of talents, assuming the character of a moral religious instructor.

As for Weishaupt and his Illuminati, they spread the idea that "adultery, assassination, poisoning and other crimes of the like infernal nature" were "lawful," even "virtuous" actions.[61]

Not everyone in New England swallowed Robison whole. Those who opposed Morse and Dwight criticized them for their inconsistence in condemning Illuminist goals which at other times they professed to support. William Bentley pointed out that Robison censured the Illuminati for thinking that "'by making men good, by enlightening their minds, by finding employment for every talent, and by placing every talent in its proper sphere of action,' they expect *a steady and just morality will be produced that will govern the world*" without recourse to princes and nobility. Bentley wryly noted that it had been "for a long time, a favorite sentiment with some of our eminent Divines, who are among the greatest admirers of Mr. Robison's Proofs, that in the *Millennium* . . . the whole world of mankind will be governed by principles of *General and Pure Benevolence*."[62] Naturally, Robison's supporters ignored such criticism. Infidels might profess high-minded ideals, but the means they used to attain their secular version of a "millennium" seemed clearly those of the devil.

61. Dwight, *Nature and Danger*, pp. 45–46; *Duty of Americans*, p. 12.

62. [William Bentley] *Extracts from Professor Robison's "Proofs . . ."* (Boston, 1799), pp. 22–23. Bentley himself professed such millennial hopes to be "in some measure chimerical."

Condemnation of "means," in fact, took a central place in prophetic rhetoric, perhaps precisely because the devil seemed to be wedding his underhanded methods to a philosophy of high ideals. "To crown such a system of falsehood and horror, all means were declared to be lawful, provided the end was good," noted Dwight. Morse declared that since the Illuminati were "governed by the maxim, borrowed from the Jesuits, 'that the end sanctifies the means,' they are prevented by none of those religious and moral principles . . . from pushing their plans by the vilest means." Theodore Dwight echoed his brother in New Haven: "The creed of this society of demons, is, *'That all means however flatigious, are to be used for the accomplishment of their favorite end.'*"[63] Voltaire and his crew were ostensibly helping to build churches, while in private their attitude toward Christ was "'Crush the wretch!'" Infidels published subversive works and attributed them to respected men who had long been dead, so as to attract the gullible through an aura of respectability. Sophists used ridicule to make their case, Dwight angrily observed. "I don't deny, that ridicule may be properly used in certain cases; but I wholly deny the propriety of using it to decide any serious concern of mankind."[64] When infidels could not sell their propaganda for profit, they tried to dispense it gratis. Sophists hawked *The Age of Reason* "at a very low rate, gave them away where they could not sell them; and slipped them into the pockets of numbers who refused to accept them."[65]

When Robison's book first appeared, Federalists used it as a stick to beat Republicans, and particularly the democratic clubs that had sprung up around the country. Republican

63. Timothy Dwight, *The Duty of Americans*, p. 12; Theodore Dwight, *An Oration Spoken at Hartford* (Hartford, 1798), p. 23; Morse, *Sermon Delivered at New North*, p. 23.

64. Dwight, *Nature and Danger*, p. 61.

65. Ibid.; John M. Mason, *A Voice of Warning, to Christians* (New York, 1800), pp. 35 ff.

polemicists replied in kind, and successfully defused the controversy when letters from a respected German scholar, Christopher Ebeling, denied Robison's accusations. But if Illuminism was dead as a political issue, it continued to reinforce the perceptions of prophetic scholars. Ebeling was "too gross a Socinian" and "too much of an equality man to judge concerning this subject as we do," confided Dwight in a letter to Morse.[66]

Thirteen years later Dwight was still warning the public that Voltaire's deists had "inserted themselves into every place," "swarmed in the palace," "haunted the church"; that "every individual illuminée, and almost, if not quite, every infidel, on the continent of Europe, lent his labours" for the accomplishment of the French Revolution. Few Yale students before or since have heard quite as scathing and vitriolic a polemic as their president delivered in 1812:

> The spirit of infidelity has the heart of a wolf, the fangs of a tyger, and the talons of a vulture. Blood is its proper nourishment: and it scents its prey with the nerves of a hound, and cowers over a field of death on the sooty pinions of a fiend. . . . Enemies to all men, they were of course enemies to each other. Butchers of the human race, they soon whetted the knife for each other's throats. . . . Knell tolled upon knell; hearse followed hearse; and coffin rumbled after coffin; without a mourner to shed a tear upon the corpse, or a solitary attendant to mark the place of the grave.

Since the coming of war in 1792, the final battle of Armageddon had begun, and it continued to rage even in 1812. "We are come upon a day of wrath," concluded Dwight.[67]

---

66. Letter to Jedidiah Morse, December 30, 1799. Morse Family Papers, Sterling Memorial Library, Yale University.

67. Timothy Dwight, *A Discourse in Two Parts*, 2d ed. (Boston, 1813), pp. 10, 13, 27 ff.

Dies Irae, the Day of Wrath: it was the logical as well as chronological end to history. If the morphology of conversion shaped history as a whole, the concept of judgment dominated its end and inevitably cast its shadow backward into contemporary events. Chapter 3 demonstrated that catastrophes—either natural or supernatural—could be understood as part of the millennial logic only when they were viewed as judgments designed either to chastise the wicked or sanctify the elect. In this sense, judgment was both present and future, within as well as at the end of history. Yet the roles of judgment future and judgment present differed in emphasis. The judgment at the end of history was final, condemning or elevating forever; it was a vindication of past wrongs, a time when evil men would finally be destroyed and the martyrs rewarded. Judgment within history was differently oriented. In the present world, saints were the ones judged, and the task was sanctification, not destruction. Gold was being tried in the fire, purified and made ready for a better world. Of course, the difference between judgment future and ment present was relative, not absolute. Some evil men were punished in the present world, and some saints rewarded. But the thrust of the Revelation's rhetoric maintained the primary distinction.

When the study of millennial chronologies fostered a sense of imminence, and the application of a conversion psychology polarized perceptions of the social situation, the temptation grew to bring down judgment future and apply it to the present. In one sense, the concept of the millennium itself illustrates that, because it hastens the process of retribution and vindication, transferring it from an otherworldly heaven and hell to a temporal thousand-year reign. The transference is most easily discerned in the more sensual, literalistic interpretations of chiliasts, but it is equally present in Joseph Mede's scenario, where judgment is coterminous with the thousand years; or even in the gradualistic hopes of nine-teenth-century postmillennialists. The millennium, whether spiritual, literal, or sensual, was by definition a time when judgment future came down to earth, elevating the saints, destroying antichrist.

Hence prophetic interpretations of the French Revolution led men to conclude that Armageddon was begun; that the righteous were finally ready for the battle when the forces of evil would *not* win. When the Bastille was stormed and the Revolution still in its early stages, the "signs of the times" seemed to indicate that the French struggle paralleled its American counterpart. Even as late as 1795, the New England clergy interpreted the Revolution as pure in spirit, though inevitably accompanied by some "false steps of political phrenzy."[68] But as the new regime seemed less and less likely to mend her ways, and as Tom Paine spread the infection of infidelity across the Atlantic, men like Morse were forced to conclude that the Revolution had sprung from "an impure origin."[69] And this shift of interpretation led to a perplexing problem. If good men were at the helm of the French Revolution, destroying the old Roman Catholic au-tocracy, then the righteous were fighting virtuously to bring judgment on the wicked, just as the prophecies of Armaged-don predicted. On the other hand, if wicked infidels were being used to bring down the papal antichrist, how could expositors square their accounts? At Armageddon, evil men were not supposed to join Christians in the fight against Rome.

68. David Osgood, *A Discourse Delivered February 19, 1795* (Boston, 1795), p. 17. For a detailed account of the clergy's reaction, see Gary B. Nash, "The American Clergy and the French Revolution," *William and Mary Quarterly* 22 (July, 1965):392–412. The prophetic commentaries of Bicheno, Crawford, and Linn all reflect this initially friendly attitude toward the French Revolution.

69. Jedidiah Morse, *A Sermon, Preached at Charlestown, November 29, 1798* (Boston, 1798), p. 32.

At first glance, the afflictive model of progress seemed to provide an answer—certainly it was the one expositors chose to take. The whole pattern of history, they noted, had been one where God brought good out of evil, which was precisely what was happening here. "God often accomplishes his purposes by his enemies," William Linn explained; and James Bicheno agreed. Even if French leaders had proved as "atrociously wicked as their enemies, . . . still the great principles of [the revolution] may demand our homage." That, after all, had been the case with the English Reformation. "What was Henry the Eighth . . . ? A monster! What were his motives? The gratification of his lusts!" But God still used him as an instrument for good.[70] As the French excesses grew worse, Morse still argued that God was bringing down antichrist, and that men ought not to confuse God's noble "end with the means" of accomplishment. "Because atheism and licentiousness are employed as *instruments*, by divine providence, to subvert and overthrow popery and despotism, it does not follow that atheism and licentiousness are in themselves good things."[71] It was just that God in his wisdom had used them to accomplish his ends.

That was the explanation of good out of evil that was offered, but was it actually the pattern at the heart of the afflictive model? The prime example of that model, the centerpiece of the history of redemption, was Christ himself. At the Crucifixion, light appeared out of darkness when evil men afflicted the good; and the model was perpetuated by suffering saints throughout history. But Morse wished to justify God's using evil men to afflict other evil men; he wished to applaud God's ends while condemning the actions of God's instruments, the means. Could the End justify the means, so long as it was God's End and God's means?

70. Linn, *Discourses*, p. 17; Bicheno, *Signs of the Times*, p. 7.
71. Morse, *Sermon Delivered at New North*, p. 26.

Apparently so. Infidels deviously sold their tracts for a song, but it was benevolence that inspired the American Bible Society to make the literature of the Gospel available at little or no charge. John Mason objected when atheists slipped their propaganda into pockets even when it was refused; but his society had no qualms about sending a missionary to the Chickasaws unbidden. Deists stooped low and used ridicule to sway the minds of men; Timothy Dwight was politic enough to remain anonymous when he published his low-brow gibes in *The New England Palladium*.[72] All these efforts were made in the service of a good cause; indeed, if ever a glorious end was needed to justify a few dubious means, could there be anything more worthy than a thousand years when men would dwell in peace?

So this is an end—only one end fortunately—to which eschatology may be taken. It is likely to leave us uncomfortable. Not because millennial logic remains recalcitrantly strange and remotely distant; precisely the opposite. So long as men can imagine, they will be capable of conceiving a future which is just and humane; so long as they can question, they will demand, with Job, a reason for the injustices and inhumanities of the present; so long as they have passions, they will in some way strive to bridge their past with that future. The urge to bring on a day of reckoning—when heaven comes down to earth—is with us still, will always be with us. The lesson of the Revelation seems to be that if we try too hard to hasten that day, we are in peril of losing our humanity. Yet surely we are equally in peril if we choose not to make the attempt at all.

72. See, in *The New England Palladium*, "Farmer Johnson's New England Catechism," March 27–May 8, 1801, especially the last number; "To the Farmers and Mechanics," May 12–June 5, 1801; and the articles by "Morpheus," November 24, 1801–March 9, 1802. For details of Dwight's involvement, see Robert Edson Lee, "Timothy Dwight and the *New England Palladium*," *New England Quarterly* 35 (June 1962):229–38.

Selected Bibliography of Primary Sources

Allen, William. *Of the State of the Church in Future Ages*. London, 1684.

Allix, Peter. *Two Treatises*. London, 1707.

Baldwin, Ebenezer. *The Duty of Rejoicing under Calamities and Afflictions*. New York, 1776.

Barnard, Thomas. *A Sermon Preached to the Ancient and Honorable Artillery Company*. Boston, 1758.

Bellamy, Joseph. *A Sermon Delivered before the General Assembly*. New London, Conn., 1762.

———. *Sermons on the Following Subjects*. Boston, 1758.

———. *The Wisdom of God in the Permission of Sin, Vindicated*. Boston, 1760.

Bicheno, James. *The Signs of the Times*. Providence, R.I., 1794.

Bray, Thomas. *A Dissertation on the Sixth Vial*. Hartford, 1780.

Burnet, Thomas. *The Sacred Theory of the Earth*. 6th ed. London, 1726.

Burr, Aaron. *A Discourse Delivered at New-Ark*. New York, 1755.

———. *A Sermon Preached Before the Synod of New York*. New York, 1756.

Byles, Mather. *Poems. The Conflagration*. Boston, 1755.

Chauncy, Charles. *The Earth Delivered from the Curse*. Boston, 1756.

———. *Earthquakes, a Token of the Righteous Anger of God*. Boston, 1755.

Cheever, Ezekiel. *Scripture Prophecies Explained in Three Short Essays*. Boston, 1757.

Colman, Benjamin. *The Judgments of Providence*. Boston, 1727.

———. *Practical Discourses*. 2d ed. Boston, 1747.

Cressener, Drue. *The Judgments of God upon the Roman Catholick Church*. London, 1689.

Cummings, Henry. *A Sermon Preached at Billerica on the 23rd of November, 1775*. Worcester, Mass. [1776].

Daubuz, Charles. *A Perpetual Commentary on the Revelation of St. John*. London, 1720.

A Discourse Addressed to the Sons of Liberty, February 14, 1766. Providence [1766].

Duffield, George. *A Sermon Preached in the Third Presbyterian Church in the City of Philadelphia*. Boston, 1784.

Dwight, Timothy. *A Discourse in Two Parts*. 2d ed. Boston, 1813.

———. *The Duty of Americans at the Present Crisis*. New Haven, Conn., 1798.

———. *The Nature and Danger of Infidel Philosophy*. New Haven, Conn., 1798.

———. *Sermon Delivered in Boston, September 16, 1813* . . . . Boston, 1813.

———. *Sermon Preached at Northampton . . . Occasioned by the Capture of the British Army*. Hartford, 1781.

———. *A Sermon, Preached at Stamford . . . December 18th, 1777*. Hartford, 1778.

———. *The Triumph of Infidelity*. "Published in the World," 1788.

———. *A Valedictory Address to the Young Gentlemen . . . July 25, 1776*. New Haven, Conn. [1776].

Edwards, John. *Brief Remarks upon Mr. Whiston's New Theory of the Earth*. London, 1697.

Edwards, Jonathan. *The Works of President Edwards*. Edited by Sereno E. Dwight. 10 vols. New York, 1830.

———. *The Works of President Edwards*. 4 vols. New York, 1849.

———. *The Works of Jonathan Edwards*. Edited by Perry Miller and John Smith (gen. eds.). 4 vols. New Haven, 1958–.

———. "Notes on the Apocalypse." MS transcribed in Stephen Stein, " 'Notes on the Apocalypse,' by Jonathan Edwards." 2 vols. Ph.D. dissertation, Yale University, 1970.

Erskine, John. *The Signs of the Times Considered*. Edinburgh, 1742.

Fleming, Robert. *The Fulfilling of the Scriptures*. Boston, 1743.

Gay, Ebenezer. *St. John's Vision of the Woman Cloathed with the Sun . . . Explained and Improved*. Boston, 1766.

Gill, John. *Three Sermons*. Boston, 1756.

Goodwin, Thomas. *The Works of Thomas Goodwin*. 12 vols. Edinburgh, 1860–66.

Hopkins, Samuel. *Sin, Thro' Divine Interposition, an Advantage to the Universe*. Boston, 1759.

———. *A Treatise on the Millennium*. Boston, 1793.

Hurd, Richard. *An Introduction to the Study of the Prophecies Concerning the Christian Church*. 2 vols. 4th ed. London, 1776.

Imrie, David. *A Letter from the Reverend Mr. David Imrie*. Boston, 1756.

Keach, Benjamin. *Antichrist Stormed*. London, 1687.

Keill, John. *An Examination of Dr. Burnet's Theory of the Earth*. Oxford, 1698.

Langdon, Samuel. *Observations on the Discourses on the Revelation of Jesus to St. John*. Worcester, Mass., 1791.

———. *A Rational Explication of St. John's Vision of the Two Beasts*. Portsmouth, N.H., 1774.

Lathrop, Joseph. *Sermon on the Dangers of the Time*. Springfield, Mass., 1798.

Lee, Samuel. *A Dissertation Concerning the Place and State of the Dispersed Tribes of Israel*. London, 1677.

———. *Ecclesia Gemens*. London, 1677.

Lightfoot, John. *The Whole Works of the Late Rev. John Lightfoot*. 13 vols. London, 1822–25.

Linn, William. *Discourses on the Signs of the Times*. New York, 1794.

Livingston, John Henry. *Two Sermons Delivered before the New York Missionary Society*. New York, 1799.

Love, Christopher. *The Strange and Wonderful Predictions of Mr. Christopher Love*. Boston, 1759.

McKnight, John. *Life to the Dead*. New York, 1799.

———. *A View of the Present State of the World*. New York, 1802.

Mason, John M. *Hope for the Heathen*. New York, 1797.

Mather, Cotton. "Biblia Americana." Manuscript, Massachusetts Historical Society, Boston.

———. *Boanerges*. Boston, 1727.

———. *A Midnight Cry*. London, 1691.

———. "Problema Theologicum." Manuscript, American Antiquarian Society, Worcester, Mass.

———. *The Stone Cut Out of the Mountain*. Boston, 1716.

———. *Theopolis Americana*. Boston, 1710.

———. "Triparadisus." Manuscript, American Antiquarian Society, Worcester, Mass.

Mather, Increase. *The Blessed Hope*. Boston, 1701.

———. *A Discourse Concerning Faith and Fervency in Prayer and the Glorious Kingdom of Jesus Christ*. Boston, 1710.

——. *A Dissertation Concerning the Future Conversion*. London, 1709.

——. *A Dissertation Wherein the Strange Doctrine . . . .* Boston, 1708.

Mayhew, Jonathan. *A Discourse on Revelation XV: 3-4*. Boston, 1755.

——. *The Expected Dissolution of All Things*. Boston, 1755.

——. *Popish Idolatry*. Boston, 1765.

——. *Two Discourses Delivered October 25th, 1759*. Boston, 1759.

——. *Two Discourses Delivered October 9, 1760*. Boston, 1760.

Mede, Joseph. *The Apostacy of the Latter Times*. London, 1641.

——. *The Key of the Revelation*. London, 1643.

——. *The Works of the Pious and Profoundly Learned Joseph Mede*. Edited by John Worthington. London, 1672.

More, Henry. *Apocalypsis Apocalypseos*. London, 1680.

Morse, Jedidiah. *A Sermon Delivered at the New North Church*. Boston, 1798.

——. *A Sermon Preached at Charlestown, November 29, 1798*. Boston, 1798.

Newton, Thomas. *Dissertations on the Prophecies Which Have Remarkably Been Fulfilled*. 2 vols. New York, 1794.

Noyes, Nicholas. *New England's Duty and Interest to Be an Habitation of Justice and Mountain of Holiness*. Boston, 1698.

Osgood, David. *The Devil Let Loose*. Boston, 1799.

Parsons, Jonathan. *Good News from a Far Country*. Portsmouth, N.H., 1756.

——. *Sixty Sermons*. 2 vols. Newburyport, Mass., 1779.

Patrick, Simon, et al. *A Critical Commentary and Paraphrase on the Old and New Testament*. 4 vols. Philadelphia, 1848.

Philpot, Thomas. *A New Systeme of the Apocalypse*. London, 1688.

Priestly, Joseph. *Two Sermons*. Philadelphia, 1794.

Prince, Thomas, Jr. *The Christian History*. 2 vols. Boston, 1744-45.

Robison, John. *Proofs of a Conspiracy*. New York, 1798.

Sewall, Joseph. *The Certainty and Suddenness of Christ's Coming*. Boston, 1716.

Sewall, Samuel. Diary of Samuel Sewall. *Collections of the Massachusetts Historical Society*. 5th series. Vols. 5-7. Boston, 1878-82.

——. Letterbook. *Collections of the Massachusetts Historical Society*. 6th series. Vols. 1-2. Boston, 1887.

——. *Phenomena Quaedam Apocalyptica*. Boston, 1697.

——. *Proposals Touching the Accomplishment of Prophecies Humbly Offered*. Boston, 1713.

Sherwood, Samuel. *The Church's Flight into the Wilderness*. New York, 1776.

Smith, William. *A Discourse Concerning the Conversion of the Heathen*. Philadelphia, 1760.

Spalding, Joshua. *Sentiments Concerning the Coming of Christ*. Salem, Mass., 1796.

Stiles, Ezra. *The United States Elevated to Glory and Honor*. New Haven, 1783.

Stillman, Samuel. *Thoughts on the French Revolution*. Boston, 1795.

Tappan, David. *A Discourse Delivered at the Third Parish in Newbury*. Boston, 1783.

———. *The Question Answered, Watchman, What of the Night?* Salem, Mass., 1783.

———. *A Sermon, Delivered to the First Congregation in Cambridge . . . April 11, 1793*. Boston, 1793.

Tennent, Gilbert. *The Good Man's Character and Reward Represented*. Philadelphia, 1756.

Torrey, William. *A Brief Discourse Concerning Futurities or Things to Come*. Boston, 1757.

West, Samuel. *An Anniversary Sermon Preached at Plymouth, December 22nd, 1777*. Boston, 1778.

———. *A Sermon Preached before the Honorable Council*. In *Pulpit of the American Revolution*, edited by John Wingate Thornton. Boston, 1876.

Wetmore, Izrahiah. *Sermon Preached before . . . the General Assembly*. New London, Conn., 1773.

Whiston, William. *The Accomplishment of Scripture Prophecies*. London, 1708.

———. *An Essay on the Revelation of St. John*. London, 1706.

———. *A New Theory of the Earth*. London, 1696.

Whitby, Daniel. *A Paraphrase and Commentary of the New Testament*. London, 1727.

Willard, Samuel. *The Checkered State of the Gospel Church*. Boston, 1701.

———. *The Fountain Opened*. Boston, 1700.

———. *The Peril of the Times Displayed*. Boston, 1700.

Winchester, Elhanan. *A Course of Lectures, on the Prophecies*. 2 vols. Norwich, Conn., 1794–95.

———. *The Three Woe Trumpets*. Boston, 1794.

———. *Two Lectures on the Prophecies*. Norwich, Conn., 1792.

Index